Learn HTML5 by Creating Fun Games

Learn one of the most popular markup languages by creating simple yet fun games

Rodrigo Silveira

BIRMINGHAM - MUMBAI

Learn HTML5 by Creating Fun Games

First published: June 2013

Production Reference: 1190613

Published by Packt Publishing Ltd.
Livery Place
35 Livery Street
Birmingham B3 2PB, UK.

ISBN 978-1-84969-602-9

www.packtpub.com

Cover Image by Duraid Fatouhi (duraidfatouhi@yahoo.com)

Credits

Author
Rodrigo Silveira

Reviewer
Thomas Mak

Acquisition Editor
Andrew Duckworth

Commissioning Editor
Shreerang Deshpande

Lead Technical Editor
Madhuja Chaudhari

Technical Editors
Veena Pagare
Priya Singh
Sampreshita Maheshwari

Project Coordinator
Apeksha Chitnis

Proofreaders
Aaron Nash
Bernadette Watkins

Indexer
Hemangini Bari

Graphics
Ronak Dhruv
Valentina Dsilva

Production Coordinator
Nilesh R. Mohite

Cover Work
Nilesh R. Mohite

About the Author

Rodrigo Silveira is a web engineer at Deseret Digital Media. His responsibilities include back-end system development, tools, and maintenance, front-end application development and design, and more recently, he's been involved in mobile development of various products on the Android platform.

He received his Bachelor's of Science in Computer Science from Brigham Young University, Idaho, as well as an Associate's Degree in Business Management from LDS Business College in Salt Lake City, Utah.

His fascination for web development began in his early teenage years, and his skills grew as he discovered the power of a library subscription, a curious and willing mind, and supportive parents and friends. Today Rodrigo balances his time between the three great passions of his life—his family, software development, and video games (with the last two usually being mingled together).

About the Reviewer

Thomas Mak, also known as **Makzan**, is a developer with a specialty in web development and game design. He has over ten years of experience building digital products, including real-time multiplayer interaction games and iOS applications.

He is currently a founder of game development learning company, 42games (http://42games.net), where he makes game development tutorials and online learning resources.

He has written two books with Packt publishing and one screencast series for building Flash Virtual World and making games with HTML5 and related web standards.

I would like to thank my family and my wife, Candy Wong, for supporting all my writings.

www.PacktPub.com

Support files, eBooks, discount offers and more

You might want to visit www.PacktPub.com for support files and downloads related to your book.

Did you know that Packt offers eBook versions of every book published, with PDF and ePub files available? You can upgrade to the eBook version at www.PacktPub.com and as a print book customer, you are entitled to a discount on the eBook copy. Get in touch with us at service@packtpub.com for more details.

At www.PacktPub.com, you can also read a collection of free technical articles, sign up for a range of free newsletters and receive exclusive discounts and offers on Packt books and eBooks.

http://PacktLib.PacktPub.com

Do you need instant solutions to your IT questions? PacktLib is Packt's online digital book library. Here, you can access, read and search across Packt's entire library of books.

Why Subscribe?

- Fully searchable across every book published by Packt
- Copy and paste, print and bookmark content
- On demand and accessible via web browser

Free Access for Packt account holders

If you have an account with Packt at www.PacktPub.com, you can use this to access PacktLib today and view nine entirely free books. Simply use your login credentials for immediate access.

Table of Contents

Preface

If you would like to write a software that can reach billions of people world-wide, then this book will help you get started on that journey. Today, most of the devices people use every day (computers, laptops, tablet computers, smart phones, and so on) are capable of running HTML5 code. What's more, as modern web browsers continue to get more and more powerful, your HTML5-based games and applications can run at or very near native application performance levels.

This book will help you learn all about HTML5, including the semantic markup elements, CSS3 styling, and the latest supporting JavaScript APIs. With this knowledge and skill, we'll be able to create fun games that can be played by anyone using a device connected to the Internet.

What this book covers

Chapter 1, An Overview of HTML5, explains what HTML5 is, and how it fits into the Open Web platform paradigm. It also introduces the three pillars of HTML5, namely the new HTML elements, CSS3, and new JavaScript APIs.

Chapter 2, HTML5 Typography, introduces the first game in the book, namely, a DOM-based typography game. The main HTML5 features described in the chapter include web forms, metadata, web fonts, transitions, animation, text shadow, box shadow, window.JSON, and querySelector.

Chapter 3, Understanding the Gravity of HTML5, builds a basic jelly-wobbling gravity game. This chapter includes a discussion of cross-browser support, polyfills, and how to get around different API implementations among different browsers. The main HTML5 features described in the chapter include web audio, SVG graphics, and drag-and-drop.

Chapter 4, Using HTML5 to Catch a Snake, creates a traditional snake game using the new HTML5 canvas element, with its accompanying 2D rendering context. Other HTML5 features described in the chapter include web workers, offline storage, and RequestAnimationFrame.

Chapter 5, Improving the Snake Game, builds on the same game created in the previous chapter, adding features such as window messaging, web storage, local storage, session storage, and IndexedDB.

Chapter 6, Adding Features to Your Game, focuses the discussion on advanced HTML5 concepts, as well as the latest features. Although no game is built in this chapter, the JavaScript and CSS APIs described represent the current state of the art in HTML5 and web development. The major features described in the chapter include WebGL, web sockets, video, geolocation, CSS shaders, CSS columns, and CSS regions and exclusions.

Chapter 7, HTML5 and Mobile Game Development, concludes the book by building a 2D space shooter game completely optimized for mobile game play. The focus of the chapter is mobile-specific considerations in web development, including a discussion about the differences between desktop and mobile platforms. The major HTML5 features described in the chapter include media queries and touch events.

Setting up the Environment, walks through the setup of a local web development environment, including installing an open source Apache server. In addition to setting up the development environment, it demonstrates how to build a web portal using the new HTML5 elements, from which we can access the games developed throughout the book. This chapter is available online at: `http://www.packtpub.com/sites/default/files/downloads/Setting_up_the_Environment.pdf`.

What you need for this book

You need the latest version of a modern web browser, which, at the time of writing' includes Google Chrome, Mozilla Firefox, Safari, Opera, and Internet Explorer (at least Version 10). You also need a basic text editor of your choice, although any code editing software you may be familiar with will also suffice. Prior knowledge of, or experience with HTML, CSS, and JavaScript is helpful, but not required.

Who this book is for

This book is primarily written for developers with prior experience with game development, who are now making the transition to HTML5. The focus of the book is not the complexities and theories of game development, but rather, it focuses on helping the reader learn HTML5, and how the Open Web platform can be a means to reaching billions of users world-wide.

Conventions

In this book, you will find a number of styles of text that distinguish between different kinds of information. Here are some examples of these styles, and an explanation of their meaning.

Code words in text are shown as follows: "We can include other contexts through the use of the `include` directive."

A block of code is set as follows:

```
[<div id="wrapper">
  <div id="header"></div>
  <div id="body">
    <div id="main_content">
      <p>Lorem Ipsum...</p>
    </div>
    <div id="sidebar"></div>
  </div>
  <div id="footer"></div>
</div>
```

When we wish to draw your attention to a particular part of a code block, the relevant lines or items are set in bold:

```
<input type="text" name="firstName" value="First Name" class="hint-on"
    onblur="if (this.value == '') {
```

New terms and **important words** are shown in bold. Words that you see on the screen, in menus or dialog boxes, for example, appear in the text like this: "clicking the **Next** button moves you to the next screen".

Warnings or important notes appear in a box like this.

Tips and tricks appear like this.

Reader feedback

Feedback from our readers is always welcome. Let us know what you think about this book—what you liked or may have disliked. Reader feedback is important for us to develop titles that you really get the most out of.

To send us general feedback, simply send an e-mail to `feedback@packtpub.com`, and mention the book title via the subject of your message.

If there is a topic that you have expertise in and you are interested in either writing or contributing to a book, see our author guide on `www.packtpub.com/authors`.

Customer support

Now that you are the proud owner of a Packt book, we have a number of things to help you to get the most from your purchase.

Downloading the example code

You can download the example code files for all Packt books you have purchased from your account at `http://www.packtpub.com`. If you purchased this book elsewhere, you can visit `http://www.packtpub.com/support` and register to have the files e-mailed directly to you.

Errata

Although we have taken every care to ensure the accuracy of our content, mistakes do happen. If you find a mistake in one of our books—maybe a mistake in the text or the code—we would be grateful if you would report this to us. By doing so, you can save other readers from frustration and help us improve subsequent versions of this book. If you find any errata, please report them by visiting `http://www.packtpub.com/submit-errata`, selecting your book, clicking on the **errata submission form** link, and entering the details of your errata. Once your errata are verified, your submission will be accepted and the errata will be uploaded on our website, or added to any list of existing errata, under the Errata section of that title. Any existing errata can be viewed by selecting your title from `http://www.packtpub.com/support`.

Piracy

Piracy of copyright material on the Internet is an ongoing problem across all media. At Packt, we take the protection of our copyright and licenses very seriously. If you come across any illegal copies of our works, in any form, on the Internet, please provide us with the location address or website name immediately so that we can pursue a remedy.

Please contact us at `copyright@packtpub.com` with a link to the suspected pirated material.

We appreciate your help in protecting our authors, and our ability to bring you valuable content.

Questions

You can contact us at `questions@packtpub.com` if you are having a problem with any aspect of the book, and we will do our best to address it.

1
An Overview of HTML5

Welcome to the fascinating world of web development! As we begin our journey towards HTML5 development, we'll take the time and review the past. After all, you can't really get anywhere unless you know where you're coming from. Unless you have been living under a rock for the past several years, you have certainly heard a lot about Web 2.0, the Open Web, and definitely HTML5. If you have heard those terms from, say, three different people, you will probably have also heard at least three different definitions of each. For this reason, we will briefly describe what those terms mean, why you should be excited about them, and how HTML5 is a game changer.

What is HTML?

The first term we need to be clear about before we start talking about the Open Web, and how HTML5 plays a central role in its success, is HTML. Simply put, HTML is a very basic markup language used to describe text files to the programs that read them. While that is possibly the most generalized definition of what it is, it is interesting how such a fundamental technology has played such a crucial part in the development of our entire society. From humble beginnings, and serving a very specific purpose at first, HTML has become the primary markup language of the Web, which in turn has found its way into almost every household throughout the world, as well as most briefcases, pockets, and other electronic devices.

Given this dramatic, widespread reach of HTML, it quickly became clear that the technology needed to do more than simply declaring the color of some block of text, or the width and height of a photograph stored in some research paper. Because of the many different ways in which the Web has been used over the years, HTML has grown and evolved, going from a simple markup language, to becoming the foundation for the development of powerful, highly complex online applications and services.

A brief history of HTML

Hyper Text Markup Language, or **HTML** for short, as we know it today was first conceived in the mind of Tim Berners-Lee in 1989. At the time, while working at the European Laboratory for Particle Physics in Geneva, Switzerland, Tim Berners-Lee thought it would be beneficial to link the various research documents written and used by scientists. That way, instead of having a large collection of individual and independent documents that one could read, each document that referenced another research paper could have a hyper link to the other document, so that the reader could navigate from one document to the next with ease, and in a timely manner.

In order to implement his idea of hyperlinking documents together, Tim Berners-Lee looked to an existing markup language as the basis for his own markup language—
Standard Generalized Markup Language or **SGML** for short—as a starting point. SGML was a simple language designed to structure text by using a tag vocabulary. For example, in order to specify that a block of text was to be interpreted as a paragraph, one would surround such text with a pair of "paragraph tags", which looked the same as today's paragraph tags in HTML. While the basic vocabulary in Tim's version of the language remained the same, one key tag was added—the hyperlink tag. Thus, HTML was born.

Keep in mind that Tim's vision for the language was very specific. Through HTML's ability to cross-reference documents together, published scientific research papers could be much more efficiently studied. It was not until many years later that HTML started being used for other purposes beyond sharing of interlinked text.

The evolution of the World Wide Web

As the computer became more common place and more people started to own their own machine, and as the Internet became more widely used, people started finding new ways to use the new technology. Instead of using the Web simply to read what others had written, people began to use it to talk to people by writing and publishing documents. It wasn't long after that until the Internet became a giant virtual society.

The Internet continued to grow in popularity through the 1990s, and different uses for it continue to emerge. With each new idea of how that amazing infrastructure could be used, new ways had to be thought of in order to bring those ideas into reality, since the technology that supported the Internet was still the same. At its core, a web application was still nothing more than a text-based document, formatted using HTML. In order to add some logic to this otherwise static data, programmers used programs stored in the web server to manipulate input from the user, and create HTML documents dynamically. Again, the actual documents that users interacted with as they navigated the Internet, were nothing more than pure HTML.

In order for the Internet to continue to grow and adapt to the way and purposes for which it was being used, changes were needed. Instead of only sending plain text data to HTML readers (web browsers), it would be more efficient if there was a way to add some sort of code to the web pages, so that it could process information while on the browser. Thus, JavaScript was born.

Today the Web continues to grow both in terms of the amount of people using it, and in the ways and purposes in which it is used. The good news is that the technologies that support and run the Web are also growing and evolving, so that new use cases can be accommodated.

What is HTML5?

You undoubtedly have heard people using the term HTML5 in different contexts, which has probably caused at least some confusion. Like most so-called technical terms that find their way into the general population, and frequently fall from the lips of not-so-technical people, HTML5 finding it's way into the general population in fact means more than one thing. At the most basic level, HTML5 refers to the next version of the markup language created by Tim Berners-Lee, which now has a governing body guiding its progress. The other meaning of the term makes reference to other technologies that compliment the markup language, as well as the idea of an Open Web, which we'll talk more about later in the chapter.

HTML5 – the next step in the evolution

Believe it or not, people have been trying to develop full-featured, complex applications intended to be executed in web browsers for a long time. For the most part, the greatest challenge has been the fact that the technologies required to accomplish this goal haven't been fully available until relatively recently. The reason why it was so difficult to create large web applications using earlier versions of HTML was that HTML was not originally designed for this. However, as the Web has evolved, so has HTML.

One of the goals of HTML5 is to accomplish exactly that — to enable developers to create powerful, non-trivial applications that run completely over the Internet. Another major goal of HTML5 is to be completely backwards compatible, so that web pages used for other purposes (namely the hyperlinking of research documents) can still function the same.

Just as Tim Berners-Lee added the hyperlink tag to SGML (among other tags), HTML5 is basically just that—more tags (or more functionality) to the previous version of the language. While that is a good, general overview of what HTML5 is, there is a bit more to the story. Beyond the new tags added to the HTML specification, the term HTML5 also refers to this next step in the evolution of the Web.

Some people have called this Web 2.0 and others have simply called it *the future*. When I refer to this next step in the history of HTML, I'll be referring to the upgrades done to HTML, CSS, and JavaScript, since these are the three major technologies behind this new Internet, where web applications (including online games) are the center of attention, as well as one of the focuses of this book.

HTML5 is not a single feature

Before providing the developer with new features, HTML5 tries to solve core problems that were exposed in previous versions of HTML, namely the programming architecture. Since HTML was not originally created with web application development in mind, as programmers started using it for such purposes, they soon found themselves with very messy code. The application data was heavily mixed with the presentation code, which was in turn tightly coupled with the application logic.

To solve this problem, developers were given **Cascading Style Sheets** (CSS), which allowed them to separate HTML markup (the information) from how the information was rendered. Thus, the term HTML5 really refers to three separate technologies, namely HTML5 (the new semantic elements or tags), CSS3, and JavaScript (all the new APIs, such as web storage, web workers, and web sockets, to name a few).

More semantic document structure

As developers see the need for, and experiment with different applications for existing technologies, they use what they have, and adapt it to the new circumstances. Such was the case with previous versions of HTML. Since only a handful of container tags existed, developers described very complex document structures with the same elements; while this accomplished the job, it also made it confusing and hard to maintain structures. Simply put, if all you have is a hammer, then everything you see will become a nail.

For example, it was common for developers to use the `<div>` tag to represent every single part of the document when describing a structure like the one represented by the following illustration:

Figure 1

The previous figure shows a very typical structure of most websites built in the last generation of web design.

Such a design could be represented by the following structure:

```
<div id="wrapper">
  <div id="header"></div>
  <div id="body">
    <div id="main_content">
      <p>Lorem Ipsum...</p>
    </div>
    <div id="sidebar"></div>
  </div>
  <div id="footer"></div>
</div>
```

While using the `<div>` tag for any purpose under the heavens was one way to get the job done, you can see how this can quickly get out of hand, and turn the document into something hard to understand without great inspection. Looking at this type of code becomes especially troublesome when you see a long series of closing `<div>` tags—how can you know what each closing tag is actually closing, since all the tags have the same name? Worse yet, how can you know if you have just the right number of closing tags?

Another major problem with designing HTML structures after the `<div>` paradigm was that each tag was completely meaningless from a semantic point of view. In order to make each `<div>` tag slightly more meaningful and self-describing, extra attributes were added, normally in the form an an ID or a class. Again, this solution only added to the problem, since larger, more complex documents required more and more of these attributes, which one had to keep track of, thus increasing the complexity of what should be a simple solution.

Thankfully, in HTML5 this problem is solved in a very elegant manner. Seeing that a lot of documents used the `<div>` tags for the same purpose, namely to define common sections such as the header, footer, navigation, and main content, new tags were added to represent such common sections. With these new tags, you are now able to visually scan a design structure, and very quickly understand the way information is to be laid out. Furthermore, the need to create endless ID attributes in order to distinguish each `<div>` tag is completely gone.

Using some of the new tags provided by HTML5, the same design concept from *figure 1* can be represented as follows:

```
<header></header>
<section>
  <article>
    <p>Lorem Ipsum...</p>
  </article>
  <nav></nav>
</section>
<footer></footer>
```

You can see how much more descriptive the code becomes. Keep in mind also, that the benefits of this more meaningful structure extend beyond better readability for humans. With the new semantic tags in HTML5, search engines (such as Google, Microsoft's Bing, and Yahoo!) are able to better understand the content of web pages, and can therefore better index your website based on its subject matter, thus making the Web a bit better. Also, by defining your HTML files with more specific tags, screen reader software is able to better understand the contents of web pages, thus allowing users who depend on such software to better use and enjoy the Internet.

Since the Internet seems to have made our world completely flat, you should never make the assumption that only your friends and neighbors will be accessing the content you publish online. Not only will your visitors come to your site from other countries and devices (such as smartphones, tablets, and even television sets), but many of the people surfing the Internet (thus, coming to your site to consume the material you make available to them) also have special needs such as visual or audio aid devices or software. For this reason, when you lay down any HTML code, keep that in mind, and consider how a screen reader program might interpret your content, and how easy it will be for that user to use and consume your work.

The following tags were added to HTML5 to accomplish this new, more streamlined semantic order. Keep in mind that each tag has several attributes, which we'll discuss in detail when we show sample usage in the next chapter. Also, because of the new data attributes, elements can be extended arbitrarily.

The following table has been taken from *HTML5 W3C Candidate Recommendation 17 December 2012*, which can be found at `http://www.w3.org/TR/2012/CR-html5-20121217/`.

Tag name	Description
`<address>`	This tag represents contact information related to its associated article element, or related to the entire document when associated with a body element.
`<article>`	This tag represents a standalone piece of content, such as an article or blog post. Article elements may be nested, in which case a child article node would be associated with its parent, yet it would still be independent of all other pieces of content in the document.
`<aside>`	This tag represents a piece of content related to other content elements within the document, yet could still be represented independently of its related elements. For example, sub-navigation sections, sidebars, and so on.

Tag name	Description
`<audio>`	This tag represents a sound or audio stream (or both) from a single source. Multiple sources may be specified, though the browser selects the most appropriate source to stream from.
`<bdi>`	This tag represents an isolated piece of text context that may be formatted in a bidirectional fashion.
`<bdo>`	This tag represents an element that controls the text direction of its children elements. The value of the `dir` attribute specifies whether text within the element is to flow from left to right (with a value of `ltr`) or from right to left (with a value of `rtl`).
`<canvas>`	This tag represents a rectangular panel that may have its contents manipulated through rendering context APIs exposed through JavaScript.
`<command>`	This tag represents a command that can be executed by the user, such as a keyboard shortcut.
`<details>`	This tag represents additional content related to some other element or content.
`<figure>`	This tag represents independent content that may be used as annotations for photos, illustrations, and so on.
`<footer>`	This tag represents a section of content with information about its elements, such as copyright information and other details about an article.
`<header>`	This tag represents a section heading, such as table of contents and navigational elements.
`<hgroup>`	This tag represents a section subheading, such as alternative titles and bylines.
`<mark>`	This tag represents a section of content marked up for referencing, similar in purpose as highlighting a block of text.
`<meter>`	This tag represents a value within a known range, such as the amount of energy left. Note that since there is a dedicated `progress` element, the `meter` element should not be used to represent a progress bar.
`<nav>`	This tag represents a navigation element with links to other documents, or links within the same document.
`<progress>`	This tag represents the amount of progress done within a known range, such as the number of steps completed in a registration process.
`<rt>`	This tag represents the text component of a ruby annotation.
`<rp>`	This tag represents the text component of a ruby annotation that is displayed by the browser when ruby annotations are not supported.
`<section>`	This tag represents a general-purpose section within the document, such as a slide, or the area of a document where a list of articles is displayed.
`<summary>`	This tag represents a summary of some content.

Tag name	Description
`<time>`	This tag represents a date and time in both human and machine-readable formats. The content displayed by the browser is meant for human consumption, whereas the data attributes are designed to be used by the browser and other applications.
`<video>`	This tag represents a video stream from a single source. Multiple sources may be specified, though the browser selects the most appropriate source to stream from.
`<wbr>`	This tag represents a line break opportunity, hinting to the browser where it would be appropriate to break a line when needed. Note that this element has no width, so that when a line break is not required, the element is not visible.

A warning about performance

Something that is often overlooked in web design and front-end web development is performance. While today's major browsers make rendering HTML seem like a trivial task, there is actually a lot of work going on behind the scenes in order to turn a collection of HTML tags and CSS into a nice looking web page. What's more, as it becomes easier to add bells and whistles to a web page through rollover effects, drop down menus, and automatic slideshows, it is easy to forget about what the browser still needs to do to get that work done.

If you think about an HTML document as a tree structure, where each nested tag is like a branch in the structure, then it's easy to understand what a deep layout would look like compared to a shallow layout. In other words, the more nested tags you have, the deeper the structure.

With that said, always keep in mind that the slightest change in an HTML node (such as the physical size a text tag takes up on the page changing because a hover effect caused the text to become bold, thus taking a few extra pixels on the screen) may trigger what is called a reflow, which essentially will cause the browser to perform many calculations on each and every branch (tag) in your HTML structure, because it will need to recalculate where each element needs to go, so it can redraw the page properly.

The more shallow you can make your HTML structures, the less calculations the browser will need to make every time it needs to redraw the page, thus causing a smoother experience. While the argument that deeply nested `<div>` tags cause HTML files to become harder to read and maintain can be subjective, there is no arguing that deep HTML structures perform much worse than flatter alternatives.

Native features of the browser

As stated earlier, one of the strengths of HTML5 is the way it reflects real-world needs, and brings elegant solutions to such needs. Features that don't get used a whole lot by developers (or that don't get wide adoption by browser makers) eventually find their way out of the spec. Likewise, repeated efforts by developers to solve recurring problems eventually cause new features to be suggested, then added to the spec. As new recommendations become accepted as part of the spec, browser makers implement these new features, and the end result is that the browser is extended, and becomes capable of doing what developers had to code by hand.

As an example, let's take a look at placeholder fields. A placeholder is the text inside an input field found in HTML forms, which take the place of a separate label. When the input field is empty, the text inside it describes the data that the field expects (such as a first name, or an e-mail address). Once the user begins to type into the field, that placeholder text disappears, and the actual input from the user replaces it.

While this technique is very intuitive, it takes more physical space to represent, which becomes especially challenging on smaller screen sizes.

A much more dynamic solution, as shown in the following screenshot, is to use a combination of JavaScript and CSS to move the field label inside the field itself:

Before HTML5, this effect took quite a few lines of boilerplate JavaScript code:

```
<style>
.hint-on { color: #ddd; }
.hint-off { color: #333; }
</style>
<input type="text" name="firstName" value="First Name" class="hint-on"
       onblur="if (this.value == '') {
                  this.className='hint-on';
                  this.value='First Name';
              }"
       onfocus="if (this.value == 'First Name') {
                  this.className='hint-off';
                  this.value='';
              }" />
```

Of course, there are many ways to achieve this same effect using JavaScript. In HTML5, this same feature, called placeholder, can be achieved with a single line of code, as shown in the following code snippet:

```
<input type="text" placeholder="Last Name" />
```

The reason that this second version works is because the attribute *placeholder* was added to the browser, as well as the logic required to make it work. While this may seem like a nice little trick that the browser has learned, let's take a closer look at some of the main benefits this provides us with:

- You, as the developer, have potentially hundreds fewer lines of code to write and test throughout the course of your entire project, since the browser exposes such a simple alternative

- Development time decreases for two reasons: you have less code to write, and you have less code to test

- Your code will be more portable and reliable, since you don't need to write specific implementations of your code logic for each browser, and you can trust that each browser will implement the feature properly (even if it takes a couple of updates for them to get there)

In other words, instead of putting a lot of your efforts into normalizing your code so it runs the same way in as many browsers as possible, or writing a lot of boilerplate code just to bring your application to the latest accepted standards, you can now invest the majority of your time building unique applications, since the repetitive code is abstracted away by the browser.

One last exciting point about this positive cycle of HTML5 that I'd like to point out is, how, since HTML5 is responsive to common use cases and real world needs, as time goes by we can only expect more and more really neat and useful features being added to the browser natively. Who can even imagine what new features the browser will support natively in the next few years?

As of this book, the following are some native features that modern browsers support (more detail about these features will be given in the following chapters, but this list should give you a good foretaste of what is to come).

Automatic form validation

You tell the browser the exact format that your want user input to be in, and the browser will enforce that format. Any invalid input provided (based on your settings), and the browser will even report back to the user, letting the user know what went wrong.

New input types

Collect data from the user in a variety of formats beyond text, lists, or checkboxes and radio buttons. For values within a given numerical range, you can use a slider input (also known as a range input). You can also take precise input related to dates, colors, telephone numbers, or e-mail addresses. All it takes to specify such restrictions in your input is a single HTML element attribute.

Telephone-friendly hyperlinks

When browsing through text documents, the browser has always been very good at navigating from one document to the next. All it takes to tell the browser where to go next is an anchor tag. Now that smart phones make up nearly half of all Internet usage in some parts of the world, a hyper link can have a different context—such as telling your device to dial a number, for example. With HTML5 you can tell that same anchor tag to treat its link as a phone number to be called, similar to how you currently tell it to treat its resource as an email address.

CSS-based DOM selectors

Unless you have lived under a rock for the past five years or so, you will have heard of, and possibly used the most popular JavaScript library today—jQuery. One of the main reasons that jQuery has become so popular, and has gained such wide acceptance by web developers, is the revolutionary way in which it allows you to access DOM elements. Before jQuery, the three most common ways of accessing DOM elements were as follows:

- `document.getElementsByTagName()`

- `document.getElementsByClassName()`

- `document.getElementById()`

Based on jQuery's solution to this limited way of accessing document nodes, you can now retrieve an element (or a collection of elements) from your document by specifying a CSS selector. Any or all nodes that match such CSS selectors are returned by the new selecting commands:

- `document.querySelector("css query goes here");`

- `document.querySelectorAll("css query goes here");`

Text-to-speech

Text-to-speech is probably one of the most exciting and powerful features being added natively to the browser. While your user can simply type some input into an input field, and you can do with that text input what you wish, the browser now gives you the ability to take voice input from your user. Whatever the user literally *tells* the browser through a microphone, the browser will use its own text analysis algorithms, and give you the equivalent text transcription. By adding a single line of code to your application (and a web-based application, no less), you can now get that much closer to the type of interface only portrayed in movies (or offline, in desktop-based applications).

CSS3

Cascading Style Sheets, most commonly known simply as CSS, is another contributing technology to the success of HTML and the World Wide Web. CSS is a style language that controls the way an HTML structure is rendered. Some of the benefits of using a style language alongside a markup language include separation of concerns, reusability of visual design, ease of maintenance, and scalability. As part of the HTML5 revolution, there were some significant updates to the CSS spec, which have also taken the language to a whole new level.

Separation of concerns

The first, and possibly most apparent benefit that CSS brings to the game is separation of concerns. By allowing HTML to describe the data that it represents, and not worry about how that data is presented, CSS is able to control the way that data is displayed. This way the CSS expert can work on styling a web application without the need to touch the HTML file. Best of all, the CSS expert needs absolutely no knowledge of any of the possibly many other technologies used in a given project. This way, no matter how complex the rest of the project is, the styling can be done independently and separately.

Reusability of visual design

There are many ways to include CSS rules into an HTML document. For example, you can write all the CSS code right into the same HTML file that uses it, you can write it inside each HTML element as you create them, or you can put the CSS style in a completely separate file, then import the stylesheet into the HTML file. Most commonly, what you'll want to do is write all your CSS code in one or more separate files (think separation of concerns), then import each file into the HTML files that you'd like to use for each set of styles. This way you can have a single stylesheet that describes a particular visual *theme*, then you can reuse that theme throughout an entire application (possibly composed of thousands of individual HTML files and pieces) simply by importing the stylesheet with a single line of code:

```
<style>
p {
    color: #cc0000;
    font-size: 23px;
}
</style>
<p>Hello, World!</p>
<p style="color: #cc0000; font-size: 23px;">Hello, World!</p>
```

The previous code is an example of CSS rules written on a specific element. In this case, only this HTML paragraph tags will use the style defined by this simple rule (which tells the browser to render the text in red, and 23 pixels height).

```
(file: /my-style sheet.css)
p {
    color: #cc0000;
    font-size: 23px;
}
(file: /index.html)
<!doctype html>
<html>
<head>
    <link rel="style sheet" href="my-style sheet.css" />
    (...)
```

The previous code is an example of CSS rules written in a separate document. In this case, any HTML paragraph tags in the file index.html will use the style defined by this simple rule (which tells the browser to render the text in red, and 23 pixels height). Other documents will not use the styling rules found in my-style sheet.css if the stylesheet is not imported into those files.

Ease of maintenance

Another tremendous benefit that you get by separating the presentation of your HTML documents through external CSS files is that maintenance becomes very easy. Imagine the scenario where you write all your styles in the same document that uses them. If you only have one document, then that's not a big problem. However, most projects include multiple HTML files. So imagine that you simply copy and paste the CSS from one file into the next, since they both share the same CSS rules. How would you go about making a change to some of these rules if you now have tens or hundreds of files to update also, since the CSS to be updated in found in all of these HTML file?

Thus, if you only have a few CSS that only contain CSS code, and all the HTML files that use them simply import the stylesheet, whenever you need to change the style for your project, you only need to update one CSS file. Once that CSS file is updated, all other HTML files that import the CSS will automatically use the new style.

Scalability

Lastly, the advantage of using CSS is that it makes the presentation layer of your project very scalable. Once the CSS code is in place, you can use it throughout hundreds of thousands of files (think of Wikipedia, for example), and the style will be consistent throughout all of them. If you then decide to upgrade your design, you only need to make changes to one file — the stylesheet.

The evolution of CSS

Although the idea of having a separate style language to handle the presentation layer of HTML documents is unarguably brilliant, CSS has been somewhat of a nightmare to most designers. Since different browsers have always tried to be unique enough from other competing browsers in order to win the favor of users, different browsers have implemented certain features of CSS differently. For examples, a CSS rule that specifies an element with a width of 500 pixels would not behave consistently in all major browsers. By specifying an element's width attribute through CSS, most browsers would only set the content width of the element, while allowing any padding, border, and margin width to make the total width of the element even larger. However, there were browsers that included the width of an element's padding and border when setting the CSS width attribute.

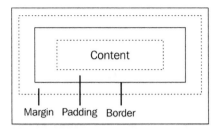

The previous figure shows an example of a CSS box model. Note that the margin space is always transparent, while any padding space inherits the background color or image of its corresponding element.

Inconsistencies like this made the success of CSS limited and slow. When a designer took on a project, one design would need to be coded with many browsers in mind, which also meant that it would need to be tested in many different browsers. Not only that, but the actual set of features that CSS offered were limited. For example, before Version 3, the only way to create an element with rounded corners through CSS was by adding a background image to the element, where this image was a box with rounded corners. This was not very practical, and often involved changing the HTML structure, which partly defeated the purpose of external stylesheets.

Thanks to the responsive nature of web standards, however, a new version of CSS was released alongside the new version of HTML. Officially named CSS Level 3, the new specification builds on CSS Level 2 modules, and includes additional modules. Given the wide acceptance and usage of CSS, major web browsers have been doing a much better job at implementing features more consistently, meaning that one code base is more likely to run consistently on different browsers.

Experimental features and vendor prefixes

As new features are added to the spec, and the spec itself progresses, browser vendors attempt to stay on top of things and provide the latest and greatest features to designers and end users. As of this book, however, not all features listed on the CSS3 specification are fully implemented by all browsers. The way you can tell if a feature is not yet fully supported by the browser (or that a feature may stop being supported by a particular browser) is that the CSS rule is prefixed by a dash, followed by the code name for the browser. For example, `-webkit-(rule name)`.

Vendor	Prefix
Google Chrome	`-webkit-`
Mozilla Firefox	`-moz-`
Microsoft Internet Explorer	`-ms-`
Opera	`-o-`
Safari	`-webkit-`

Eventually, the specification will stabilize even more, and all browsers will implement the CSS specification the same, and no vendor prefix will need to appear in your stylesheet code. But until then, you'll need to repeat some CSS Level 3 rules so that each browser will recognize the feature.

CSS preprocessors

It can sometimes be difficult to keep up with all the CSS features and their corresponding browser support. Some features have already gone out of the prefix (meaning that all major browsers support the rule without the vendor prefix keyword in front of the rule keyword). Still, many others haven't completely outgrown this experimental stage, and only some of the major browsers support them without any vendor prefix.

Some brave developers make the effort to stay on top of the latest browser updates, and update their code accordingly, by removing superfluous vendor prefixes from their stylesheet code. Others find this proactive effort to be counter productive, and instead include all possible versions of the rule to their code, in which case they would only need to update their stylesheet code one day in the far future, if at all.

Of course, repeating the same rule with each vendor prefix in front of it, followed by the non-prefixed rule, quickly makes your stylesheet files very large, and a nightmare to maintain. Find an approach that works best for you. There are also various tools available that help you maintain your CSS files, especially with regards to this evolving situation with the vendor prefix.

The two most popular such tools (also known as CSS preprocessors) are LESS (see `http://lesscss.org/`) and SASS (see `http://sass-lang.com/`). Although each preprocessor is slightly different, they all accomplish the same thing, namely, taking plain CSS stylesheets, then adding all the required vendor prefixes where needed.

CSS3 modules

The new CSS Level 3 modules can be divided into several modules, namely, **style attributes**, **selectors**, **colors**, and **media queries**.

Style attributes tell the browser how an element is to be rendered (or styled). This could be anything from a string of text being styled with a font size of 23 px, to styling a list of images rotated 45 degrees about their y-axis and placed above its own reflection, to styling various HTML nodes to animate every half a second using keyframe animation.

Selectors are the way you tell the browser what elements are to be styled. That is, through the special expression language of CSS selectors, you can address one or more elements whose styling rules follow the selector declaration. The new CSS3 selectors basically extend this expression language, making it possible to target different elements in different, more flexible ways.

Colors, as the name implies, hints to the browser how an element is to be shaded. Colors can be applied to the actual text on a web page, to the border surrounding text or other elements, as well as the background of elements, following the box model scheme.

Finally, media queries allow the stylesheet to target the document (or parts of it) based on various conditions. What's more, media queries are triggered in real time by the browser. In other words, if, for example, you specify a media query that defines CSS rules that should only apply when the browser window is no wider than a certain width, the browser will update the web page automatically as needed as the window is resized. This way a web page can be *responsive*, meaning that it responds immediately to any changes in its environment that causes any media query to become valid.

A brief definition of these modules will follow, but a more in-depth discussion, along with usage examples, can be found in subsequent chapters as each model is added to our games.

Style attributes

Within the style attributes module, we can subdivide the features into smaller modules that deal with custom fonts, text effects, other effects, and animation.

Attribute	Definition
border-radius	This specifies how much to round each corner or a box
border-image	This specifies an image to render over the border of a box
box-shadow	This specifies the direction and size of a drop shadow relative to a box
background-size	This specifies the size of a background image
background-origin	This specifies the offset position of background images
background-clip	This specifies how much to draw a background image
animation	This specifies various aspects of animation, such as keyframes, timing, effect, and so on
transform	This specifies various types of 2D and 3D transformations
transition	This specifies how two attributes should transition from one to the other
text-shadow	This specifies the direction and size of a drop shadow relative to text
@font-face	This specifies a font file that the browser can download into the user's system and use as a native font

Selectors

CSS selectors, first introduced in CSS Level 1, have always been fairly powerful and comprehensive.

Attribute	Definition
E[foo^="bar"]	It selects an E element with an attribute foo has a value that begins with bar
E[foo$="bar"]	It selects an E element with an attribute foo has a value that ends with bar
E[foo*="bar"]	It selects an E element with an attribute foo has a value that contains bar
E:root	It selects an E element at the root of the document
E:nth-child(n)	It selects the Nth E child element
E:nth-last-child(n)	It selects the Nth E child element counting from the last child element
E:nth-of-type(n)	It selects the Nth E sibling element of its type

Attribute	Definition
`E:nth-last-of-type(n)`	It selects the *N*th E sibling element of its type, counting from the last child element
`E:last-child`	It selects the last E element
`E:first-of-type`	It selects the first E sibling element of its type
`E:last-of-type`	It selects the last E sibling element of its type
`E:only-child`	It selects an E element if this is the only child node of its parent element
`E:only-of-type`	It selects an E element if this is the only sibling node of its type of its parent element
`E:empty`	It selects an E element if it has no child nodes and no text content
`E:target`	It selects an E element whose ID attribute matches the URL hash symbol
`E:enabled` `E:disabled`	It selects an E element that has been disabled through its corresponding attribute
`E:checked`	It selects an E element that has been checked through its corresponding attribute, or through appropriate user interaction
`E:not(S)`	It selects an E element that does not match a selector expression S
`F ~ E`	It selects an E element preceded by an F element

Source: Cascading Style Sheets (CSS) Snapshot 2010, W3C Working Group Note 12 May 2011
http://www.w3.org/TR/CSS/

Colors

The two main additions to colors in CSS Level 3 are the adoption of HSL colors, and an additional alpha channel. Before, you could specify a color using RGB by specifying a value between 0 and 255 for each channel (red, green, and blue). Now the extra alpha channel can be appended to the end of the attribute, allowing you to control the level of transparency:

```
div { background: RGBA(255, 255, 255, 0.5);
```

This CSS rule specifies a completely white background, with an opacity of 50 percent (half transparent) represented by the decimal fraction:

```
div { background: RGBA(100%, 100%, 100%, 50%);
```

Alternatively, you can specify the same CSS rule using percentages for all values, which might be easier to read, and make the expression more consistent.

Specifying colors using **Hue, Saturation, and Lightness (HSL)** is similarly easy, and arguably much more intuitive. Instead of using the RGB or RGBA keyword, you simply specify a color as HSL by using the keyword HSL (or HSLA if you would like to add the extra and optional alpha channel). Another benefit to using HSL over RGB is that RGB is hardware-oriented, whereas HSL is not.

```
div { background: HSL(359, 100%, 50%);
```

Here you specify a very bright red background color by setting the saturation to its limit, and lighting the color half way. Remember that setting the lightness channel to 100% will cause the color to be completely white (as a super bright light would do), while setting it to 0% will cause it to be completely black, as you would expect in a dark room; for example, see the following line of code:

```
div { background: HSLA(359, 100%, 50%, 50%);
```

Alternatively, you can specify the same CSS rule with a semi-transparent look by adding the alpha channel, and setting it to the 50% opacity.

The hue channel of HSL is a number between 0 and 359, which represents an angle in the color wheel, with red being 0 degrees, green being 120, and blue being 240. Note that this number wraps (since it's an angle value), so that 360 represents the same location in the wheel as 0. The saturation and lightness channels represent the percentage between being fully represented, and not at all.

Media queries

Media queries allow you check for specific features of the device rendering your HTML file. This is most commonly used in determining in real time the width and height of the window viewing your site. A common use case for this powerful feature is to determine whether the user is on a mobile device or not. A simple way to understand media queries is to think of them in terms of conditional statements, such as, "if the media is (...)". For example, as illustrated in the following screenshot, when a media is at least 500 pixels wide, one set of CSS rules gets applied. When the media is less than 500 pixels wide, an alternative set of CSS rules are used:

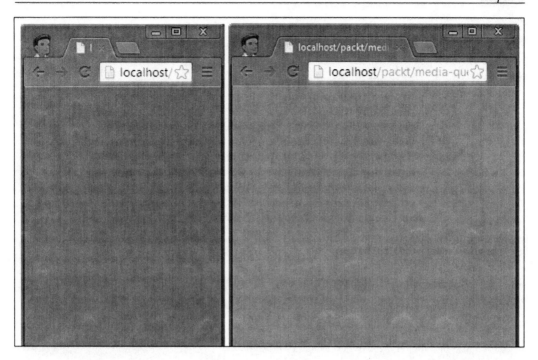

The same HTML structure is rendered differently based on the current state of the browser, thanks to media queries.

```
@media (orientation: portrait) {
    body {
        background: RGB(100%, 0%, 0%);
    }
}
```

This simple example specifically targets any device in portrait mode, and defines the CSS rule that specifies a red background color to the body element.

> Behind the scenes, the way that browsers implement this particular media query (the portrait mode) is by calculating the width of the window viewing the page with respect to the window's height. If the window happens to be higher than it is wider, then for all practical purposes, the page is considered to be in the portrait mode. Similarly, if you manually resize the window, or if it just happens to be in a position where it is wider than higher, then the browser will consider the page to be in the landscape mode, and any media queries targeting the mode will be triggered.

```
@media (max-width: 240px) {
    body {
        background: RGB(100%, 100%, 100%);
    }
}
```

In the previous example, we tell the browser to check if the window is less than or equal to 240 pixels wide. If it is, we define the CSS rule that tells the body tag to render itself with a white background.

```
@media (min-width: 800px) and (max-width: 1200px), (min-height:
5000px) {
    body {
        background: RGB(0%, 100%, 0%);
    }
}
```

As a last example for now, we tell the browser to check for a few different conditions in the previous code snippet. If at least one of the conditions evaluates to true, then the CSS rules inside that media query block will be made available to the page. This can be very helpful when reusing rules for different conditions, or when simply creating different rules to be applied in different situations. In this particular case, we set the background color of the body tag to a bright green whenever one of two (or both) conditions are true: the window is at least 5000 pixels tall, or the window's width is between 800 pixels and 1200 pixels (both values inclusive).

JavaScript APIs

As stated earlier, when HTML was created, it was not meant to be used for the development of large enterprise applications. When JavaScript was first created back in 1995, its main goal was to provide a simple scripting language that would allow web designers to add some logic to their web pages. This too was not meant to be a foundation tool from which large, complex applications would be developed.

However, as we have seen with HTML itself, as well as CSS, JavaScript has become very widely used, and developers have outgrown its limited capabilities. Seeing the direction in which developers were taking the language, in an attempt to leverage the Web as a platform, browser vendors started to make improvements to JavaScript as much as was in their power. As a result, very powerful JavaScript engines have emerged. So, as JavaScript become even more used, and as browser became even more powerful, a new set of additions has been added to JavaScript.

Today JavaScript is the most popular scripting language used on the Web. Given its capabilities and the latest tooling available for it, JavaScript has become a very good option for the development of large applications, especially for games. The latest JavaScript APIs allow for 2D and 3D graphics rendering, thread-like behavior, sockets, embedded databases, and a whole lot more. Best of all, this new functionality is built with security in mind, and is not only available on desktop computers, but can also be used in most devices connected to the World Wide Web.

New JavaScript APIs

While the following is not a comprehensive list of all the new and upcoming APIs and language features, it does cover the most significant, stable additions to JavaScript, especially ones that we can leverage for game development. A more detailed explanation of each of the APIs listed in the following list, as well as usage examples, are available in subsequent chapters:

API	Definition
Canvas API	It renders 2D or 3D graphics
Web Audio API	It controls playback of audio files
Web Video API	It controls playback of video files
Geolocation API	It provides access to geographical location of hosting device
Web Socket API	It provides a protocol for two way communication with a remote server
Web Workers API	It provides a thread-like, background worker for concurrent execution

API	Definition
Messaging API	It provides mechanism for communication between different browser contexts
Web Storage API	It provides a key-value pair persistence mechanism
Indexed Database API	It provides a NoSQL object storage mechanism
Drag and Drop API	It provides a native mechanism for dragging and dropping objects
Selector API	It provides a mechanism to select DOM elements using CSS selectors

There was another persistence API in HTML5 that was known as WebSQL. The spec for this API defined an asynchronous way to store and query data in the client using an actual built-in SQL-based database engine. The specification has been deprecated, and was replaced in its entirety by the more robust and more accepted IndexedDB API.

The Web as a platform

One of the most exciting things about HTML5 is that it is the main language of the World Wide Web. In other words, just about any device connected to the Web is able to run any games or applications you write in it. That makes the Web a very unique platform.

Doubtlessly, you have heard about or experienced such things as "the console war", where different video game console manufactures fight to win a larger percentage of the market over their competitors. While some people own more than one video game console, the majority of gamers own only one system. So what that means for a game developer is that, in order for their games to sell well, or in other words, in order for their games to be played and enjoyed by the largest possible amount of players, they need to develop the same version of a game for multiple platforms. This is an expensive and very time consuming process. Creating one game is already expensive and time consuming, let alone duplicating all that work for one or two other platforms.

Today, with more and more users world wide using the Internet, you don't have to go through what console video game developers do. As long as your game runs properly in a standard, modern web browser, it will run the same in just about any other browser across the world. In other words, your same code base can be enjoyed by over a billion people because they all run browsers that conform to HTML5. This makes the Web the largest, and greatest platform of all time. And the best part about it—it's totally free to develop for it. You don't need to have a special license or pay royalties to anyone in order to develop games or other applications for the Web.

The Open Web

As we mentioned earlier in the chapter, there are many buzz words in circulation today, whose meaning is unclear at best. Depending on who is telling you about the future of the human race, the specific definition of the term Open Web may vary.

Most commonly, the term *Open Web* refers not to a collection of technologies, but rather to a philosophy, if you will. The word open is meant in the sense that the Web is not closed up to a select few, or restricted by someone, or to a certain purpose. The World Wide Web is designed to be a place where all are welcome to come, create, innovate, consume, and enjoy. There is no centralized governing body over the Web. In reality, everybody owns the Web, especially in the sense that without the millions of individual servers and files, the Web would not be what it is.

You may be asking yourself what this all has to do with HTML or HTML5, or what is it in for you. Simply put, everything. Really. The reason the Open Web is such an exciting thing (and such a success so far) is because for the most part, everybody is on equal ground there. While there are dozens of different server-side languages and technologies, the part of the application that users interact with is written in three basic technologies, namely HTML, CSS, and JavaScript. The reason that now is such an exciting time to be a part of the Open Web, and the reason that you should consider yourself lucky to be able to be a part of it, is that these technologies are ripening and getting more mature.

HTML5 is built for the Open Web. It has enough power to leverage the distributed paradigm of the Web, and allows you, whether you're an independent developer or a member of a very large corporation with hundreds of other programmers, to create a desktop-like experience right on a browser, instantly reaching hundreds of millions of people world wide, all the time.

HTML5 – a game changer

Back when the World Wide Web was first introduced, its founders had one thing in mind—information exchange. Later, HTML was developed, with the goal of describing text documents. Again, the main aim was to aid the exchange and distribution of text documents.

Although HTML5 is fully backwards compatible, and still provides a terrific paradigm for information distribution, it is also designed with applications in mind. Today the Web is no longer used only for information exchange. People are now using the Web as a means to find entertainment—to watch movies, listen to the radio, and especially to play complete, full-featured video games.

HTML5 is a game changer in at least three ways, namely its wide adoption, its powerful capabilities, and the fact that it brings its features right to the browser—no plug-ins required. These three ways are explained as follows:

- **Wide adoption**: Not only are there over a billion people using the World Wide Web, but just about any device connected to it is able to execute HTML5 code. That means your program HTML5 games to be played on desktop computers, laptops, smart mobile phones, tablets, and even television sets.

- **Powerful capabilities**: Before HTML5, many commonly used tasks and features had to be programmed every time by developers—the drag-and-drop functionality, form validation, custom font faces, and so on. With HTML5, all of those things (and much more) are done for you by the web browser. You no longer need tens or hundreds of lines of code to create a drag-and-drop effect. The browser makes that job trivial for you, the developer.

- **No plug-ins**: While many of the features that HTML5 bring to the table had already bee seen before by means of third-party software, such as Macromedia Flash (which was later acquired by Adobe), or Java applets. The challenge with using these technologies as part of your web applications was that users had to install (and frequently upgrade) plug-ins that extended the browser's native capabilities. No only that, but developers also needed to learn and maintain at least two separate code bases, written in different languages. HTML5 solves that problem by cooking its own powerful feature set, allowing users to have a similar, and often better experience with the software, and best of all, without installing or worrying about a single plug-in.

In summary, the Web has gone from being a place to exchange information, to a place where users go to find quality entertainment. Responsive to this change, HTML5 has been designed to empower you to create the entertainment that users are looking for on the Web, in the form of fun video games.

Learning HTML5 through game development

In this book we will learn all about HTML5. We'll learn what each feature is meant to do and how you can use them. More than that, however, we want to make this teaching process fun, simple, and memorable. Thus, our approach might be somewhat different than most other books.

If you pay close attention to the way most teachers and authors teach new concepts, you will notice the following pattern: first the topic is explained, then, in an attempt to solidify the student's understanding of the material just covered, an example is given in order to show how the subject may be applied. The problem is that often this example is neither useful nor usable. For example, in computer programming books, you will see a common theme describing animals, food, or other abstract concepts that do not lend themselves well in real-world application. Thus, the student may become frustrated by the lack of real-world applications.

The key to effective learning, then, is a good example or use cases where the student may apply the newly acquired information. This way, when the student finds himself or herself in a real-world situation when their new skill could indeed be applied, they may readily recognize the opportunity and use the knowledge just gained. Furthermore, if the learning process is too abstract and theoretical, the student tends to get distracted or even bored. If the teaching process is involving and fun, on the other hand, the student is more likely to remember the concepts, but better yet, he or she is more likely to understand what is being taught.

Our approach in this book will be slightly different than what you might be accustomed to, in that we will focus most of our efforts not in listing as much theoretical information as we can about HTML5 and all that it involves, but rather in illustrating each topic through a fun game.

Why teach HTML5 through game development, you ask? There are many reasons for this. For starters, games are fun. Game development, although some of your friends might disagree, is also fun and very rewarding. Also, it just so happens that most of the features of HTML5 lend themselves so well to game development, that teaching HTML5 and not making the application for games is also rude. Finally, games are so fun, that learning a new programming technology through game development will provide the learner with both a very exciting set of examples to show each concept in action, and also a powerful physical product as the outcome of the learning process.

Our goal in this book is not, however, to teach you how to develop video games. What we're setting out to do is to teach you HTML5 first and foremost. If you already know game development, and have some experience in this arena, you will not only learn the latest and greatest features of HTML5, but also learn how they can be applied directly to designing and programming video games. If you're not a very experienced game developer, or haven't done any game development at all as a matter of fact, do not fear! You will still learn some techniques of game development, since we'll walk you through the concepts involved, but keep in mind that the focus of the book is HTML5.

The games we will be writing in the book will be fun, complete, and easy to extend. We will be building each game in layers, so that adding more capabilities or refactoring parts of it will be simple enough. At the end of each chapter you will have your own HTML5 game, which because of the Open Web, you will be able to share with all your friends with access to the Internet, as well as with hundreds of millions of people world wide.

Finally, since HTML is nothing more than text markup, and JavaScript is a dynamic, interpreted language, we will not be needing expensive or complex tools in order to develop our games. If you have a text editor program in your computer, and a modern web browser such as Google Chrome, Mozilla Firefox, Opera, Safari, or the latest Internet Explorer, then you are good to go. You will also need one type or another of a web server, which we'll go into more details about in the next chapter.

Thanks to the nature of the Open Web and HTML5, it doesn't matter one bit what kind of computer system you have. Whatever HTML5 code you write on your particular system will run just the same on somebody else's different computer. Best yet, there will be no installations required, which further lowers any barriers that could keep your games from being enjoyed by hundreds of millions of people world wide.

Summary

In this chapter we took a look at what HTML is, where it came from, and where it's headed. We discussed how the Open Web is a place where anyone with at least some knowledge of the technologies that make it work, and a lot of ambition (or enough curiosity) can reach an unprecedented audience at a virtually non-existent cost.

Although HTML5 is an upgrade of previous versions of HTML, the term also makes reference to the upgrade of other technologies that go hand in hand with the markup language, such as CSS and JavaScript. All three of these languages have been upgraded in response to current needs, and in order to take the Web to the next level. Many of the new features added to the languages attempt to shift the hard work of implementing commonly used functionality from the developer to the browser. What was once done by many developers through arduous, time consuming, and often expensive work, can now be done by the browser with minimal effort by the programmer. Also, many of the new features and capabilities of HTML5 make the web platform a very aggressive opponent to the desktop paradigm. The idea of individual desktop computers running in complete isolation from each other, each running program from its own central storage system is steadily going away. The replacement is a cloud-based paradigm, where the software in question is sent to each user from one central server connected to the Web. And since these web applications are executed in the users' browser, some of the major parts of the application are written in pure HTML5.

HTML5 is the perfect technology to master right now because it is at the core of the Open Web. Thanks to the responsive and evolving nature of HTML5, we can only wait to see what the future has in store for us, as browsers continue to get more powerful, and the cost of computing continues to decline.

We will explore the exciting world of HTML5, and cover its major concepts and building blocks by designing and developing fun and engaging games. We're taking this approach not only because games are fun, but also because many of the new capabilities in HTML5 lend themselves so well to the complex problems of programming video games. Also, by successfully programming full games in pure HTML5 technology, we will be able to test and prove the true capacity of HTML5 and the Open Web.

In the next chapter we will take the first step towards building awesome web-based games. First we'll set up a development environment by installing a web server. Next we will build an HTML5 web portal from which we can access our games, as well as get a bit of practice using the new semantic elements.

2
HTML5 Typography

Now that we have our environment set up, we're ready to take a deep dive into the actual code behind HTML5. This is where the book begins to take off, since no matter how much theory you learn, it's very difficult to master a programming language without some keyboard time.

The game we'll be developing in this chapter will be a typing game, with some emphasis in the typography aspect of it. Again, I remind you that the focus of this book is not to teach game development, but rather to teach you all about HTML5. Thus, the general approach we'll take to coding the games will not necessarily be most optimal for general game development, although all of the games covered in the book will perform fairly well in most major browsers.

The game

For lack of creativity, and to steer away from a possible lawsuit from a grumpy game company, we'll name this first game simply `Typography Game`. I know, that's not the most impressive game you've heard of, but at least it does a great job of explaining what the game is generally about.

The overall storyline for the game, as well as its general point, goes as follows: correctly type a phrase that is shown to you word-by-word, and win your dream boat. If you don't type each character correctly and fast enough then **Snooty McSnootington** wins the boat and you lose the game skills.

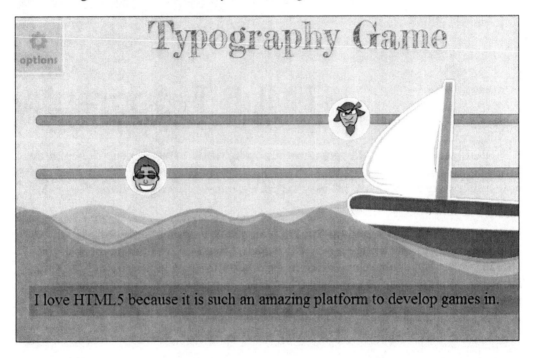

It's hard to convey all the details about this user interface from a single screenshot, but the waves in that beautiful ocean are actually very smoothly animated, as well as the boat, which floats freely and is tossed about by the waves. Also, although there are exactly six images in the entire game, all of the components used in this game are DOM elements. The boat, the waves, and the characters are done using divs, images, and other semantic HTML5 elements. All of the animations are done using native CSS3 features.

The rest of the chapter will list all of the HTML, CSS, and JavaScript features used in the game, show examples of how to use them, and how they were used in the game. The coding style used is geared towards simplicity, so don't mind the global variables, the inconsistent use of object oriented principles, and the overall rudimentary graphics. With the basic HTML5 concepts in place, you can take the game to the next level by applying whatever additional improvements you may feel are necessary to make the game more polished or scalable from a development perspective.

We'll organize the game into three separate files: an `index.html` file, where we'll host all of the HTML structures and bring together the other two files, namely a CSS file and a JavaScript file. This should be a pretty standard file structure but feel free to adjust things to best fit your needs and habits.

Following the file structure convention we created last chapter when we built our web portal, we'll need to create a directory inside the root directory of our project, and call it typography. Inside this directory, we'll create the following files and directories:

- `packt/typography`
- `packt/typography/index.html`
- `packt/typography/fonts`
- `packt/typography/css`
- `packt/typography/css/style.css`
- `packt/typography/js`
- `packt/typography/main.js`
- `packt/typography/img`

 I'll walk you through the process of finding and downloading custom fonts, when we get to that section later in the chapter. As for the images, you can draw or buy your own, or download the same ones I drew for the game from the website `http://www.CHANGE-THIS-FOR-A-REAL-WEBSITE`.

Game elements

There were nine HTML5 elements used in this game. Each will be explained within its main category of either HTML, CSS, or JavaScript. The game itself is composed of roughly 15 elements, as depicted in the illustrations as follows:

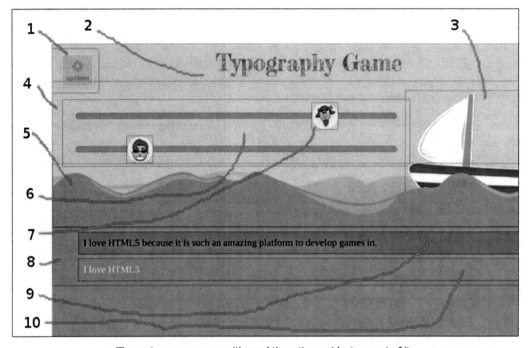

The main game screen, with a subtle options widget as part of it.

After a game is finished, whether or not the player wins the game, a score board is shown, where the player is given the opportunity to enter his or her name as well as start a new game.

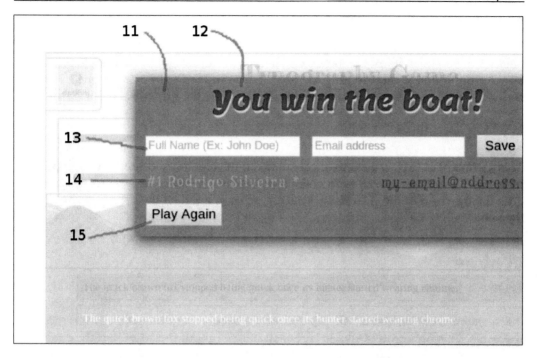

The preceding screenshot shows a messaging widget to indicate that the player has won or lost, as well as a leaderboard widget.

In order for us to easily identify each of the major visual game components, we'll list them as follows:

The options widget

This widget allows the player to select a preset difficulty level. Selecting a harder difficulty level will make the enemy move faster across his track towards the boat. Additionally, we could have made it so that the phrases that the player would need to type would be harder or easier based on the difficulty setting. However, we have left this implementation detail as an exercise to the reader.

The game title

This text based widget simply displays the main title of the game. Note that the type face used there is pure text (no images), using a custom web font. Its only purpose is to decorate the user interface.

Boat

This animated widget serves the purpose of strengthening the user interface by helping to tell the story of the game. The boat is a simple HTML element (div), with a background image representing the boat. The animated path that the boat follows is done strictly in CSS, and is managed completely by the browser.

Sky

This section of HTML is used to encapsulate all the elements located on the top half of the user interface, as well as to make it possible to animate the sky. As the game goes on, the color of the sky changes subtly, so as to emulate the setting and rising of the sun.

Waves

There is a section of HTML classed as *ocean*, which is a section that encapsulates the area where the waves are stored. Each wave (there are two in use in this case) is a div element with a width of 100 percent, and a background image that represents the wave. This background image is repeated throughout the entire width of the div element, and is animated through CSS in order to give the illusion of motion, following a pattern of waves in the ocean.

Tracks

This widget is a section of HTML that encapsulates the individual track widgets, along with the player that uses that track.

Players

Each of those icons represent the individual players in this game. To keep things as simple as possible, there are only two players in the game: you (the hero), and Mr. Snooty McSnootington (the enemy). Additionally, we could have very easily added functionality to the options widget to allow the player to choose specific icons for both, the hero and the enemy, since the code that controls what icons are used is a simple CSS class that can be added to or removed from the icon objects.

The main container

This section of HTML holds the elements that control the game, which is everything below the sky widget.

Words to write

Here is where we display the words that the user must type when the game starts. Behind the scenes, this is a simple block-level HTML element, whose only purpose is just to display a few words.

Words written

Although, this widget is identical to the words to write widget (with slightly different styling, of course), this widget is a bit more dynamic, as it will respond to user actions. When a user presses a key on the keyboard, that input will be displayed there. If the character typed matches the expected character based on whatever is shown in the Words to write widget, then the character is displayed in white. If the character is incorrect, it'll be displayed in red, with a line through it, indicating very strongly that a mistake was made. The user can use the *Backspace* key to delete any or all characters displayed in this widget. As each correct character is typed in, the hero will move to the right proportionally to the percentage of characters entered, relative to the total amount to be typed.

The message container

This section of HTML is displayed atop a semitransparent element to give the appearance of an overlay box. The widget is primarily meant to be a generic communication tool, through which we can inform the player of events, such as letting them know that the game is over, or that he or she won or lost the game. Additionally, we have added four other elements to it in order to make the game more engaging.

The message title

Very similar in styling and purpose to main game title widget, this element simply notifies the user of the contents of the rest of the message container widget.

The new champion form

The idea behind this form is to simulate those old-school leaderboards used in old arcade games. Once you win a game against Mr. Snooty McSnootington, you are given the opportunity to enter your name and e-mail address to be shown in the leaderboard as in the following screenshot. Of course, that information is symbolic, and only serves the purpose of illustrating how we can use HTML5's web forms. The information generated by the form is not saved anywhere, and thus, it goes away after each page refresh (or when the game is closed or navigated away from). Again, it would be a trivial task to either email the contents of that form, save it to a backend server, or even stored it locally in the browser, through any one of the many persistence or storage APIs that we'll discuss in *Chapter 4, Using HTML5 to Catch a snake*, later in the book.

Leaderboard

Any data entered in the new champion form (provided that the data entered is valid) is displayed here. The number next to each name simply shows the order that each name was entered. The asterisk to the right of the name indicates the difficulty level that the game was played (level 1 — easy; in this particular case). For a more engaging experience, we could have kept track of how long it took the player to complete the game, how many mistakes were made, or somehow calculate an overall score and display it here. The reason we chose a full name and an email address was to show how to perform form validation in HTML5. This alone is probably the most powerful and exciting feature of HTML5 used in this game. What used to take developers hundreds of lines of code, and often lots of repeated code, now only takes a couple of HTML attributes that the browser enforces.

Game controls

Finally, the message container widget includes controls that allows the player to start a new game.

In order to make the code more concise and easier to explain, we'll be aiming at less portable code, where the only requirement will be that the code runs properly in at least one browser.

Most of the APIs used are indeed very portable (meaning that the code executes the same in most major browsers), but certainly not all of it, especially any experimental CSS APIs that require vendor prefixes. For maximum compatibility with the following examples, I recommend you use the latest version of Google **Chrome** or Google **Chromium**, or at least any webkit-based browser, such as Apple Safari.

The reason for this approach, first and foremost, is to simplify the teaching process. There's no need to explain a given feature, then show code example that is 99 percent identical, but differs only in the first part of the feature name, which is the vendor name. The reasoning behind selecting webkit as the browser engine of choice is also very simple; we had to choose something, so why not webkit? Besides, Google Chrome and Apple Safari have great market penetration, as well as an incredible set of tools to help us in the development process (such as Google Chrome's Developer Tools).

Finally, the *nine* HTML5 elements used in the game, along with their corresponding category:

HTML

Both of the HTML features used in this game can be used in JavaScript or by the browser directly. The web form elements and attributes add great functionality to the browser out of the box, while the data attributes are more meaningful when tied to the JavaScript. In the game of our `Typography Game`, we have built these elements within a context that made sense, but we could certainly have used other techniques (such as storing the data represented by the data attributes strictly in code), or used the elements and attributes we did use in different ways.

The web form

The new form API added in HTML5 is one of the most visible additions to the language. With it you have access to 13 new input types, as well as countless new attributes that make form development fast, fun, and fascinating. Most of the additions will probably look familiar to you visually, since the effects that they add natively to the browser had already been done for a long time. These effects include things such as placeholder text, form validation, auto focusing fields, and so on so forth.

Two of the 13 new input types were used in the game, along with a handful of attributes for each of them, including form validation and field placeholders. Following is a brief explanation of how these elements were used in the game. An in-depth discussion of how they work and how to use them is found the the next section.

Range input

The new range input type is a slider that allows the user to select a value by moving the slider horizontally. In the game, we used the range input as a means to select a difficulty level. The range specified in this game is from 1 to 3, with 1 being the easiest difficulty level and 3 being the toughest.

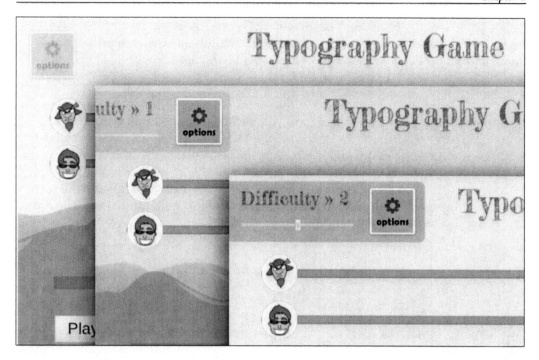

The container that holds the input type range uses CSS to toggle the options menu and fade it out when not in use.

Email input

The email input type looks exactly the same as the old text input type, but with a few benefits. First, when used in a mobile device, the input type hints to the operating system what kind of information it expects, in which case the operating system can display a special keyboard to the user. For example, if the user attempts to enter data into a number input type, where only numbers are allowed, a mobile operating system can display a keyboard that only has numbers. In the case of the email type, the keyboard displayed is normally one that includes the @ symbol which makes it easier and more convenient for the user to enter the information into the web form.

The second benefit of using the email input type, which is also a benefit to desktop users, is that the browser itself can validate the data entered by the user. If the field is set to be validated and the data in the field does not match the basic format of an email address, the browser will tell the user that there is a problem and the form will not be submitted.

In the game, we use this feature whenever a player wins, by asking the user to enter his or her full name and email address. That information is used in a leaderboard, like you have probably seen in older games. While the user is not forced to enter any of the information asked for in the form, if the user does choose to input any information the data will be validated automatically by the browser.

The exciting thing about automatic form validation is that you can customize your form through the HTML attributes included, making only required fields validated, what the error message says, and so on so forth. Also, even if the user disables JavaScript functionality in the browser the form will still be validated and handled by the browser. Of course, as you well know, one of the main rules about taking input from the user is that you should never trust the user and always validate and sanitize any, and all user input in the server as well.

If no data is entered or is in the wrong format, the browser will tell you about it and keep the form from being submitted.

Data attributes

As part of the effort, for more semantic document structure, HTML5 allows us to create our own, custom element attributes. Before HTML5, most browsers simply ignored element attributes that it did not understand (for example, a custom attribute made specially for one's application) but the downsides to this practice included the fact that the document could not be validated, the behavior was somewhat unpredictable, and there was a chance that a new release of the language introduced attributes of the same name, thus making your old custom attributes invalid. Now, we can safely create custom attributes for elements and none of the downsides just mentioned would apply.

In our game, we used data attributes to do two things, namely to specify the minimum speed that a player can move across the track and to specify that a generic button should trigger a new game (so that any button with that data attribute did not need any extra logic within JavaScript in order to act like a special button).

CSS

Since this game was intended to show off the more visual aspects of HTML5, we focused most of our efforts in making the interface of the game a real eye-candy. Since CSS is all about that visual presentation, most of the featured employed fall under this category.

Web fonts

Prior to HTML5's ability to handle custom fonts, web designers and developers were limited to a handful of type faces that could be used in a website or web application. Over time, there were a few solutions developed to solve this problem, but none were particularly impressive and most (if not all) broke some of the browser's functionality. For example, one common technique to display custom text involved the use of JavaScript to dynamically replace each character in a string with an actual image of that character using the custom font. The problems with this approach included the fact that one needed to create and manage all of those images. The user had to download all of those images, and worst of all, the resulting text could not be selected, copied, resized, and the color could not be changed.

Now we can simply specify the name of a font, along with the actual font file, which the browser can download if the user's operating system doesn't have that font installed and use just as any other font.

In the game, we use three different custom fonts to create just the right visual effect and make the texts in the game match the desired visual theme. The three fonts used are open source fonts, which can be downloaded from the internet and used for free. The fonts used were Lemon, Mystery Quest, and Fredericka the Great. Amazing names, don't you agree?

Prior to looking for some fonts for the game, I had no idea that these fonts existed. Best of all, it only took me a couple of minutes to go through a large collection of open source fonts (from Google's Web Fonts tool) and find just what I wanted.

Since a font file is an external asset just like anything else that is downloaded from the server, there is a period of time between the time the browser starts downloading a font file and the time when the page is ready to be rendered. Different browsers handle this situation differently. For example, webkit hides the text until the font asset is ready. Other browsers may render the text with a fallback or default font until the web font file is ready, then swap the fonts and re-render the text.

Transitions

A CSS transition attribute tells the browser what attributes it applies to and how long the transition should last. Once those properties change, the browser will interpolate the beginning and end states and generate a very smooth transition for the duration specified. Of course, this can only be applied to attributes represented by some numerical value, such as font size, background color (represented by either an RGB or HSL value, or a hexadecimal number, all of which can be converted to percentages), element position, and so on. Values that do not get smoothly interpolated in CSS transitions include font-family, background images, or any other attribute that don't have in-between values, such as display block and display none.

In the game, the only uses of transition were with the options menu, the message container, and in moving the players across the tracks. The options menu is set to be pushed off the left side of the screen and the main icon that represents it is 75 percent transparency. Once the user hovers the mouse over that icon, it transitions to zero percent transparency (fully visible) and the rest of the menu transitions onto its left side to move to the right until its left edge snaps to the left edge of the browser.

The message container uses a similar effect, and that it is always positioned at the top of the screen, its width being 100 percent the window viewport and its height is set to zero by default (when the container is `closed`). When we want to display a message to the user, add the CSS class `open` to the container widget which sets the container's height to 100 percent, thus triggering a smooth transition that simulates a slide-in effect.

Finally, we used transitions to move the players from right to left within the tracks to which they are each bound. This was a very easy task to accomplish, even though the hero and the enemy are controlled slightly different. The way the enemy moves is simple: at every tick of the game timer we increment the enemy's horizontal position (by changing its left style attribute) by whatever value is set in its data-speed data attribute. The smooth transition between the two points is handled by the browser. The way the hero moves is similar, with the exception that the data-speed is always set to zero (otherwise it'd be moving automatically without the user having to type anything) and at each key press we check whether the character typed in was what was expected, in which case we advance the hero a percentage of the way to the end of the track, which is relative to the percentage of characters typed in properly and relative to the total amount of characters. For example, if the user correctly typed in the tenth character of a phrase that has 100 characters, then we move the hero 10 percent of the way across its track. Both, the hero and the enemy, have checks in place so that they can't be moved beyond the width of their respective tracks.

Animations

Probably the most powerful feature of CSS3, the animation attribute, allows for named keyframe animation very similar to the formerly popular Adobe Flash. The way it works is incredibly simple: you create an animation sequence, give it a name, and specify one or more CSS attributes to be applied at each keyframe. Each keyframe represents a moment in time when those attributes should be added to whatever element you associate with that animation sequence. Then, every moment in time between two keyframes are smoothly interpolated by the browser and the illusion of animation is achieved.

In the game, we use animations to give life to the ocean waves, to move the boat in its path, and to make the sky fade darker and lighter with the passing of time, thus simulating the rising and setting of the sun. Although this may seem like a complicated task, animating elements is so easy that the main limitation you're likely to run into may be creativity. If you're somewhat familiar with CSS and how to use it to apply various styles to elements, then learning and using the animation API should be a natural next step.

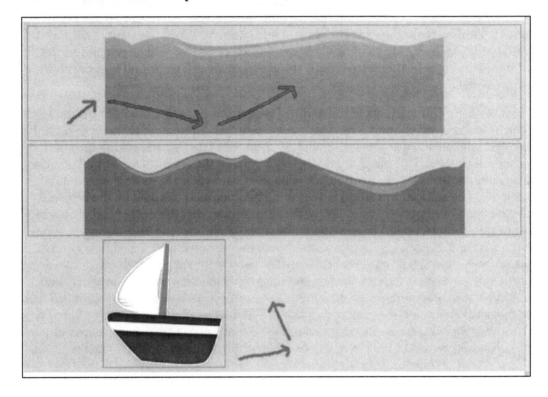

Each animated object was nothing more than a `div` element with a background image set to it. The waves' background image was set to repeat about the x axis, whereas the boat's background image was set to no-repeat. The boat's width and height was set to match the image it represented, whereas the waves had a different height set for each of them (the wave positioned behind everything was a bit taller so that it could be seen behind the other wave), but with a width of 100 percent, so that it always fills the width of the monitor viewing the app, no matter how wide that monitor is. At the end of this animation cycle, the objects follow that same path, but in reverse, making the animation seem continuous and always smooth.

The easiest element to animate was the sky, since it only had two keyframes. At the first keyframe, the `div` element that represented the sky was set to have a light blue color for its background. The last keyframe changed that background color to a slightly darker blue. For a more dramatic effect, we could have had this last keyframe define a very dark color for the background. For an even more drastic effect representing this night fall, we could also have added another `div` on top of this sky element, with its background image being a transparent image with white dots scattered about it. Each dot would represent a star. Then, at the same pace that the sky gets darker, we set the opacity of this element to become more visible (less transparent), so that it animates from fully transparent to fully opaque. The final effect would be that as the sky gets darker, then stars would appear.

The boat was animated with three keyframes: the first placed it at some position slightly above the waves, the second moved it to the right and up, and the third keyframe moved it significantly higher, and a bit to the left. The trick to making the animation between these points seem somewhat natural, and more like something would move on the ocean in real life, is to make the distance the object moves between two different keyframes different. For example, the horizontal distance the boat moves between the first and second keyframe is different than the horizontal displacement used between the second and third keyframes. The vertical displacement between those keyframes are even more drastic. If the distances were all the same, our eye would get used to the same familiar pattern of motion, and the animation would soon appear too repetitive and uninteresting.

Animating the waves was equally easy. Although there were two sets of waves, they both use the same animation set. The only difference is that the set of waves positioned behind the other (the back wave) was set to move slower, so that it looked like it was farther away, and the animations didn't seem to be the same.

All that was animated in these wave elements (remember, a wave element is just a `div` with a repeating background image) was the position of the background image. The `div` elements themselves were always static and absolutely positioned atop each other. Since the elements were transparent wherever their background images were transparent, we were able to apply a background color to the element holding all three of these elements (both waves and the boat), which we set to be the sky element, which animated the background color.

Although the final result looks fun and slightly complex, the work required to put this sort of thing together is really no more complicated or difficult than setting up any other design using plain CSS, especially because this is nothing more than plain old CSS.

At the time of this writing, there were a handful of tools aimed at helping developers create and manage keyframe animations. While many of these tools were free and many are completely cloud-based (written using HTML5 technologies), if you're looking for an enterprise level tool to help you build professional animations truly similar to what we're used to seeing with Adobe Flash, you'll need to invest in some cash in more advanced and fine tuned tools. Although some of these tools may not be the best option for a developer on a budget (or one with no budget at all), their quality and power are normally orders of magnitude beyond whatever any of the free tools can provide.

If you're only developing for fun, or for the learning experience, the plethora of free tools available online should be more than enough to get you going with CSS3 keyframe animations. However, if your goal is to build high-end applications and you need the high precision and control over the animations, then a professional tool might be well worth your investment.

One particularly popular free web-based CSS animation generator can be found at `http://www.css3maker.com/`. On the other hand, Adobe makes a terrific product called Adobe Edge Animate, which can be purchased at `http://html.adobe.com/edge/animate/`.

The text shadows

This new text attribute in CSS allows you to simulate a shadow effect around text. Behind the scenes, what the browser really does is create a copy of the text that the shadow is being applied to, then displace it behind the original text based on the values you specify as the vertical and horizontal offset. You can also tell the browser how much to blur this "shadow" version of the text by specifying a values between zero and whatever integer value you desire. After a point, depending on the size of the original text, the blur is so high that the text is virtually invisible, so supplying very large numbers can be counter productive.

The only instance in the game where text shadow is used is in the message container's title. Since the rest of the user interface for the game used pretty flat graphics with very subtle or no gradients at all, I thought I'd use text shadows to add a solid, lighter shadow to give continuation to the theme of flat, single dimensional graphics.

The CSS3 text shadow API allows you to specify an arbitrary number of displaced and blurred copies of a text string.

The box shadows

Similar to text shadows, box shadows place one or more boxes behind a particular element, with a vertical and horizontal offset specified as parameters, with a third parameter being the amount of blur to be applied to the shadow. You can specify solid colors or use the optional alpha channel in order to add varying levels of opacity to it. Alternatively, the shadow can be applied to the inside of the container to which it is bound. Note that any box shadow applied to elements, if they're placed behind the box, are placed outside the border, if one is available, ignoring any margin the element may have. Shadows placed inside an element are placed just inside the border, if one is present, ignoring any padding added to the element.

In the game, there are two instances of a CSS box shadow. One shows off the traditional shadow behind an element, and is applied to the message container. The other instance of box shadow in the game is applied to the tracks that hold each player. In this case, the shadow is intended to convey the effect that the tracks are pressed in into the page, which is done by using the attribute that places the shadow inside the box. If the shadow is placed outside the box, the effect given is that of the box being stacked over the page.

The white line on the bottom of each track is just a bottom border, but the same effect could have been accomplished by adding a second box shadow.

The border radius

Before the border radius property was available, the same effect it provides could be achieved by positioning images of rounded corners to the corners of elements. This was a tedious task to do and the final effect was rarely as impressive as intended. With the CSS3 border radius property, we can apply an arbitrary amount of roundness to one or more corners of a container element.

Keep in mind that, although it is possible to make a
`container` element look completely round by specifying
a border radius value to all four corners large enough
proportional to each side's length, the element is still a
rectangle to the browser. In other words, if you float two or
more elements that have been made to look round through
CSS, they will behave like rectangles and not circles.

The flow of elements and text in HTML5 is still rectangular
based, although there are experimental APIs that allow us to
specify arbitrary shapes through which text flows. For more
information about these particular CSS APIs (called **regions**
and **exclusions**), see *Chapter 6, Adding Features to Your Games*.

There was only one use of CSS border radius in the game, which was on the right
side of the navigation options widget. The API allows us to specify which specific
side to apply a border radius to, and to demonstrate this feature, only two of the four
sides of the container were rounded.

The player icons could have been more HTML5-ish instead of just being a transparent
image applied to the background of the element. One possibility could be to have
each icon be a rectangular image, which we could apply to the background of the
container representing each player, then we could have used border radius to make
the element look completely circular. An optional box shadow could also have been
added to create the same shadow effect achieved by the photo editing software used
to create the images. One benefit of using this technique would be that the native
effects would scale much better, meaning that if you zoom the page in or out, the
image will eventually look distorted and pixelated, whereas any border radius, box
shadow, or borders added to the element would always look smooth and fresh.

JavaScript

Although the logic that drives this game is fairly simple, and quite a bit limited, there
is still a decent amount of JavaScript code in order to make the game work. Since
we're trying to focus on HTML5 features, we'll only look at one particular API used
in the code that can more or less be considered HTML5. This is the **selectors API**,
which was first drafted by the W3C back on May of 2006.

Query selectors

If you have been doing any web development at all in the last several years, you've certainly heard or, used, and have fallen in love with the popular JavaScript library jQuery. Among its many powerful features, one of jQuery's most useful tools is its amazing DOM selector API, which allows you to retrieve the DOM elements by simply using CSS selectors and pseudo selectors, as opposed to using the limited `document.getElementById()`, `document.getElementsByClassName()`, and `document.getElementsByName()` methods, among other equally limited ones.

The good news is that this powerful nodes selector API is now all native to modern browsers. Since the feature is native to the browser, it is much faster and more stable. Furthermore, since the feature is native to the browser, there is no need to import a library to handle the task.

This game, as well as all the others described in this book, uses the new selectors API level 1. Since there are no visual elements that can be seen form query selectors, we'll deepen the discussion about its usage in the next section, where we'll also take a look at some code examples.

API usage

Now that we've discussed what all of the game elements are and how each HTML5 feature was used to fulfill that role, let's take a deeper look at how to make the most out of each of these APIs. For each of the following APIs, we'll provide a more concrete definition of the feature, what its intended use is, and a code example will follow. You may also refer to the complete source code attached at the end of the chapter in order to fill the gap between the code sample and how that feature fits in with the rest of the game code base. It is also recommended that you code along and play with the various settings and values in order to experiment with and more fully understand each API.

Web forms

The new HTML5 web forms API adds 13 new input types that allows for a much more flexible and powerful experience. What's more, web forms are also able to validate themselves requiring zero JavaScript intervention.

New input types

The following are the new input types defined in the new web forms chapter of the HTML5 specification:

Date

The date input type allows the user to select a specific date from a browser-supplied calendar. The specific format and styling of this calendar is unique to the browser and platform used. The data that results from a date selection is of the form YYYY-MM-DD.

```
<input type="date"
  min="1935-12-16"
  max="2013-08-19"
/>
```

The optional attributes min and max can be used to force validation of the date selected by the user to be within a given range. Other valid attributes for the date input type include the following:

- name (value must be a string): Identifies a particular field by the string value associated with the attribute

- disabled (acceptable values include disabled, "", or empty): Specifies that the element is disabled and cannot receive control

- autocomplete (acceptable values include on or off): Specifies whether the browser should store values entered by the user, so inputting a stored value in the future can be automatically completed by the browser upon hint by user

- autofocus (acceptable values include autofocus, "", or empty): Specifies to the browser that the element must receive focus immediately after the document finishes loading

- min (value must be a valid date in the form of "yyyy-mm-dd"): Specifies the lowest date allowed to be selected by the user

- max (value must be a valid date in the form of "yyyy-mm-dd"): Specifies the highest date allowed to be selected by the user

- readonly (acceptable values include readonly, "", or empty): Specifies that the value of this element cannot be changed by the user

- step (acceptable values include any or any positive integer): Specifies how the value attribute of the element is to change

- required (acceptable values include required, "", or empty): Specifies that this element must have a valid value in order for the form to be allowed to submit

- value (value must be a valid date in the form of "yyyy-mm-dd"): Specifies the actual date represented by this element

Month

The month input type allows the user to select a specific month and year from a browser-supplied calendar. The specific format and styling of this calendar is unique to the browser and platform used. The data that results from a date selection is of the form YYYY-MM.

```
<input type="month"
  min="1935-12"
  max="2013-08"
/>
```

Other valid attributes for the date input type include the following:

- name (value must be a string): Identifies a particular field by the string value associated with the attribute

- disabled (acceptable values include disabled, "", or empty): Specifies that the element is disabled and cannot receive control.

- autocomplete (acceptable values include on or off): Specifies whether the browser should store values entered by the user so inputting a stored value in the future can be automatically completed by the browser upon hint by user

- autofocus (acceptable values include autofocus, "", or empty): Specifies to the browser that the element must receive focus immediately after the document finishes loading

- min (value must be a valid date in the form of "yyyy-mm"): Specifies the lowest date allowed to be selected by the user

- max (value must be a valid date in the form of "yyyy-mm"): Specifies the highest date allowed to be selected by the user

- readonly (acceptable values include readonly, "", or empty): Specifies that the value of this element cannot be changed by the user

- step (acceptable values include any or any positive integer): Specifies how the value attribute of the element is to change

- required (acceptable values include required, "", or empty): Specifies that this element must have a valid value in order for the form to be allowed to submit

- value (value must be a valid date in the form of "yyyy-mm"): Specifies the actual date represented by this element

Week

The week input type allows the user to select a specific week of a year from a browser-supplied calendar. The specific format and styling of this calendar is unique to the browser and platform used. The data that results from a date selection is of the form YYYY-Www (for example, 2013-W05).

```
<input type="week"
  min="1935-W51"
  max="2013-W34"
/>
```

Other valid attributes for the date input type include the following:

- name (value must be a string): Identifies a particular field by the string value associated with the attribute

- disabled (acceptable values include disabled, "", or empty): Specifies that the element is disabled and cannot receive control

- autocomplete (acceptable values include on or off): Specifies whether the browser should store values entered by the user so inputting a stored value in the future can be automatically completed by the browser upon hint by user

- autofocus (acceptable values include autofocus, "", or empty): Specifies to the browser that the element must receive focus immediately after the document finishes loading

- min (value must be a valid date in the form of "yyyy-Www", where "ww" must be a two digit representation of the week number): Specifies the lowest date allowed to be selected by the user

- max (value must be a valid date in the form of "yyyy-Www", where "ww" must be a two digit representation of the week number): Specifies the highest date allowed to be selected by the user

- readonly (acceptable values include readonly, "", or empty): Specifies that the value of this element cannot be changed by the user

- step (acceptable values include any or any positive integer): Specifies how the value attribute of the element is to change

- required (acceptable values include required, "", or empty): Specifies that this element must have a valid value in order for the form to be allowed to submit

- value (value must be a valid date in the form of "yyyy-Www", where "ww" must be a two digit representation of the week number): Specifies the actual date represented by this element

Time

The time input type allows the user to select a specific time of day. The data in this element is of the form HH:MM:SS.Ms.

```
<input type="time"
  min="16:23:42.108"
  max="23:59:59.999"
/>
```

Other valid attributes for the date input type include the following:

- name (value must be a string): Identifies a particular field by the string value associated with the attribute
- disabled (acceptable values include disabled, "", or empty): Specifies that the element is disabled and cannot receive control
- autocomplete (acceptable values include on or off): Specifies whether the browser should store values entered by the user so inputting a stored value in the future can be automatically completed by the browser upon hint by user
- autofocus (acceptable values include autofocus, "", or empty): Specifies to the browser that the element must receive focus immediately after the document finishes loading
- min (value must be a valid partial time in the form of "HH:MM:SS.Mss", "HH:MM:SS", or "HH:MM"): Specifies the lowest date allowed to be selected by the user
- max (value must be a valid partial time in the form of "HH:MM:SS.Mss", "HH:MM:SS", or "HH:MM"): Specifies the highest date allowed to be selected by the user
- readonly (acceptable values include readonly, "", or empty): Specifies that the value of this element cannot be changed by the user
- step (acceptable values include any or any positive integer): Specifies how the value attribute of the element is to change
- required (acceptable values include required, "", or empty): Specifies that this element must have a valid value in order for the form to be allowed to submit
- value (value must be a valid partial time in the form of "HH:MM:SS.Mss", "HH:MM:SS", or "HH:MM"): Specifies the actual date represented by this element

Datetime

The datetime input type allows the user to select a specific date and time (including time zone) from a browser-supplied calendar. The specific format and styling of this calendar is unique to the browser and platform used. The data that results from a date selection is of the form YYYY-MM-DDTHH:MM:SS-UTC.

```
<input type="datetime"
  min="1935-12-16T16:23:42-08:00"
  max="2013-08-19T23:59:59-09:00"
/>
```

Other valid attributes for the date input type include the following:

- name (value must be a string): Identifies a particular field by the string value associated with the attribute

- disabled (acceptable values include disabled, "", or empty): Specifies that the element is disabled and cannot receive control

- autocomplete (acceptable values include on or off): Specifies whether the browser should store values entered by the user so inputting a stored value in the future can be automatically completed by the browser upon hint by user

- autofocus (acceptable values include autofocus, "", or empty): Specifies to the browser that the element must receive focus immediately after the document finishes loading

- min (value must be a valid date time, as defined in the RFC 3339): Specifies the lowest date allowed to be selected by the user

- max (value must be a valid date time, as defined in the RFC 3339): Specifies the highest date allowed to be selected by the user

- readonly (acceptable values include readonly, "", or empty): Specifies that the value of this element cannot be changed by the user

- step (acceptable values include any or any positive integer): Specifies how the value attribute of the element is to change

- required (acceptable values include required, "", or empty): Specifies that this element must have a valid value in order for the form to be allowed to submit

- value (value must be a valid date time, as defined in the RFC 3339): Specifies the actual date represented by this element

Datetime-local

The datetime-local input type allows the user to select a specific date and time (not including time zone) from a browser-supplied calendar. The specific format and styling of this calendar is unique to the browser and platform used. The data that results from a date selection is of the form YYYY-MM-DDTHH:MM:SS.

```
<input type="datetime-local"
  min="1935-12-16T16:23:42"
  max="2013-08-19T23:59:59"
/>
```

Other valid attributes for the date input type include the following:

- name (value must be a string): Identifies a particular field by the string value associated with the attribute

- disabled (acceptable values include disabled, "", or empty): Specifies that the element is disabled and cannot receive control

- autocomplete (acceptable values include on or off): Specifies whether the browser should store values entered by the user so inputting a stored value in the future can be automatically completed by the browser upon hint by user

- autofocus (acceptable values include autofocus, "", or empty): Specifies to the browser that the element must receive focus immediately after the document finishes loading

- min (value must be a valid partial time in the form of "YYYY-MM-DDTHH:MM:SS.Mss", "YYYY-MM-DDTHH:MM:SS", or "YYYY-MM-DDTHH:MM"): Specifies the lowest date allowed to be selected by the user

- max (value must be a valid partial time in the form of "YYYY-MM-DDTHH:MM:SS.Mss", "YYYY-MM-DDTHH:MM:SS", or "YYYY-MM-DDTHH:MM"): Specifies the highest date allowed to be selected by the user

- readonly (acceptable values include readonly, "", or empty): Specifies that the value of this element cannot be changed by the user

- step (acceptable values include any or any positive integer): Specifies how the value attribute of the element is to change

- required (acceptable values include required, "", or empty): Specifies that this element must have a valid value in order for the form to be allowed to submit

- value (value must be a valid partial time in the form of "YYYY-MM-DDTHH:MM:SS.Mss", "YYYY-MM-DDTHH:MM:SS", or "YYYY-MM-DDTHH:MM"): Specifies the actual date represented by this element

Color

The color input type allows the user to select a specific color from a browser-supplied color picker. The specific format and styling of this color picker widget is unique to the browser and platform used. Although some implementations of the widget may provide values in different format (RGB or HSL), the data that results from a color selection is a hexadecimal representation of the color in the form #RRGGBB.

```
<input type="color"
  value="#900CC1"
/>
```

Other valid attributes for the date input type include the following:

- `name` (value must be a string): Identifies a particular field by the string value associated with the attribute.

- `disabled` (acceptable values include `disabled`, `""`, or empty): Specifies that the element is disabled and cannot receive control.

- `autocomplete` (acceptable values include `on` or `off`): Specifies whether the browser should store values entered by the user so inputting a stored value in the future can be automatically completed by the browser upon hint by user.

- `autofocus` (acceptable values include `autofocus`, `""`, or empty): Specifies to the browser that the element must receive focus immediately after the document finishes loading.

- `value` (value must be a valid hexadecimal color with exactly seven characters in length and of the form "#rrggbb" or "#RRGGBB"): Specifies the actual color represented by this element. Keywords, such as Color, are not allowed.

Email

The email input type allows the user to input an e-mail address. In mobile devices where a digital keyboard is provided for data entry, this input type hints to the system that the keyboard to be provided should be the most appropriate for entering an e-mail address.

```
<input type="email"
  placeholder="Enter an email address"
  pattern="\w{3,}@packtpub\.com"
  maxlength="23"
/>
```

Other valid attributes for the date input type include the following:

- `name` (value must be a string): Identifies a particular field by the string value associated with the attribute.

- `disabled` (acceptable values include `disabled`, `""`, or empty): Specifies that the element is disabled and cannot receive control.

- `autocomplete` (acceptable values include `on` or `off`): Specifies whether the browser should store values entered by the user so inputting a stored value in the future can be automatically completed by the browser upon hint by user.

- `autofocus` (acceptable values include `autofocus`, `""`, or empty): Specifies to the browser that the element must receive focus immediately after the document finishes loading.

- `maxlength` (value must be a non-negative integer): Specifies the maximum length of characters that the element can contain.

- `pattern` (value must be a valid regular expression pattern as defined by ECMA 262): Specifies a pattern that the browser must validate the specified input against.

- `size` (value must be a positive integer): Specifies the maximum number of characters displayed by the element, although more characters may be allowed to be entered.

- `placeholder` (value must be a string): Specifies a string to be shown to the user as a hint as to what information the field expects. This string disappears when data is entered into the field and is shown when the field becomes empty.

- `multiple` (acceptable values include `multiple`, `""`, or empty): Specifies that multiple values are allowed in this element.

- `readonly` (acceptable values include `readonly`, `""`, or empty): Specifies that the value of this element cannot be changed by the user.

- `required` (acceptable values include `required`, `""`, or empty): Specifies that this element must have a valid value in order for the form to be allowed to submit.

- `value` (value must be a valid e-mail address and must adhere to any further restrictions specified by the pattern attribute, if any): Specifies the actual e-mail address represented by this element or a comma-separated list of valid e-mail addresses when the multiple attribute is present.

For those not familiar with JavaScript's regular expression language, or who need a refresher, following is a summary of the syntax:

[rodig] (brackets): used to match anything found within the brackets. For example: match any one of the letters within the brackets.

[^rodig] (negative brackets): Used to match anything not found within the brackets. For example, match any character except one of the letters within the brackets.

[D-M] (range): Used to match a range of characters or numbers. For example, match any characters between the capital letters D and M.

(me|you|us) (pipe): Used to match alternative options. For example, match either of the words within the parenthesis.

. (period): Match any characters, expect for a new line character or a line terminator character.

\w (word character): Match any letter, number, or an underscore.

\W (non-word character): Match any character that is not a word characters.

\d (digit): Match any single digit.

\D (non-digit): Match any non-digit character.

\s (space): Match a white space.

\S (non-space): Match any character that's not a space character.

\b (word boundary): Find a match at the beginning or end of a word.

\B (non-word boundary): Find a match that is not a word boundary.

\0 (null character): Matches the NULL character in a string.

\n (new line character): Matches the new line character.

\f (form feed character): Matches the form feed character.

\r (return carriage character): Matches the form carriage character.

\t (tab character): Matches the tab character.

\v (vertical tab): Matches a vertical tab character.

+ (plus quantifier): Matches the previous expression or character one or more times.

* (star quantifier): Matches the previous expression or character zero or more times.

? (question mark quantifier): Matches the previous expression or character zero or one time.

{3,5} (bracket quantifier): Matches the previous expression a minimum and maximum of times respectively. If the maximum digit is missing, the matches will continue until a non-match is found. For example: \d{1,} matches one or more digits.

^ (hat modifier): Matches an expression at the beginning of a string.

$ (dollar modifier): Matches an expression at the end of a string.

Number

The number input type allows the user to select number from any mechanism provided by the browser or to simply enter a numerical value if only a standard input field is provided by the browser. The value is validated by the browser to ensure that a number is indeed entered by the user. In mobile devices, where a digital keyboard is provided for data entry, this input type hints to the system that the keyboard to be provided should be the most appropriate for entering numbers.

```
<input type="number"
  min="42"
  max="108"
  step="2"
/>
```

Other valid attributes for the date input type include the following:

- name (value must be a string): Identifies a particular field by the string value associated with the attribute.

- disabled (acceptable values include disabled, "", or empty): Specifies that the element is disabled and cannot receive control.

- autocomplete (acceptable values include on or off): Specifies whether the browser should store values entered by the user so inputting a stored value in the future can be automatically completed by the browser upon hint by user.

- autofocus (acceptable values include autofocus, "", or empty): Specifies to the browser that the element must receive focus immediately after the document finishes loading.

- min (value must be a floating point number): Specifies the lowest number allowed to be selected by the user.

- max (value must be a floating point number): Specifies the highest number allowed to be selected by the user.

- `readonly` (acceptable values include `readonly`, `""`, or empty): Specifies that the value of this element cannot be changed by the user.

- `placeholder` (value must be a string): Specifies a string to be shown to the user as a hint as to what information the field expects. This string disappears when data is entered into the field and is shown when the field becomes empty.

- `step` (acceptable values include `any` or any positive integer): Specifies how the value attribute of the element is to change.

- `required` (acceptable values include `required`, `""`, or empty): Specifies that this element must have a valid value in order for the form to be allowed to submit.

- `value` (value must be a floating point number): Specifies the actual floating point number represented by this element.

Range

The range input type allows the user to select a number from a specified range using a browser-supplied slider widget. The specific format and styling of this slider widget is unique to the browser and platform used. The data that results from a range selection is a floating point number.

```
<input type="range"
  min="42"
  max="108"
  step="0.5"
/>
```

Other valid attributes for the date input type include the following:

- `name` (value must be a string): Identifies a particular field by the string value associated with the attribute.

- `disabled` (acceptable values include `disabled`, `""`, or empty): Specifies that the element is disabled and cannot receive control.

- `autocomplete` (acceptable values include `on` or `off`): Specifies whether the browser should store values entered by the user so inputting a stored value in the future can be automatically completed by the browser upon hint by user.

- `autofocus` (acceptable values include `autofocus`, `""`, or empty): Specifies to the browser that the element must receive focus immediately after the document finishes loading.

- `min` (value must be a floating point number): Specifies the lowest number allowed to be selected by the user.

- `max` (value must be a floating point number): Specifies the highest number allowed to be selected by the user.

- `readonly` (acceptable values include `readonly`, `""`, or empty): Specifies that the value of this element cannot be changed by the user.

- `placeholder` (value must be a string): Specifies a string to be shown to the user as a hint as to what information the field expects. This string disappears when data is entered into the field, and is shown when the field becomes empty.

- `step` (acceptable values include `any` or any positive integer): Specifies how the value attribute of the element is to change.

- `required` (acceptable values include `required`, `""`, or empty): Specifies that this element must have a valid value in order for the form to be allowed to submit.

- `value` (value must be a floating point number): Specifies the actual floating point number represented by this element.

Search

The search input type allows the user to enter a string intended for a search. Overall, the search input type looks and behaves very much like a regular text input type. Some browsers might add miscellaneous behavior to this field, such as built-in icons or widgets to instantly clear the field, but none of these are officially part of the specification.

```
<input type="search"
  placeholder="Search"
  pattern="[^!\?]"
/>
```

Other valid attributes for the date input type include the following:

- `name` (value must be a string): Identifies a particular field by the string value associated with the attribute.

- `disabled` (acceptable values include `disabled`, `""`, or empty): Specifies that the element is disabled, and cannot receive control.

- `autocomplete` (acceptable values include `on` or `off`): Specifies whether the browser should store values entered by the user so inputting a stored value in the future can be automatically completed by the browser upon hint by user.

- `autofocus` (acceptable values include `autofocus`, `""`, or empty): Specifies to the browser that the element must receive focus immediately after the document finishes loading.

- `maxlength` (value must be a non-negative integer): Specifies the maximum length of characters that the element can contain.

- `pattern` (value must be a valid regular expression pattern as defined by ECMA 262): Specifies a pattern that the browser must validate the specified input against.

- `size` (value must be a positive integer): Specifies the maximum number of characters displayed by the element although more characters may be allowed to be entered.

- `placeholder` (value must be a string): Specifies a string to be shown to the user as a hint as to what information the field expects. This string disappears when data is entered into the field and is shown when the field becomes empty.

- `multiple` (acceptable values include `multiple`, `""`, or empty): Specifies that multiple values are allowed in this element.

- `readonly` (acceptable values include `readonly`, `""`, or empty): Specifies that the value of this element cannot be changed by the user.

- `required` (acceptable values include `required`, `""`, or empty): Specifies that this element must have a valid value in order for the form to be allowed to submit.

- `value` (value must be a string with no line feed or carriage return character): Specifies the actual search query represented by this element.

Tel

The tel input type allows the user to enter a telephone number.

```
<input type="tel"
  placeholder="Enter your phone number"
  required
/>
```

Other valid attributes for the date input type include the following:

- `name` (value must be a string): Identifies a particular field by the string value associated with the attribute.

- `disabled` (acceptable values include `disabled`, `""`, or empty): Specifies that the element is disabled and cannot receive control.

- `autocomplete` (acceptable values include `on` or `off`): Specifies whether the browser should store values entered by the user so inputting a stored value in the future can be automatically completed by the browser upon hint by user.

- autofocus (acceptable values include autofocus, "", or empty): Specifies to the browser that the element must receive focus immediately after the document finishes loading.

- maxlength (value must be a non-negative integer): Specifies the maximum length of characters that the element can contain.

- pattern (value must be a valid regular expression pattern as defined by ECMA 262): Specifies a pattern that the browser must validate the specified input against.

- size (value must be a positive integer): Specifies the maximum number of characters displayed by the element although more characters may be allowed to be entered.

- placeholder (value must be a string): Specifies a string to be shown to the user as a hint as to what information the field expects. This string disappears when data is entered into the field and is shown when the field becomes empty.

- multiple (acceptable values include multiple, "", or empty): Specifies that multiple values are allowed in this element.

- readonly (acceptable values include readonly, "", or empty): Specifies that the value of this element cannot be changed by the user.

- required (acceptable values include required, "", or empty): Specifies that this element must have a valid value in order for the form to be allowed to submit.

- value (value must be a string with no line feed or carriage return character): Specifies the actual phone number represented by this element.

Url

The url input type allows the user to enter a website url.

```
<input type="url"
  placeholder="Enter your website address"
  required
/>
```

Other valid attributes for the date input type include the following:

- name (value must be a string): Identifies a particular field by the string value associated with the attribute.

- disabled (acceptable values include disabled, "", or empty): Specifies that the element is disabled, and cannot receive control.

- autocomplete (acceptable values include on or off): Specifies whether the browser should store values entered by the user so inputting a stored value in the future can be automatically completed by the browser upon hint by user.

- autofocus (acceptable values include autofocus, "", or empty): Specifies to the browser that the element must receive focus immediately after the document finishes loading.

- maxlength (value must be a non-negative integer): Specifies the maximum length of characters that the element can contain.

- pattern (value must be a valid regular expression pattern as defined by ECMA 262): Specifies a pattern that the browser must validate the specified input against.

- size (value must be a positive integer): Specifies the maximum number of characters displayed by the element although more characters may be allowed to be entered.

- placeholder (value must be a string): Specifies a string to be shown to the user as a hint as to what information the field expects. This string disappears when data is entered into the field and is shown when the field becomes empty.

- multiple (acceptable values include multiple, "", or empty): Specifies that multiple values are allowed in this element.

- readonly (acceptable values include readonly, "", or empty): Specifies that the value of this element cannot be changed by the user.

- required (acceptable values include required, "", or empty): Specifies that this element must have a valid value in order for the form to be allowed to submit.

- value (value must be a string with no line feed or carriage return character): Specifies the actual url represented by this element.

Form validation

Although a form submission will automatically validate data inserted into the form and alert the user of any possible errors, there is a nicely defined API that gives us much more control over the validation process and reporting, than just the default.

Validity state object

Each `form` element has an object attached to it of type **ValidityState**, which contains a list of properties related to the validation status of that node. You can access this object directly from a `form` element and inspect its properties manually:

```
var firstName = document.querySelector("#myForm
input[name='firstName']");
//firstName.validity == ValidityState {
  valid : false,
  customError : false,
  badInput : false,
  stepMismatch : false,
  rangeOverflow : false,
  rangeUnderflow : false,
  tooLong : false,
  patternMismatch : false,
  typeMismatch : false,
  valueMissing : false
}
```

With these properties, we're able to inspect each `form` element and really customize the validation routine for the form. However, seeing that automatic validation is such an attractive feature designed to save time and effort, we'll focus on the functionality that can best help us with respect to this auto validation.

Custom validation

One of the properties of **ValidState** is the Boolean `customError`, which specifies whether a custom error message has been set to the field element or if the browser is to display a generic error message for this element in case the form does not validate. To set a custom error message, we can call the `setCustomValidity()` method of the `form` element itself and assign a message for the browser to use when needed, as follows:

```
var email = document.querySelector("#myForm input[type='email']");
email.pattern = "\\w{3,}@packtpub\\.com";
email.setCustomValidity("Please enter a valid Packt email
address...");
```

The first entry in the form just seen is invalid because it doesn't contain the string packtpub.com. The second form is valid because it conforms to the pattern specified. Note the customized error message on the first form, which is guaranteed to be the same in any browser that supports the features, as opposed to having a generic error message which can vary from browser to browser.

Used in the game

There were two separate instances in the game where the web forms API was used. The first was in the game options widget, where a range input type was used to allow the user to select the difficulty of the game, and the other was used in the new champion form, allowing the user to enter his or her full name along with an email address.

```
<nav id="navOptions">
  <div>
    <p>Difficulty &raquo; <span>1</span></p>
    <input type="range" step="1" min="1" max="3" value="1" />
  </div>
  <img src="img/options-icon.png" />
</nav>
```

Here we set up a basic range input, specifying the maximum value as 3. By default, most browsers will set the value for the step, min, and value attributes all to 1, but just to be safe, we'll specify those values in case a browser handles that differently in case the attributes aren't specified.

```
<form>
  <input type="text" name="fullName"
    pattern="\w{2,16}\s\w{2,16}"
    placeholder="Full Name (Ex: John Doe)"
    autofocus
  />
  <input type="email" name="email"
    placeholder="Email address"
  />
  <input type="submit" value="Save" />
</form>
```

Normally, you'll want to have two separate fields in your forms when asking for a first and last name. However, asking for a full name in a single field makes the field a great candidate for a custom pattern attribute.

The pattern used to validate a full name in this case is pretty simple; we look that the input as a word between 2 and 16 word characters (letters, and in this case possibly even numbers), followed by a single white space, which is in turn followed by another word of length greater than two, but less than 16 characters.

A placeholder string is added to both input field elements to avoid the need for extra labels in the form. This way the form can be nice and concise, yet descriptive enough that the user is never confused about what the form is asking.

Data attributes

When you need to need to store data in an HTML element and there is no other attribute that would be more appropriate to hold that data, the HTML5 specification provides a special attribute for this very situation. Although the specification specifically refers to this attribute a custom data attribute, most people simply call them as the data attributes.

The way these `custom data` attributes work is very simple. Simply create the attribute name of your choice starting the name keyword with the prefix `data-`, then using any keyword of your choice that is at least one character in length. The only restriction is that the keyword must not contain any uppercase letters, although all HTML element attributes get lowercased automatically by default. You may add an arbitrary amount of such custom attributes to a single element. Finally, any `custom data` attributes may have any value of your choice, have the empty string as its value, or be empty, in either case the attribute is considered to have the value true (and the value false in its absence).

```
<!-- Indicates an element that display some sort of score -->
<input type="text" id="scoreDisplay"
  <!-- Indicates that this score is not yet a new high score -->
  data-is-high-score="false"
  <!-- Indicates the current high score -->
  data-score-to-beat="891,958"
  <!-- Not a good use of data attributes, since the disabled
    attribute is a better choice -->
  data-enabled="false"
/>
```

In the example code just seen, we have some DOM node that happens to be an `input` tag and represents the score for some game. The first two sample data attributes, `data-is-high-score` and `data-score-to-beat`, are good examples. Just by looking at the names chosen for each attribute, we can infer the context in which they were meant to be used.

The first attribute is meant to hold a Boolean value that represents whether or not the score displayed by the heading element is a new high score. Since it currently holds the value false, then obviously the current score is not yet a new high score.

The second attribute stores the current high score, meaning that if the player gets a score higher than that value, his or her score will become a new high score and the attribute `data-is-high-score` should be updated to hold the value true. Keep in mind that these attributes are static and meaningless and the logic of your application is in charge of adding meaning to them based on their context as well as handling any updates to them, such as the example described previously.

Finally, note the third `data` attribute example. This is not a very practical use of data attributes because there exists another HTML element attribute that exists for that very purpose, namely, to specify that an element is disabled.

To add, remove, and check for an element's attributes and their values programmatically, you can use the following JavaScript APIs:

```
var myInput = document.getElementById("scoreDisplay");

// Check for the presence of an attribute
if (myInput.getAttribute("data-is-high-score") == null) {

  // If attribute is not present, add it to the element with some
    default value
  myInput.setAttribute("data-is-high-score", false);
}

// If attribute is present, check its value
else {

  var isHighScore = myInput.getAttribute("data-is-high-score");

  if (isHighScore) {
    // Do something with this new high score
  } else {
    // The current score is not yet a new high score
  }
}
```

Used in the game

There were a couple of usages of custom `data attributes` in the game with different purposes and for different reasons. As mentioned previously, one use was to specify a player's current speed. Two other instances of the attribute were used to identify and distinguish a player from the other and to group separate buttons that were intended to behave the same way.

While the official specification states that you should always use the most appropriate attribute to store data in a DOM element, you should also keep in mind that the line that separates a possible `custom data` attribute and some other existing attribute may at times become gray. When this happens, you should prioritize your specific needs and goals.

For example, if you are trying to use a `custom data` attribute to name a group of related elements, the question might arise that a simple CSS class can achieve the same result. Some people might argue that since CSS classes already exist and their purpose is to group related elements, others may also argue that if no specific style is shared among these elements, then use of such a custom data attribute is well justified. However, the overruling factor should be the specific application goals and needs, so if, for example, adding a symbolic CSS class to group these elements would make it confusing, since no real corresponding CSS class exists, then the use of the custom data attribute is indeed well justified.

```
<section class="tracks">
  <div class="track">
    <span data-name="badGuy" data-speed="0"></span>
  </div>

  <div class="track">
    <span data-name="goodGuy" data-speed="0"></span>
  </div>
</section>
```

Note that each span element inside the `div.track` element has both, a data attribute of name, which distinguishes the hero player from the enemy player, and a data attribute of speed, which specifies how much each element moves by on each tick of the game timer. Whether that number represents pixels, percentages, or any other unit is irrelevant, since both players have the value set to zero, meaning that they move nothing per timer cycle.

Whether the data attribute name could be better represented by a CSS class can be argued in either direction. In this case, I chose to use a data attribute because then the styling can be independent of anything, and that concern can be delegated to another part of the application without any hesitation.

```
<button data-intent="play">Play Again</button>
<section id="mainContainer">
  <div id="wordsToWrite"></div>
  <div id="wordsWritten"></div>
  <button data-intent="play">Play</button>
</section>
```

Here we have two separate buttons that share the same data attribute intent = "play". With that attribute present, and that value assigned, we can then some JavaScript logic to handle those, and any other buttons, making their behavior predictable and universal.

```
// Select all buttons with a custom data attribute of intent and
   a value of play
var playBtns = document.querySelectorAll
   ("button[data-intent='play']");
// Assign the same click handler to all of these buttons
for (var i = 0, len = playBtns.length; i < len; i++) {
   playBtns[i].addEventListener("click", doOnPlayClicked);
}

// Now every button with data-intent="play" executes this
   function when clicked
function  doOnPlayClicked(event) {
   event.preventDefault();

   // Play button click behavior goes here
}
```

Query selectors

There are two different, yet very similar, APIs as part of the new selectors interface. One selects a collection of elements that match the query used and the other only matches one. If multiple nodes are matched by a query used in the single selector version, only the first occurrence is returned.

To use this interface, you call the appropriate function on the document object and supply a string representing a CSS query. Now you can stop selecting an element by its ID, then navigating weird sub paths, in order to finally get to the element you want to target programmatically.

Before this feature was available, it was common for developers to clutter their document structure with ID and class attributes just to make targeting those elements programmatically a bit easier. While using CSS expressions to target specific nodes may be easy enough that you may feel that you no longer need to add a unique ID or a class to an element just so it's easier to target that element through code, keep in mind that long CSS expressions might be so complex that the performance of your application might be compromised because of the time it takes to navigate to those elements. Remember that the shorter the CSS query, the easier it is for the browser to match the elements involved.

Consider the following code snippet from the game, where we try to register a click event listener to the image element found inside a navigation menu holding the game options:

```
<nav id="navOptions">
  <div>
    <p>Difficulty &raquo; <span>1</span></p>
    <input type="range" step="1" min="1" max="3" value="1" />
  </div>
  <img src="img/options-icon.png" />
</nav>

<script>
// 1. Capture the image element inside that nav structure
   with id="navOptions"

// ---------------------------------
// Without query selectors:
// ---------------------------------
var nav = document.getElementById("navOptions");
var img = null;

// Iterate through every child node of nav instead of
   directly targeting the current
// position of that image element in case the structure
   of #navOptions change,
// in which case this code wouldn't need to be updated.
for (var i = 0, len = nav.children.length; i < len; i++) {
  if (nav.children[i].tagName == "IMG") {
    img = nav.children[i];
    break;
  }
}

// ---------------------------------
// With the query selectors:
// ---------------------------------
var img = document.querySelector("#navOptions img");

// 2. Set the click handler
if (img) {
  img.addEventListener("click", doOnOptionsClicked);
}
</script>
```

You will note that the demonstration of the old way of selecting elements uses a very defensive programming style. While trivial selections may not need such paranoiac measures, a large application would definitely benefit from such an approach in case a particular element is not found in the DOM, and an event listener is attempted to be added to a variable holding a null reference. Either way, you can see how the new selectors API solves this problem in this particular situation, since no matter what other elements are possibly added to, or taken away from that #navOptions subtree, the CSS query used in the querySelector("#navOptions img") statement would still hold true, whereas nav.children[1] might not refer to the same element, should the structure of #navOptions change.

Also, you will note that the call to querySelector will return null if no elements are matched with the CSS query provided. When using the querySelectorAll interface, remember that a list will be returned whenever a match is found, whether one or more elements are selected. Thus, if only a single element is matched, you would still need to index into the result set in order to match the only element returned.

```
<div id="wordsWritten">
  <span class="correct">I</span>
  <span class="correct">love</span>
  <span class="correct">HTML5</span>
  <span class="wrong">?</span>
</div>

<script>
var correctWords = document.querySelectorAll("#wordsWritten
.correct");
// correctWords == [
//   <span class="correct">I</span>,
//   <span class="correct">love</span>,
//   <span class="correct">HTML5</span>]

var wrongWords = document.querySelectorAll
  ("#wordsWritten .wrong");
//   wrongWords == [
//     <span class="wrong">?</span>]
</script>
```

Used in the game

As mentioned previously, every node selection was done using query selectors in the game. It is worth mentioning that it is not possible to register an event listener to a collection of nodes at once. You will need to iterate through the entire list (or at least a part of it) in order to touch one or more individual nodes in the list.

```
// Select a collection of zero, one, or more buttons
var playBtns = document.querySelectorAll
  ("button[data-intent='play']");

// Assign the same click handler to all of these buttons
for (var i = 0, len = playBtns.length; i < len; i++) {
  playBtns[i].addEventListener("click", doOnPlayClicked);
}

// This does not work >> TypeError: Object [object Array] has
  no method 'addEventListener'
  playBtns.addEventListener("click", doOnPlayClicked);
```

If you attempt to call any function that would normally call on an individual node directly on a result set from a `querySelectorAll` call, you will get a `TypeError` since the function called is applied to the array element and not each and all of its elements.

Web fonts

The new web fonts API is particularly exciting and liberating to all those web developers out there who have had to rely on images in order to make the web truly beautiful up until now.

To use custom fonts, we use the CSS property `@font-face` and specify a few attributes, such as the name of the font and the font file, which the browser will follow and download to the client much like it does with assets such as images, videos, and sound files that are called by the client.

```
@font-face {
  font-family: "Lemon",
  src: url("/fonts/lemon.woff") format("woff");
}

h1 {
  font-family: "Lemon", Arial, sans-serif;
}
```

The only caveat with web fonts is that not all browsers support the same font types. The solution, though simple, can be a bit of a pain, since it involves uploading the different file format to your server then specifying each and all of them in the font-face declaration. When a browser comes across your custom font declaration, it can then download the file format that it can handle and serve that to the client.

```
@font-face {
  font-family: "Lemon",
  src:url("/fonts/lemon.woff") format("woff"),
      url("/fonts/lemon.eot") format("eot"),
      url("/fonts/lemon.ttf") format("truetype"),
      url("/fonts/lemon.svg#font") format("svg");
}
```

As of this writing, Google Chrome, Firefox 3.6, and Microsoft Internet Explorer 9 accept the `.woff` font files, while Safari, Opera, and Android support the `.ttf` files. Apple's iOS only supports the `.svg` font files.

Alternatively, you can encode the entire font file into a `Data-URI` string and embed that into your CSS.

```
@font-face {
  font-family: "Lemon";
  src: url("data:font/opentype;base64,d09GRgABAAAA...");
}
```

One great resource for free, open source, web fonts is Google's Web Fonts project. There you can find a directly with several hundred different font files that you can search from and import right into your projects. Each file is hosted on Google servers, which means that the availability of these fonts is very high and the delivery speed is Google fast. What's more, through their service, once you find a font that you'd like to import into your project, Google provides you with three options to import it: a standard link `rel="stylesheet"` tag, a CSS `@import` statement, or a JavaScript alternative. Either choice you make, the font file that eventually gets served to your end users is the exact format that the requesting browser supports. This way you don't need to specify the multiple `src: url` attributes in your CSS file.

Transitions

CSS transitions is a great and simple way to add that special effect to any existing website. It is likely that your existing projects already use some sort of state change to elements based on different events, such as a hover effect, which may cause elements to change size, color, or position.

By adding a CSS transition attribute to these elements, you can more closely control the various states between the original state and the final state. For example, if a link is set to have a blue color by default and the font color changes to purple when the user moves the mouse cursor over that text, a CSS transition would cause the text to smoothly and gradually change the blue into the purpose color, instead of simply changing the color property in the blink of an eye.

Remember, only properties that can possibly have intermediate states can transition between states. Normally, you can determine if that is the case with a particular attribute by looking at the value assigned to the attribute. If the value is a number, such as 10px, 2.5em, or 50%, then you can be sure that a transition property would result in an incremental change into the final state. Since colors are ultimately represented by numbers, whether they're hexadecimal values or something else, we are able to apply transition properties to colors as well.

```
#navOptions {
  position: relative;
  top: 10px;
  left: -230px;
  width: 325px;
  overflow: auto;
  padding: 10px;
  border-radius: 0 10px 10px 0;
  -webkit-transition: all 0.3s;
}

#navOptions.open {
  left: 0;
  background: rgba(100, 100, 100, 0.5);
  padding-right: 15px;
}
```

In this example, the element with the ID property of navOptions is given a transition attribute. By default, that element has a left position of -230px, a patting of 10px, and no background color. Then we define a class called open, and specifically associate it with the name #navOptions element. This class specify different values for the left, padding, and background properties. Thus, whenever the #navOptions element gets assigned to the class .open, those three properties will change gradually from the default into the new values.

Note that the transition property is assigned with a browser-specific prefix. This was done for simplicity, but in your production code you might want to check the status of each browser in regards to that specific property, and specify all values possibly needed, along with a plain, non-prefixed version for when the prefix is removed from a browser:

```
#navOptions {
  position: relative;
  top: 10px;
  left: -230px;
  width: 325px;
  overflow: auto;
  padding: 10px;
  border-radius: 0 10px 10px 0;

  -webkit-transition: all 0.3s; /* Webkit-based browsers */
  -moz-transition: all 0.3s;     /* Mozilla Firefox */
  -o-transition: all 0.3s;        /* Opera */
  transition: all 0.3s;            /* One day, every browser. Today,
any browser not in experimental */
}
```

The example just seen uses short hand to define all four possible properties, but they can also be declared individually:

```
#navOptions {
  position: relative;
  top: 10px;
  left: -230px;
  width: 325px;
  overflow: auto;
  padding: 10px;
  border-radius: 0 10px 10px 0;

  transition-property: padding;
  transition-duration: 0.3s;
  transition-timing-function: linear;
  transition-delay: 1s;
}
```

In short hand, the order of these parameters are: `property`, `duration`, `timing function`, and `delay`. You can also specify multiple properties in the same declaration by using a comma-separated list of properties:

```
#navOptions {
  position: relative;
  top: 10px;
  left: -230px;
  width: 325px;
  overflow: auto;
  padding: 10px;
  border-radius: 0 10px 10px 0;

  transition: padding 0.3s ease-out 0.1s, left 0.5s linear,
    background ease-in 1s 1s;
}
```

Note that you can have any arbitrary number of properties specified, or simply use the keyword `all`. Also, as shown in the previous example, not all values need to be the same (each property can have a different duration, timing function, or delay). The default delay is `0` (meaning that the transition starts right away as soon as the property change is triggered), and the default value for the timing function is ease.

Animations

The animations API is somewhat similar to the transitions API, but the main difference is that we get to specify two or more keyframes and the browser transitions between these keyframes. A keyframe is simply a point in time, with a series of properties specified for that particular point.

To use a CSS animation, you'll first need to create a named keyframe sequence, specify all the properties for each keyframe, then assign that keyframe sequence to some element. Similar to transitions, when you specify the keyframe sequence to an element, you also specify the configurations for that sequence, such as animation name, duration, timing function, delay, iteration count (how many times to play the entire keyframe sequence), direction (whether the animation plays from the first keyframe to the last or from the last to the first), and the play state (indicating whether the animation is running or paused).

To set up a keyframe sequence, simply use the `@keyframes` keyword, followed by a string identifying that sequence.

```
@keyframes myAnimation {
}
```

Then, in a way slightly different from other CSS properties, we nest other expressions inside this declaration, where each sub-expression is an individual keyframe declaration. Since each keyframe is a point in time (where the total time is specify when the animation sequence is applied to an element, as we'll see shortly), we specify each keyframe in one of two ways: we can either specify a percentage of the time for when a keyframe is called into action, or we can use the keywords from and to, indicating the point in time when 0 percent and 100 percent of the total animation time has elapsed.

```
@keyframes myAnimation {
  from {
    background: #ffffff;
  }

  to {
    background: #000000;
  }
}
```

Note that the from keyword behaves the exact same way as 0 percent and the to keyword the same as 100 percent. Whether to use one over the other is purely a matter of preference.

```
@keyframes myAnimation {
  0% {
    left: 0px;
    top: 0px;
  }

  25% {
    left: 0px;
    top: 50%;
  }

  50% {
    left: 50px;
    top: 100%;
  }

  75% {
    left: 50px;
    top: 100%;
  }

  100% {
    left: 0px;
    top: 0px;
  }
}
```

Needless to say, the same issues regarding vendor prefixes apply to the animations interface.

```
-webkit-@keyframes myAnimation {
  from {
    background: #ffffff;
  }

  to {
    background: #000000;
  }
}

#sky {
  -webkit-animation-name: myAnimation;
  /* This is how you link a keyframe sequence to an element */
  -webkit-animation-duration: 3s;
  /* Can be a value in seconds (s) or milliseconds (m) */
  -webkit-animation-timing-function: ease-out;
  /* Can be linear, ease, ease-in, or ease-out */
  -webkit-animation-iteration-count: 23;
  /* Can be any non-negative integer or "infinite" */
  -webkit-animation-direction: alternate;
  /* Default is "normal" */
  -webkit-animation-play-state: running;
  /* Can also be "paused" */
}
```

The text shadow

The text shadow interface is much simpler to use than the transition or animation APIs since it only has four basic parameters, but can be equally as powerful in adding beautiful visual elements to make the user experience great. The parameters are the horizontal and vertical offset of the shadow relative to where the text is, the amount of blur to apply to the shadow, and finally, the color of the shadow, which can have the optional alpha channel for added opacity.

```
h1 {
  text-shadow: -5px 5px 0 #000;
}
```

Multiply shadows may be added to the same element by adding them in a comma-separated listed:

```
h1 {
  text-shadow: -5px 5px 0 #000, 5px -5px 0 rgba(50, 50, 50, 0.3);
}
```

Also, text shadows may be added to custom fonts embedded onto the page through HTML5's web fonts:

```
h1 {
   text-shadow: 1px 1px 5px #000;
   font-family: "Lemon";
}
```

The box shadow

Box shadows are identical to text shadow, except for a few very important distinctions. First and for most, they are not applied to text but only to box elements. You could in fact apply a box-shadow property to a text element (such as a p tag, h1, h2, h3, and so on), but the effect would be drastically different. While the text shadow effect, essentially, simply renders an offset and blurred copy of the text to which the shadow is applied, a box shadow effect is simply a copy of the rectangle created by the elements width, height, margin, and border which is rendered with the specified color, offset, and blur values assigned in CSS.

```
div {
   box-shadow: 5px 5px 3px #aaa;
}
```

Again, just like with text shadows, we can apply multiple box shadows to the same element through a comma-separated list of shadow declarations.

```
div {
   box-shadow: 5px 5px 3px #aaa, -10px -10px 30px rgba
      (255, 255, 255, 0.01);
}
```

If you apply multiple shadows as just shown, any subsequent shadows should be drawn behind shadows drawn earlier, should they so happen to overlap. For example, the following set of shadows would display as a single, red shadow, since the red (#cc0000) was declared first and they both just so happen to cover the same area. Should the shadows have any amount of blur, the effect would be a mixture of the shadows. Since in this particular example, the shadows are completely solid, no blending takes place and the shadow in front takes precedence (since it's drawn higher in the rendering stack).

```
div {
   box-shadow: 5px 5px 0 #cc0000, 5px 5px 0 #0000cc;
}
```

There is also a fourth value that can be specified in a box shadow, which specifies the spread (or size) of the shadow. The default value is zero, which means the blur will begin right at the edge of the container created by the containing element. The effect created by a shadow spread is similar to a border placed between the blur of the shadow and the container created by the containing element.

Finally, the optional `inset` keyword tells the browser to draw the shadow from the border of the container inwards, as opposed to from the border (or where the border would be, had there been a border width greater than zero) outwards in the direction of the horizontal and vertical offsets.

```
div {
    box-shadow: inset 5px 5px 3px #aaa;
}
```

Note that in a multiple shadow declaration, each shadow can specify its own rendering orientation.

```
div {
    box-shadow: inset 5px 5px 3px #aaa,
    /* This shadow is drawn inside the div */
        5px 5px 3px #aaa; /* And this shadow is drawn outside it */
}
```

The border radius

The border radius property allows us to round the corners of the container formed by an element's dimensions. If there is any content where the rounding of the corner reduces the physical area of the container, that content is not drawn. Finally, the border radius declaration can be specified by a single value, where that value is applied to all corners (observe that here we refer to corners, not sides, as in a border declaration), by supplying four different values (where the corners would be targeted in the order top-left, top-right, bottom-right, and bottom-left), or by targeting each corner individually.

```
div.one {
    border-radius: 5px; /* Make all four corners round by 5px */
}

div.two {
    border-radius: 5px 10px
    /* Top left and bottom right = 5px, top right and
        bottom left = 10px */
```

```
div.three {
  border-top-left-radius: 4px;
  border-top-right-radius: 8px;
  border-bottom-left-radius: 15px;
  border-bottom-right-radius: 16px;
}
```

The code

Now that you are familiar with the HTML5 APIs used in this fun game, let's look under the covers and see how the game was put together. Due to brevity and ease of explanation, only the main portions of the source code for this game will be listed or explained here. Be sure to download the complete source code for the game at the book's website.

The HTML structure

The first component of this game was the HTML structure. The main pieces of it are the tracks where each player moves, along with each individual player, and the containers that show the text that needs to be typed by the user. There is also a second container that displays whatever text the player actually types in. For customization, there is an input type range that allows the player to change the difficulty level of the game, which for all practical purposes, only increases the speed attribute of the enemy player.

```
<section class="tracks">
  <div class="track">
    <span data-name="badGuy" data-speed="0"></span>
  </div>

  <div class="track">
    <span data-name="goodGuy" data-speed="0"></span>
  </div>
</section>

<section id="mainContainer">
  <div id="wordsToWrite"></div>
  <div id="wordsWritten"></div>
  <button data-intent="play">Play</button>
</section>
```

Other elements only add to the experience, either visually (through animations and other visual components) or with more interaction. But these are the basic game components without which the game cannot work.

JavaScript and logic

The logic for this game is separated into three very basic components, namely, a `Player` class that encapsulates the behavior of each player, a game loop function that is called at a regular interval based on a game timer, and a few global functions that encapsulate various pieces of logic used throughout the life cycle of the application.

The `Player` class holds a reference to the DOM nodes that represent the player, the track where the player runs, and defines some basic behavior to control the player.

```javascript
function Player(query) {
  // Hold a reference to the DOM element that they player
    will control
  var element = document.querySelector(query);
  var trackWidth = parseInt(element.parentElement.offsetWidth);
  var minLeft = 0 - parseInt(element.offsetWidth / 2);
  var maxLeft = trackWidth - parseInt(element.offsetWidth / 2);

  // Move the player based on whatever speed is set in
    its custom data attribute
  this.move = function() {
    var left = parseInt(element.style.left);
    var speed = parseInt(element.attributes.getNamedItem
      ("data-speed").value);

    element.style.left = (left + speed) + "px";

    if (left > maxLeft) {
      this.moveToFinish();
    } else if (left < minLeft) {
      this.moveToStart();
    }
  };

  // Manually move the player to a certain point along its track,
    independent of
  // what its speed data attribute is.
  this.moveToPercent = function(percent) {
    element.style.left = parseInt(percent * maxLeft) + "px";
```

```
      if (percent >= 100) {
        this.moveToFinish();
      } else if (percent <= 0) {
        this.moveToStart();
      }
  };

  // Determine if the player has reached the end of its track
  this.isFinished = function() {
    return parseInt(element.style.left) >= maxLeft;
  };

  // Place the player at the beginning of its track
  this.moveToStart = function() {
    element.style.left = this.getMinLeft() + "px";
  };

  // Move the player to the very end of its track
  this.moveToFinish = function() {
    element.style.left = this.getMaxLeft() + "px";
  };
}
```

In the global scope, we create two instances of this player class, one representing the hero of the game and the other the enemy that we try to defeat.

```
var hero = new Player("[data-name='goodGuy']");
var enemy = new Player("[data-name='badGuy']");
```

When the game starts, we initialize some code, which is among a few other things, means that we determine how fast the game timer is to run, how fast the enemy player is to move, what phrase the user is to type in, and most importantly, we register a keyboard event on the body element of our HTML structure. In other words, we listen to every key press anywhere on the page, so that we can detect what the user has typed in after the game has begun.

This is probably the most complex function in the game because we have to handle every key press by ourselves. This means that we need to take into account whether or not the user has pressed a key while holding the *Shift* key (in which case they have entered a capital letter), or whether a special key combination was pressed. For example, if the user presses the *Backspace* key, by default the browser will respond to this event by navigating the web page back to the last page navigated. Obviously, we don't want the browser to navigate away from our game. Instead we want the last character typed in by the user to be deleted. Thus, small details such as this must be taken into account.

Finally, at each letter typed in by the user, we must check whether that letter was the same letter we were expecting (the correct letter) or whether the user has typed in a wrong letter. Based on this decision, we output to the screen the letter just typed, along with some HTML that allows us to render that letter differently based on whether or not it was the right key.

```
function handleKeyPress(event) {

  var keyCodes = {
    SHIFT_KEY: 16,
    BACKSPACE_KEY: 8,
    SPACEBAR_KEY: 32,
    COMMA_KEY: 188,
    PERIOD_KEY: 190
  };

  var wordsLen = wordsWritten.children.length;

  // If the Shift key was entered, just ignore it
  if (event.keyCode == keyCodes.SHIFT_KEY)
    return false;

  // If the backspace key was entered, don't let the
    browser navigate away
  if (event.keyCode == keyCodes.BACKSPACE_KEY) {
    event.preventDefault();

    // If we have deleted every letter entered by the user,
      don't do anything else
      if (wordsLen < 1)
        return false;

      // If the user has pressed the backspace key, and
        there is at least one letter
      // that the user had typed in before, delete that
        letter from where it was output.
      // Note that some browsers might not support
        the .remove() function on a node,
      // but rather use the removeChild() function on
        the node's parent element.
    wordsWritten.children[wordsLen - 1].remove();
    return false;
  }
```

```
// Determine what character the user has typed in
var letter = String.fromCharCode(event.keyCode);

// If the charactered enterd by the user is a letter,
  capitalize it if the Shift key was pressed
if (!event.shiftKey && event.keyCode >= 65 &&
  event.keyCode <= 90)
  letter = String.fromCharCode
    (event.keyCode + keyCodes.SPACEBAR_KEY);

// Convert special character codes into their corresponding
character
  if (event.keyCode == keyCodes.COMMA_KEY)
    letter = ",";

  if (event.keyCode == keyCodes.PERIOD_KEY)
    letter = ".";

// Determine if they letter entered is right or wrong,
  and print special HTML to
// indicate that. Move the hero if the letter
  entered was correct.
if (letter == words[wordsLen]) {
  wordsWritten.innerHTML += "<span class='correct'>"
    + letter + "</span>";
  var correct = document.querySelectorAll
    ("#wordsWritten .correct").length;
  var percent = correct / words.length;
  hero.moveToPercent(percent);
} else {
  wordsWritten.innerHTML += "<span class='wrong'>"
    + letter + "</span>";
}

// By returning false from a key press event,
  we further prevent the browser
// from taking any default action based on the
  key combination entered.
return false;
}
```

At every tick of the main game timer, which we can make faster or slower based on the difficulty that the player has selected, we call our main game loop, which performs some basic tasks. First we move each player, then check if any of them has reached the end of their track. This is done by calling each player's isFinished() function, defined by the Player class. If that is the case, then we know that the game is over. If that is so, we unregister the keyboard event we had bound to the body element, so that we no longer inspect any keyboard input from the user. After we've determined that the game is over, we determine if the user has actually won or lost the game. If they have won, we record their victory. If they have lost, we tell them so, and allow them to play a new game. If the game is not yet over, we simply wait for the game loop to run again.

```
function tick() {

  hero.move();
  enemy.move();

  if (isGameOver()) {
    document.body.removeEventListener("keydown", handleKeyPress);

    if (hero.isFinished()) {
      gamesWon++;
      showWinPanel();
    } else if (enemy.isFinished()) {
      showLosePanel();
    }
  } else {
    setTimeout(tick, tickPeriod);
  }
}
```

Summary

In this chapter, we finally jumped off the spring board we set up in the previous chapter, and dove headfirst into the very deep world of HTML5 game development. We started out by setting up the project structure used in constructing this game and discussed the main goals and objectives of the game. Next, we looked at each of the components used in the game and discussed how and why they were used. Finally, we look a deeper look at each of the HTML5 APIs, that make up each of these components, and looked at some code examples to make them work.

Since the complete source code for the game is fairly lengthy, we only took a brief peek at the main structure of the code, so that when you download the full source from Packt's website, the code looks somewhat familiar to you. Again, I want to remind you that because the focus of this book is not game development but rather HTML5, the methods and techniques used to make this game may or may not be the most optimal approach to game development. Although, the way this game was coded in pure HTML5, it works and performs great in any modern webkit-based browser. A discussion in game development as well as more sophisticated techniques is beyond the scope of the book.

3
Understanding the Gravity of HTML5

Before we dive into the game that we'll build in this chapter, we will examine why writing applications in HTML and JavaScript can be difficult when deploying in multiple different browsers. We will focus on simple and practical solutions to these problems, especially with regards to HTML5 and the latest APIs used today.

The game we will build in this chapter will be a basic jelly wobbly gravity game. It will make use of HTML5's new API for vector graphics, native audio manipulation, and drag-and-drop. As the backbone of the rendering system for this game, we will use the old JavaScript timer, which, as we will see, is not at all appropriate for games such as this one where we need multiple updates per second. Thankfully, modern browsers have solved this issue, and taken into account the need we have for highly efficient rendering engines. However, we won't be discussing this new feature until the next game. Just for completion, this new feature is known as **requestAnimationFrame**.

Browser compatibility

Anyone who has done any web development at all has quickly developed a very deep, profound, and thorough hatred towards the way different browsers interpret and render the same code. However, if we dig a bit deeper into this phenomena, and look for the root cause of these discrepancies, it will surprise some people to realize that the problem is not what it seems. While finding the cause for rendering differences is easy, for example, some browsers define the box model differently, finding the cause for differences in code may not be so clear. Surprisingly, some developers seem to despise the JavaScript language because some code runs differently in some browsers. However, the truth of the matter is that JavaScript is actually quite portable, and its API is quite stable and consistent.

Believe it or not, most of these headaches are caused by the DOM API, and not JavaScript itself. Some browsers register DOM-related events one way, while other browsers don't acknowledge that method, and instead use their own variation for it. The same goes for manipulating DOM elements and subtrees.

For example, one way to remove a node from the DOM is to call the `remove` method on the node itself. However, as of this writing, only a very limited handful of browsers expose this functionality. Most commonly, browsers allow us to remove a node from a DOM tree by calling the `removeChild` method on a parent node, passing a reference to the child node to be removed from the parent.

The key point to be made here is this; JavaScript itself is very consistent across browsers, but the way that browsers allow us to programmatically interact with the DOM, although this is most commonly done via JavaScript, may vary from browser to browser. While none of this is news to anybody, and certainly is not unique to HTML5, it is still important to remember that the main tool we have for programming the web platform, that is, JavaScript, is a very powerful and consistent one. The problem that we need to keep in mind is the DOM API (as well as CSS, although this particular issue is becoming less and less of an issue, as browsers are beginning to agree on common standards related to that).

Supporting different browsers

There are different approaches that we can take when developing an HTML5 application in order to ensure that the code runs the same in different browsers, and that the design is rendered the same as well. Some of these practices are painful and tedious, others are unreliable, and others are simply good enough. Unfortunately, as long as there are so many browser differences as there are today, there will never be one single silver bullet that completely makes the problem disappear.

The two main goals when it comes to writing code that runs practically identical in different browsers are; write as little unique code to each browser as possible, and write code that degrades gracefully. It is one thing to specifically target a couple of unique features specific to a particular browser, but it is a completely different issue to maintain two or more separate code bases. Remember this, that the best code you can possibly write, both in terms of efficient execution and security, is the code that you never have to write at all. The more code you write, the more subject to errors and faults your code will be. Thus, avoid writing too much code that does the same thing as other code you're also writing, but writing it uniquely for a different browser.

While being a perfectionist can be a great attribute, we must be realistic that we won't achieve perfection any time soon. Not only that, but in most cases (certainly in all cases where a video game is involved) we don't need to write software that is anywhere near perfect. At the end of the day, whether you agree with it or not, the goal of software development is to produce software that is good enough. As long as the program solves the problem for which it was written, and does so in a reasonable fashion, then for all practical purposes, we can say that the software is good.

With that introduction behind us, keep those two principles in mind as you develop HTML5 applications, including games, aimed at reaching hundreds of millions of people world wide. True, there are some browser-specific functionalities that may make a game unplayable, or at least make the user experience significantly different, that the final result might not be desirable. But, pay close attention to what you're really trying to accomplish, so as to discern what browser differences are good enough. It may very well be that a feature targeted to a particular browser is used by so few users that there is no cost benefit to the feature. What we never want to do, however, is to deploy an unusable product.

HTML5 libraries and frameworks

In our quest for multiple browser support in cost efficient ways, we can find comfort in knowing that we're not alone in this struggle. Today, there are so many open source projects aimed at solving this same problem of browser compatibility that we can possibly play the alphabet game, where we name a different HTML5 library or framework for each letter of the alphabet.

There are normally two reasons for the existence of such tools, namely to abstract away browser differences, and to speed up development. While most abstractions provided by today's JavaScript tools attempt to provide the client with a single interface that unifies browser discrepancies, a lot of these libraries also provide functionality that simply speed development time and effort.

jQuery

By far, the most popular JavaScript library is one called jQuery. If you haven't heard of jQuery before, chances are that you just woke up from a very deep and profound hibernation, while your body traveled through distant galaxies. Some of the main benefits for using jQuery includes a very powerful DOM query and manipulation engine, a very simple, unified **XHR (XML HTTP Request** also known as Ajax) interface, and the ability to extend it through a well defined plugin interface.

One example of how using a JavaScript library, particularly jQuery, can save you development time and effort is trying to make an asynchronous request to your server. Without jQuery, there is a bit of boilerplate code that we'd need to write so that different browsers all behave the same. The code is as follows:

```
var xhr = null;

// Attempt to create the xhr object the popular way
try {
  xhr = new XMLHttpRequest();
}
// If the browser doesn't support that construct, try a different one
catch (e) {
  try {
    xhr = new ActiveXObject("Microsoft.XMLHTTP");
  }
  // If it still doesn't support the previous 2 xhr constructs, just
give up
  catch (e) {
    throw new Error("This browser doesn't support AJAX");
  }
}

// If we made it this far, then the xhr object is set, and the rest
// of the API is identical independent of which version we ended up
with
xhr.open("GET", "//www.some-website.com", true);
xhr.onreadystatechange = function(response) {
  // Process response
  // (...)
};

xhr.send();
```

Now, in contrast, that exact functionality can be achieved with the following code using jQuery:

```
$.ajax({
  type: "GET",
  url: "//www.some-website.com",
  async: true,  /* This parameter is optional, as its default value is
true */
  complete: function(response) {
    // Process response
    // (…)
  }
});
```

One of the awesome things about jQuery's XHR functionality is that it is highly flexible. At a bare minimum, we can achieve the same behavior as in the previous code, in a completely cross-browser fashion, as shown in the following code:

```
$.get("//www.some-website.com", function(response) {
  // Process response
  // (...)
});
```

In conclusion, much can be done with very little effort, time, and code, with jQuery. All of this also comes with the added benefit that the library is developed by a very dedicated team, with a very involved and active community behind it. For more information about jQuery, check out the official website at `http://www.jquery.com`.

Google Web Toolkit

Another popular and extremely powerful JavaScript tool is **Google Web Toolkit (GWT)**. First of all, GWT is not a mere library that provides a handful of abstractions on top of JavaScript, but rather a full blown development toolkit that uses the Java language (which itself comes with all of its benefits), then compiles and translates the Java code into highly optimized, browser-specific JavaScript code.

It is silly to try to compare jQuery with GWT, as each solve different problems, and take a completely different look at web development. However, it is worth saying that while jQuery is a great tool that is currently found in the toolbox of nearly every web developer today, it is not intended for, nor is it a very good fit for actual game development. Google Web Toolkit, on the other hand, while not the most appropriate tool for small, trivial HTML and JavaScript projects, lends itself very well to game development. In fact, the popular game Angry Birds used Google Web Toolkit in the development of the Google Chrome version of the game.

In conclusion, while GWT is enough a subject to occupy its own book, it is a great tool to consider when you take on your next large web development project, where one of the goals is to provide multiple browser support to your application. For more information about Google Web Toolkit, check out the official website at `https://developers.google.com/web-toolkit/`.

Supporting browsers with limited HTML5 features

As was previously mentioned, none of the browser-caused development headaches mentioned above are new with, or specific to, HTML5. However, it is important to know that this same problem has not gone away with HTML5 (yet). Furthermore, HTML5 brings with it a whole new level of cross-browser nightmares. For instance, while most HTML5 related APIs are well defined in a documented specification, there are also many APIs that are currently in an experimental stage (for a discussion on experimental APIs and vendor prefixes, refer back to the online chapter, *Setting up the Environment*, and *Chapter 2*, *HTML5 Typography*, where the topic is more thoroughly discussed). On top of that, there are also browsers that don't yet support some HTML5 features, or currently offer limited support, or worse yet, they provide support through a different interface than other browsers.

Again, as web developers we must always have the user at the top of the list of priorities when creating a new application. Since the problem of browser compatibility is still among us, some people feel that HTML5 is still a thing for the future, and the usefulness of its new features remain yet to be seen. The rest of this section will describe ways that we can use HTML5 today without having to worry about less desirable browsers, and yet provide a functional application to users using such browsers.

Gracefully degrade

If you pay close attention to the previous code snippet where we attempted to create an **XHR** object that works in many different browsers, you will notice that the code deliberately halts execution if the browser executing the code doesn't support one of the two options the code searched for. That is a great example of what we should not do, if at all possible. Whenever a specific feature is not available to a certain browser, the first option should be to provide an alternative construct, even if this alternative method doesn't quite provide the same behavior. We should do all that we can to at least provide a functional experience in the worst case scenario, where the browser has zero support for what we're trying to accomplish.

For example, HTML5 provides a new storage mechanism that's similar to a cookie (in other words, a simple key-value pair storage), but with the main difference being that this storage mechanism stores the data completely in the client, and that data is never sent back and forth to the server as part of the HTTP request. While the specifics of what this storage system is and how it works will be covered later in the book, we can summarize it by saying that this storage system (called Local Storage) stores key-value pairs, and does so through a well defined interface, and from a property of the Window object named localStorage.

```
localStorage.setItem("name", "Rodrigo Silveira");
```

```
localStorage.length == 1; // true
localStorage.getItem("name"); // "Rodrigo Silveira"
localStorage.removeItem("name");
localStorage.length; // == 0
```

One powerful application for Local Storage is to cache asynchronous requests made by the user, so that the subsequent requests can be fetched directly from the browser's local storage, thus avoiding the round trip to the server. However, if a browser doesn't support local storage, the worst case scenario in this particular case would be that the application would need to fetch a subsequent request from the server again. While not practical or efficient, this is by far a problem one should not lose sleep over, except if that means that we'll need to write lots of extra code to test for the presence of the localStorage object every time we need to use it, thus polluting the code base with many repetitive conditional statements.

A simple solution to a problem such as this is to use polyfills, which we'll discuss more in depth next. In short, though, a polyfill is a JavaScript alternative that the browser can use when the original implementation is not yet available. This way, you can load the polyfill if the browser needs it, and the rest of the code base can use the functionality through the original interface, and never know which implementation it is working with. In the case of localStorage, we could simply check whether the authentic API is available, and write code that mimics its behavior if it is not available. The following code snippet shows this behavior:

```
// If the browser doesn't know anything about localStorage,
// we create our own, or at least an interface that respond
// to the calls we'd make to the real storage object.
if (window.localStorage === undefined) {
  var FauxLocalStorage = function() {
    var items = {};
    this.length = 0;

    this.setItem = function(key, value) {
      items[key] = value;
      this.length++;
    };

    this.getItem = function(key) {
      if (items[key] === undefined)
        return undefined;

      return items[key];
    };
```

```
        this.removeItem = function(key) {
          if (items[key] === undefined)
            return undefined;

          this.length--;
            return delete items[key];
          };
      };


      // Now there exists a property of window that behaves just like
      // one would expect the local storage object to (although in
      this example
      // the functionality is reduced in order to make the point)
      window.localStorage = new FauxStorage();
    }


    // This code will work just fine whether or not the browser
      supports the real
    // HTML5 API for local storage. No exceptions will be thrown.
    localStorage.setItem("name", "Rodrigo Silveira");
    localStorage.length == 1; // true
    localStorage.getItem("name"); // "Rodrigo Silveira"
    localStorage.removeItem("name");
    localStorage.length; // == 0
```

Although the preceding polyfill really doesn't store any data beyond the current session, this particular implementation of a local storage polyfill can be enough for the needs of a given application. At the very least, this implementation allows us to code to the official interface (calling the real methods defined by the specification), and no exceptions are thrown by the browser, since the methods are indeed present. Eventually, whenever the browser that didn't support the HTML5 API, and thus used our polyfill because of the conditional that checked for browser support of the feature, that conditional will no longer trigger the polyfill to be loaded, thus the client code will always refer to the original implementation and no changes will be needed to the main source code.

While it is quite exciting to consider what polyfills can do for us, the observant student will quickly notice that writing complete, secure, and accurate polyfills is slightly more complicated than adding simple CSS hacks to a style sheet in order to make a design compatible with different browsers. Even though the sample local storage polyfill shown previously was relatively complicated, it does not completely mimic the official interface, and neither does it behave 100 percent the same with the little functionality that it did implement. Soon the organized student will ask how much time he or she should expect to spend writing bullet-proof polyfills. The answer, which I'm glad to report is a positive one, is given and explained in the next section.

Polyfills

To answer the preceding question, that is, how much time should you expect to spend writing your own robust polyfills in order to be able to start using HTML5 features today, and still have your code run on multiple different browsers is, zero. Unless you really want the experience of writing a fallback for different browsers, there is no reason to cook your own libraries and such, since much work has already been done on this area by hundreds of other developers who have shared their work with the community.

With polyfills, there really isn't a single JavaScript import that we can use at the top of our HTML5 project that will magically extend every deficient browser, and make them 100 percent HTML5 ready. However, there are many separate projects available, so that if you're trying to use a particular element, you can simply import that particular polyfill. While there is no definitive source where all of these polyfills can be found, a simple Google or Bing search for the particular functionality you want should quickly connect you to an appropriate polyfill.

Modernizr

One particular tool that is worth mentioning is Modernizr. This JavaScript library inspects the page that loads it, and detects which HTML5 features are available in the user's browser. This way, we can very easily check whether or not a particular API is available, and take action accordingly.

As of this writing, the current version of Modernizr allows us to test for a particular API or feature, and load specific polyfills in the case that the test returns positive or negative, which makes adding polyfills when needed very easy and effortless.

Furthermore, Modernizr also includes HTML5 Shiv, which is a very small piece of JavaScript that allows us to use all of the HTML5 semantic tags in browsers that don't recognize them. Note that this will not add the actual functionality of the tags, but will merely allow you to style those tags through CSS. The reason is that in Internet Explorer Version 8 and below, if we try to style an element that the browser doesn't recognize, it will simply ignore any CSS applied to it. With Modernizr, however, those elements are created (using JavaScript), so that the browser then knows about the tags, and thus allows CSS to be applied to them.

For more information about Modernizr, check out the official website at `http://modernizr.com/`.

The game

The project game we'll build in this chapter is simply called *Basic Jelly Wobbling Gravity Game*. The goal of the game is to feed our main hero enough jelly that he gets sick and drops to the floor with a severe tummy ache. The main character is controlled through the left and right arrow keys on the keyboard, and in order to eat a jelly, you simply have to direct the hero underneath a falling jelly. Every time you feed the hero a jelly, his health meter decreases slightly. Once enough jelly has been fed, and the health meter reaches zero, the hero gets too sick and faints. If you let a jelly drop on the floor, nothing happens except that the jelly splashes everywhere. This is a Basic Jelly Wobbling Gravity Game. Can you serve Prince George enough jelly until he passes out?

In order to demonstrate a few principles about HTML5 game development, we'll build this game completely with DOM elements. While this approach is normally not the desired approach, you will notice that many games still perform quite nicely on most modern browsers, and on the average desktop or laptop computer today. However, as we'll learn in the chapters to follow, there are a few techniques, tools, and APIs available to us in HTML5 that are far more appropriate for game development.

Also, as is common to this book, most game elements will be kept to a minimum in terms of complexity, so that it can be explained and understood easily. Specifically in this game, we'll only use SVG graphics as a proof of concept instead of diving deeply into the potential and opportunity available to us through the SVG standard. The same goes for drag-and-drop, as there is so much more that can be done with it.

Code structure

The way this code is structured is very straightforward. Every element in the game is absolutely positioned through CSS, and each element is made up of some HTML container styled with a background image or some CSS3 properties that give it a fresh look with rounded corners, drop shadows, and so on. Also, although some people might prefer object oriented programming to functional programming, and better cohesion instead of global variables everywhere, we'll take exactly that approach in this game, and focus on the HTML5 aspects instead of the design of the game. The same goes for the style and quality of the graphics. All that you see in this game was created by myself using a free photo editor program, and it took me no longer than 30 minutes to create all of the graphics you see in the game. This was mostly to show that fun games can be built even if you're on a budget, or don't have a dedicated graphics design team.

Since we're loading all of the SVG entities right inline with our HTML structure, we place them inside a `div` container that is hidden from the user, then we clone each entity that we need a copy of and use it on the game. We use this technique for all of the jellies and the hero. The hero SVG is left the same as what was exported from the vector editor software. The jelly SVG is slightly modified by removing all of the colors that they were designed with, and replaced with CSS classes. This way we can create different CSS classes that specify different colors, and each new instance of the jelly SVG is assigned a random class. The final result is one single SVG model hidden inside the invisible `div` container, and each instance of it, using zero extra code, is given a different color to add variety to the game. We could also have randomly assigned a different size and rotation to each jelly instance, but this was left out for an exercise to the reader.

```
<body>
  <div class="health-bar">
    <span></span>
  </div>

    <h1 id="message"></h1>

    <div id="table"></div>
    <div id="bowl"></div>
    <div id="bowl-top-faux-target"></div>
```

```
        <div id="bowl-top" class="dragging-icon bowl-closed"
          draggable="true"
          ondragstart="doOnDragStart(event)"
          ondragend="doOnDragEnd(event)"></div>
        <div id="bowl-top-target"
          ondrop="startGame()"
          ondragover="doOnDrop(event)"
          ondragleave="doOnDragLeave(event)"></div>

        <div class="dom-recs">
          <svg class="hero-svg">
          (...)
          </svg>
          <svg class="jelly-svg">
          (...)
          </svg>
        </div>
    </body>
```

Although we could have used data attributes instead of ID attributes for all of those elements, there would have been no real benefit over using them over the IDs, just as there is really no benefit in using IDs over data-attributes in this situation.

Note how there are two targets where the bowl-top can be dragged onto. Actually, there is really only one, which is the element bowl-top-target. The other element that looks like a target, which was cleverly given an ID of bowl-top-faux-target, is only there for the visual effect. Since a real drop target (an element where a draggable element can be placed at the end of a drag option) is only activated once the mouse pointer moves over it, there wasn't enough room on that table to accomplish the desired effect of showing a small outlined area where bowl-top appears to be dropped.

Finally, there is one global timer used in the game, which controls the frequency at which we call the game loop function, named tick(). Although this is not a chapter on proper game design, I will point out that you should avoid the temptation to create multiple timers for different purposes. Some people out there won't think twice before firing off an event through a unique timer separate from the main game timer. Doing so, especially in HTML5 games, can have negative side effects both in performance and in synchronizing all of the events.

API usage

The three APIs used in this game are audio, SVG, and drag-and-drop. A brief explanation of how each of these APIs were used in the game will follow, where only a general overview of the feature is given. In the next section, however, we'll take a detailed look at what each of these features actually do, and how we can use it in this and other situations. For the complete source code for this game, check out the book's page from Packt Publishing's website.

Web audio

Audio was used both for a never-ending loop used as a background song, as well as individual sound effects that are fired off when a jelly is launched up, bounces off the walls, splatters on the floor, or is eaten by the hungry hero. An old school sound effect is also fired off when the hero finally dies from eating too much jelly.

The way that each audio entity is managed in the game is through a simple encapsulation that holds references to individual sound files, and exposes an interface allowing us to play a file, fade sound files in and out, as well as add new sound files to the list of audios managed by this class. The code for the same is as follows:

```
// ** By assigning an anonymous function to a variable, JavaScript
// allows us to later call the variable's referenced function with
// the keyword 'new'. This style co function creation essentially
// makes the function behave like a constructor, which allows us
   to
// simulate classes in JavaScript
var SoundFx = function() {
  // Every sound entity will be stored here for future use
  var sounds = {};

  // -----------------------------------------------------------
  // Register a new sound entity with some basic configurations
  // -----------------------------------------------------------
  function addSound(name, file, loop, autoplay) {

    // Don't create two entities with the same name
    if (sounds[name] instanceof Audio)
      return false;

    // Behold, the new HTML5 Audio element!
    sounds[name] = new Audio();
    sounds[name].src = file;
    sounds[name].controls = false;
    sounds[name].loop = loop;
```

```
      sounds[name].autoplay = autoplay;
  }


  // -----------------------------------------------------------
  // Play a file from the beginning, even if it's already
playing
  // -----------------------------------------------------------
function play(name) {
  sounds[name].currentTime = 0;
  sounds[name].play();
}


  // -----------------------------------------------------------
  // Gradually adjust the volume, either up or down
  // -----------------------------------------------------------
function fade(name, fadeTo, speed, inOut) {
  if (fadeTo > 1.0)
    return fadeOut(name, 1.0, speed, inOut);

  if (fadeTo < 0.000)
    return fadeOut(name, 0.0, speed, inOut);

    var newVolume = parseFloat(sounds[name].volume + 0.01 *
inOut);

  if (newVolume < parseFloat(0.0))
    newVolume = parseFloat(0.0);

    sounds[name].volume = newVolume;

  if (sounds[name].volume > fadeTo)
    setTimeout(function(){ fadeOut(name, fadeTo, speed, inOut);
}, speed);
  else
    sounds[name].volume = parseFloat(fadeTo);

    return sounds[name].volume;
}


  // -----------------------------------------------------------
  // A wrapper function for fade()
  // -----------------------------------------------------------
  function fadeOut(name, fadeTo, speed) {
    fade(name, fadeTo, speed, -1);
  }
```

```
// ----------------------------------------------------------
// A wrapper function for fade()
// ----------------------------------------------------------
function fadeIn(name, fadeTo, speed) {
  fade(name, fadeTo, speed, 1);
}


// ----------------------------------------------------------
// The public interface through which the client can use the
  class
// ----------------------------------------------------------
return {
  add: addSound,
  play: play,
  fadeOut: fadeOut,
  fadeIn: fadeIn
};
};
```

Next, we instantiate a global object of this custom SoundFx type, where every sound clip used in the game is stored. This way, if we want to play any type of sound, we simply call the play method on this global reference. Take a look at the following code:

```
// Hold every sound effect in the same object for easy access
var sounds = new SoundFx();

// Sound.add() Parameters:
// string: hash key
// string: file url
// bool: loop this sound on play?
// bool: play this sound automatically as soon as it's loaded?
sounds.add("background", "sound/techno-loop-2.mp3", true,  true);
sounds.add("game-over",  "sound/game-over.mp3",     false, false);
sounds.add("splash",     "sound/slurp.mp3",         false, false);
sounds.add("boing",      "sound/boing.mp3",         false, false);
sounds.add("hit",        "sound/swallow.mp3",       false, false);
sounds.add("bounce",     "sound/bounce.mp3",        false, false);
```

Scalable Vector Graphics (SVG)

As mentioned previously, the way SVG is used in the game is limited simply because the SVG spec is so robust and can get fairly complex. As you'll see in the in-depth description of the SVG API, there were a lot of things that we could have done to each individual primitive shape drawn through SVG (such as natively animating the hero's facial expressions, or making each jelly jiggle or rotate, and so on).

The way we switch the sprite that represents a jelly into a splashed out jelly, when a jelly hits the floor is pretty clever. When we draw the jelly vectors using the vector editor software, we create two separate images, each representing a different state of the jelly. Both images are stacked on top of each other, so that they line up properly. Then, inside the HTML code, we assign a CSS class to each of these images. These classes are called jelly-block and splash, representing a jelly in its natural state, and a jelly splashed on the floor. In both of these classes, one of the vectors is hidden and the other is not. Depending on the state of each jelly element, these two classes are toggled back and forth. This is all done by simply assigning one of the two classes `jelly-svg-on` and `jelly-svg-off` to the parent svg element holding these two vector groups, as shown in the following code:

```
.jelly-svg-off g.jelly-block, .jelly-svg-on g.splash {
    display: none;
}

.jelly-svg-off g.splash, .jelly-svg-on g.jelly-block {
    display: block;
}
```

The way the preceding styles are driven is simple. By default, every jelly element is given a CSS class of `jelly-svg-on`, meaning that the jelly is not splashed. Then, when a jelly is calculated to have hit the floor, we remove that class, and add the CSS class of `jelly-svg-off`, as seen in the following code snippet:

```
// Iterate through each jelly and check its state
for (var i in jellies) {

  // Don't do anything to this jelly entity if it's outside the
    screen,
  // was eaten, or smashed on the floor
  if (!jellies[i].isInPlay())
    continue;

    // Determine if a jelly has already hit the floor
    stillFalling = jellies[i].getY() + jellies[i].getHeight() *
      2.5 < document.body.offsetHeight;

    // If it hasn't hit the floor, let gravity move it down
    if (stillFalling) {
      jellies[i].move();
    } else {
```

```
        // Stop the jelly from falling
        jellies[i].setY(document.body.offsetHeight -
          jellies[i].getHeight() - 75);

          // Swap the vectors
          jellies[i].swapClass("jelly-svg-on", "jelly-svg-off");
          jellies[i].setInPlay(false);

          // Play the corresponding sound to this action
          sounds.play("splash");
        }
    }
```

Drag-and-drop

Similar to the way SVG was used in the game, drag-and-drop made its way into the final product taking a backseat to web audio. Yet, the role that drag-and-drop plays in the game is arguably the most important one, it starts the game. Instead of having the game start playing right away when the page first loads, or instead of having the user press a button or hit a key to start game play, the player needs to drag the lid away from the bowl where all the jellies are stored, and place it next to the bowl on the table where it sits.

The way drag-and-drop works in HTML5 is simple and intuitive. We register at least one object to be a draggable object (the one you drag around), and at least one other object to be a drop target (the object where the draggable can be dropped into). Then we register callback functions for whatever events we want that apply to the dragging and dropping behavior.

In the game, we only listen for five events, two on the draggable element, and three on the drop target element. First, we listen for when the draggable is first dragged by the user (on drag start), which we respond to by making the bowl lid image invisible and placing a copy of the lid behind the mouse pointer, so that it appears that the user is truly dragging that lid.

Next, we listened for the event that is triggered when the user finally releases the mouse button, indicating the end of the dragging action (on drag end). At this point, we simply restore the bowl lid back to where it was originally, on top of the bowl. This event is fired whenever the dragging action is finished, and the drop was not done inside a valid drop target (the user didn't drop the lid where it was expected), which essentially restarts the process.

The three events that we listen for on the drop target are the onDragLeave, onDragOver, and onDrop. Whenever a draggable is dropped inside a drop target, the target's onDrop event is fired. In this case, all we do is call the startGame() function, which sets the game in motion. As part of the set up for this startGame function, we move the bowl lid element into the exact pixel position where it was dropped, and remove the draggable attribute, so that the user can no longer drag that element.

The functions onDragOver and onDragLeave are triggered whenever the mouse pointer is moved on top of, and hovered out of the target object, respectively. In our case, all we do in each of those functions is toggle the visibility of the bowl lid and the image that shows behind the cursor while the dragging is happening. This can be seen in the following code:

```
// ----------------------------------------------------------
// Fired when draggable starts being dragged (onDragStart)
// ----------------------------------------------------------
function doOnDragStart(event) {
  if (bowlTop.isReady) {
    event.target.style.opacity = 0.0;
    event.dataTransfer.setDragImage(bowlTop, 100, 60);
  }
}


// ----------------------------------------------------------
// Fired when draggable is released outside a target (onDragEnd)
// ----------------------------------------------------------
function doOnDragEnd(event) {
  event.target.style.opacity = 1.0;
  document.querySelector("#bowl-top-faux-target").style.opacity = 0.0;
}


// ----------------------------------------------------------
// Fired when draggable enters target (onDragOver)
// ----------------------------------------------------------
function doOnDragOver(event) {
  event.preventDefault();
  document.querySelector("#bowl-top-faux-target").style.opacity = 1.0;
}


// ----------------------------------------------------------
// Fired when draggable is hovered away from a target (onDragLeave)
// ----------------------------------------------------------
function doOnDragLeave(event) {
  document.querySelector("#bowl-top-faux-target").style.opacity = 0.0;
}
```

```
// -----------------------------------------------------------
// Fired when draggable is dropped inside a target (onDrop)
// -----------------------------------------------------------
function startGame() {

  // Keep the game from starting more than once
  if (!isPlaying) {

    // Register input handlers
    document.body.addEventListener("keyup", doOnKeyUp);
    document.body.addEventListener("keydown", doOnKeyDown);

    // Reposition the bowl lid
    var bowlTop = document.querySelector("#bowl-top");
    bowlTop.classList.remove("bowl-closed");
    bowlTop.style.left = (event.screenX - bowlTop.offsetWidth + 65) +
"px";
    bowlTop.style.top = (event.screenY - bowlTop.offsetHeight + 65 *
0) + "px";

    // Disable dragging on the lid by removing the HTML5 draggable
attribute
    bowlTop.removeAttribute("draggable");
    bowlTop.classList.remove("dragging-icon");

    newJelly();
      isPlaying = true;

      // Start out the main game loop
      gameTimer = setInterval(tick, 15);
    }
};
```

Web audio

The new web audio API defines a way to play audio right into the browser without the need for a single plugin. For a high level experience, we can simply add a few audio tags throughout our HTML page, and the browser takes care of displaying a player for the user to interact with and play, pause, stop, rewind, fast forward, and adjust the volume. Alternatively, we can use the JavaScript interface available, and either control the audio tags on the page with it, or achieve much more powerful and complex tasks.

One key detail to remember about browser support and the web audio API, is that different browsers support different file formats. When defining an audio tag, similar to an image tag, we specify the path to the source file. The difference is that with audio, we can specify multiple sources for the same file (but different formats), then the browser can choose the file it supports, or the best option it has, in case it supports multiple file formats. Currently there are three audio formats supported by all major browsers, namely `.mp3`, `.wav`, and `.ogg`. As of this writing, no single audio format is supported in all major browsers, which means that whenever we use the web audio API, we'll need at least two versions of each and every file we play through the API, if we wish to reach the greatest possible audience.

Finally, keep in mind that although we can (and should) specify multiple audio files per each audio element, each browser only downloads one of these files. This is a very handy (and obvious) feature because downloading multiple copies of the same file would be awfully inefficient and bandwidth heavy.

How to use it

The simplest way to get started with the web audio API is with an inline HTML5 element. The code for it is as follows:

```
<audio>
  <source src="sound-file.mp3" type="audio/mpeg" />
  <source src="sound-file.ogg" type="audio/ogg" />
</audio>
```

Adding the above snippet to a page will not result in anything visible. In order to add more control to the tag, including adding a player to the page so that the user can interact with it, we can choose from the elements associated with the tag. These attributes are as follows:

- **autoplay**: It starts playing the file right away as soon as the browser has downloaded it
- **controls**: It displays a visual player with buttons through which the user can control audio playback
- **loop**: It is used to continuously play the file indefinitely
- **muted**: It is used when audio output is muted
- **preload**: It specifies how the audio resource is to be preloaded by the browser

To achieve a similar result through JavaScript, we can create a DOM element of type audio, or instantiate a JavaScript object of type Audio. Adding the optional attributes can be done the same way we would to any other JavaScript object. Note that creating an instance of Audio has the exact same effect as creating a reference to a DOM element:

```
// Creating an audio file from a DOM element
var soundOne = document.createElement("audio");
soundOne.setAttribute("controls", "controls");

soundOneSource = document.createElement("source");
soundOneSource.setAttribute("src", "sound-file.mp3");
soundOneSource.setAttribute("type", "audio/mpeg");

soundOne.appendChild(soundOneSource);

document.body.appendChild(soundOne);

// Creating an audio file from Audio
var soundTwo = new Audio("sound-file.mp3");
soundTwo.setAttribute("controls", "controls");

document.body.appendChild(soundTwo);
```

Although the JavaScript Audio object may seem easier to deal with, especially since it takes that awesome constructor argument that saves us a whole line of code, they both behave exactly the same, and can only be told apart at run time if you really want to be picky and distinguish them from each other. One small detail that you should know is that when we create that audio reference in JavaScript, it is not necessary to append it to the DOM in order to play the file.

However you decide to approach this setup step, once we have a reference to an audio object in JavaScript, we can control it with any one of the many events and attributes associated with the object. The audio objects are as follows:

- **play()**: It starts playing the file.
- **pause()**: It stops playing the file, and maintains the currentTime.
- **paused**: Is a Boolean representing the current play state.
- **canPlayType**: Is used to find out whether the browser supports a particular audio type.
- **currentSrc**: It returns the absolute path to the file currently assigned to the object.

- **currentTime**: It returns the current play position in seconds, as a floating point number.

- **duration**: It returns the total play time in seconds, as a floating point number.

- **ended**: Is a Boolean indicating whether the currentTime is equal to duration.

- **readyState**: It indicates the state of the download of the source file.

- **volume**: It indicates the current volume of the file, ranging from 0 to 1 both inclusive. This number is relative to the current system volume.

SVG

Scalable Vector Graphics (SVG) for short, is an XML based format that describes graphics. This format may seem complicated enough to be confused with a full blown programming language for 2D graphics, but in truth it is just a markup language. While SVG may seem new to some web developers, the specification was first developed back in 1999.

The main difference between a vector graphic and a raster graphic (in other words, a bitmap) is the way that the graphic is described. In a bitmap, each pixel is essentially represented by three or four numbers, representing the color of that individual pixel (RGB), along with a possible opacity level. Looking at it from a broader sense, a bitmap is nothing more than a grid of pixels. Vectors, on the other hand, are described by a series of mathematical functions that describe lines, shapes, and colors, instead of each individual point on the entire image. To put it in simple terms, vector graphics do a fantastic job of scaling its dimensions, as illustrated in the following screenshot:

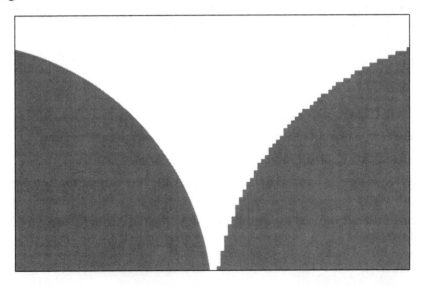

If you zoom in or try to stretch a vector graph, it will always be as smooth as the original, since the shape is defined (and scaled) using the same mathematical functions (as exemplified on the image on the left). Raster graphics, on the other hand, are only defined by the same grid of pixels. Scaling that grid just means multiplying the dimensions of the grid, resulting in the blocky, pixelated image represented by the image on the right.

Now, the SVG standard does much more than simply define shapes, lines, paths, and colors. The specification also defines transformations and animations that can be applied to any single primitive, a group of primitives, or the entire SVG context. The specification also allows for SVG to be a very accessible format, meaning that it is possible to include text and other meta data right into the file, so that other applications can understand the file in other ways besides just the graphics. For example, search engines can crawl and index, not only your web pages, but also any SVG graphic.

Since SVG is text based (as opposed to storing binary data, such as an audio file, for example), it is also possible to compress an SVG image using such compression algorithms as the popular Gzip, which is so prevalent in the world of web development these days. When an SVG file is saved as its own, standalone file, it is given the extension `.svg`. If the file is Gzip compressed, that extension should be `.svgz`, so that the browser knows to uncompress the file before processing it.

SVG files can be used in an HTML file in a few different ways. Since the file itself can be saved as its own file, it is possible to embed the entire file on a page using the object tag, using an ordinary image tag, or even using an XHR object to fetch its contents from a server, and injected right into the HTML document. Alternatively, the contents of an SVG file can be manually copied into the host HTML file, so that its contents are imported inline.

To import an SVG graphic inline into an HTML document, we simply insert an `svg` tag, with all of its contents as children nodes of it. As of this writing, the XML namespace attribute is required, along with the version number, as shown in the following code:

```
<body>
  <svg
    xmlns="http://www.w3.org/2000/svg"
    version="1.1"
    width="150"
    height="150">

    <circle
      cx="75"
      cy="75"
```

```
        r="50"
        stroke="black"
        stroke-width="2"
        fill="red"></circle>
    </svg>
</body>
```

While this may seem easy enough for a simple red circle, once the image gets to be more complex, it gets a bit hard to manage all of it in one file. Thus, it may be more convenient to simply save all of the SVG files externally, then import them individually. This approach also lends itself much better to resource sharing and reuse, as we can import the same graphic in multiple files without having to copy the entire file every time.

```
<body>
    <object type="image/svg+xml" data="red-circle.svg"
      width="100" height="100">
    </object>

    <img src="red-circle.svg" width="100" height="100" />
</body>
```

One final note about SVG before we dive into some hands on examples, is that every node inside the parent svg tag (including that parent node) is managed by the browser. Thus, every one of these nodes can be styled through CSS. If that's not enough, every node inside an SVG graphic can have browser events registered to them, allowing us to interact with the graphic and all of its individual components the same way as most other DOM elements. This makes SVG a very dynamic, highly flexible graphics format.

If the SVG instance is inlined with the HTML, then we can simply get a direct reference to the parent svg node, or to any child node direct though JavaScript. Once we have that reference, we can act on the objects just like any other DOM elements. However, if the SVG is external to the HTML, we need to take one extra step and load in the actual SVG file into the JavaScript variable. Once this step is done, we can work with the SVG's subtree as though it is local to the file.

```
<body>
    <object type="image/svg+xml" data="red-circle.svg"
      width="100" height="100">
    </object>

    <script>
      var obj = document.querySelector("object");
```

```
      // Very important step! Before calling getSVGDocument, we must
register
        // a callback to be fired once the SVG document is loaded.
    obj.onload = function(){
      init(obj.getSVGDocument());
    };

    function init(svg) {
      var circles = svg.getElementsByTagName("circle");

      // Register click handler on all circles
      for (var i = 0, len = circles.length; i < len; i++) {
        circles[i].addEventListener("click", doOnCircleClick);
      }

      // When a circle element is clicked, it adds a CSS class
        "blue"
            // to itself.
    function doOnCircleClick(event) {
      this.classList.add("blue");
    }
  }
  </script>
</body>
```

A few important details about the preceding code snippet that you should always remember are:

- The imported SVG Document is treated as an external document (similar to an Iframe), meaning that any CSS outside of that document (such as the host document) is outside of its scope. Thus, if you want to apply a CSS class to an SVG node from a `getSVGDocument()` call, that CSS class must be defined within the same SVG file that was imported originally.

- The CSS attributes for SVG are slightly different. For example, instead of defining a background color you would define a fill color. Basically, the same attributes that are used on the SVG elements themselves, are the same ones you'd use in a corresponding stylesheet declaration.

- Any browser-specific CSS attributes can be applied to SVG nodes (for example, transition, cursor, etc.)

Thus, the preceding example is completed with the following `.svg` file as the corresponding `red-circle.svg` file, as used in the following code snippet:

```svg
<svg
  xmlns="http://www.w3.org/2000/svg"
  version="1.1"
  width="150"
  height="150">

<style type="text/css">
.blue {
  /* CSS Specific to SVG */
  fill: #0000ff;

  /* CSS Specific to the browser */
  cursor: pointer;
  -webkit-transition: fill 1.25s;
}
</style>
  <circle
    cx="75"
    cy="75"
    r="50"
    stroke="black"
    stroke-width="2"
    fill="red"></circle>

</svg>
```

How to use it

Although it is highly recommended that you use a professional vector editor software when composing complex SVG graphics, such as Inkspace or Adobe Illustrator, this section will walk you through the basics of SVG composition. This way you can draw basic shapes and graphs by hand, or at least be familiar with the fundamentals of SVG drawing.

Remember that whether you are importing your SVG graphics into your HTML through any of the methods described previously, drawing them inline, or even creating them dynamically through JavaScript, you will need to include the XML namespace to the root `svg` element. This is a common mistake made by newcomers to SVG, which may result in your graphics not showing up on the page.

The primitive shapes we can draw with SVG are rectangle, circle, ellipse, line, polyline, polygon, and path. Some of these primitives share attributes (such as width and height), while others have attributes that are unique to that shape (such as the radius of a circle). Everything you see in an SVG graphic is a result of these primitives used together in some combination.

Everything in SVG is drawn inside an SVG canvas, which is defined by the parent svg tag. This canvas is always rectangular, even though the shapes inside it can be of any shape that can be created by any of the primitives. Also, the canvas has its own coordinate system, which places the point origin at the top left corner of the canvas. The width and height of the canvas (determined by the parent svg tag) determines the dimensions of the drawing area, and all the (x, y) points reference inside the canvas (by all the child elements of svg) are relative to that point.

As a boilerplate for the following examples, we'll assume an external svg file, where we'll set the canvas size to 1000 x 1000 pixels, and draw away inside it. To view the final result of each example, you can use any one of the methods described in the previous section on how to load an SVG image into an HTML file. the following code snippet shows how the svg tag is defined:

```
<svg xmlns="http://www.w3.org/2000/svg" version="1.1" width="1000"
height="1000">
</svg>
```

Drawing a rectangle is as simple as it can get with SVG. Simply specify a width and height to a rect element, and that's it. Optionally, we can specify a stroke width and stroke color (where a stroke is the same thing as a border), along with a background color. Take a look at the following code:

```
<svg xmlns="http://www.w3.org/2000/svg" version="1.1" width="1000"
height="1000">
  <rect
    width="400"
    height="150" />
</svg>
```

By default, every shape is rendered at the origin (x = 0, y = 0), with no stroke (stroke-width = 0), and a background color (fill) set to all black (hexadecimal value of #000000, and RGB value of 0, 0, 0).

The circle is drawn with a `circle` tag by specifying at least three attributes, namely an *x* and *y* position (denoted by `cx` and `cy`), along with a radius value (denoted by the letter `r`). The center of the circle is placed at position (`cx`, `cy`), and the radius length does not take into account the width of the stroke, if one is present.

```
<svg xmlns="http://www.w3.org/2000/svg" version="1.1" width="1000"
height="1000">
  <circle
    cx="0"
    cy="0"
    r="300"
    fill="#ff3" />

  <circle
    cx="200"
    cy="200"
    r="100"
    fill="#a0a" />
</svg>
```

You will notice that by default, just like positioned DOM elements, every node has the same z-index. Thus, if two or more elements overlap, whatever element was drawn last (meaning that it is positioned farther from the parent than its sibling element) is rendered on top.

Ellipses are very similar to circles, with the only difference being that they have a radius for each direction (vertical and horizontal). Other than that minor detail, drawing an ellipse is the exact same as drawing a circle. Of course, we can simulate circles by drawing ellipses that have both radii of the same length.

```
<svg xmlns="http://www.w3.org/2000/svg" version="1.1" width="1000"
height="1000">
  <ellipse
    cx="400"
    cy="300"
    rx="300"
    ry="100"
    fill="#ff3" />

  <ellipse
    cx="230"
    cy="200"
    rx="75"
    ry="75"
    fill="#a0a" />
```

```
  <ellipse
    cx="560"
    cy="200"
    rx="75"
    ry="75"
    fill="#a0a" />
</svg>
```

With those basic shapes out of the way, we will now proceed to drawing more complex shapes. Instead of just following a few predefined points and lengths, we now get to choose exactly where each point goes in the shapes we'll be drawing. While this makes it slightly harder to draw shapes by hand, it also makes the possibilities much more extensive.

Drawing a line is both simple and fast. Simply specify two points within the SVG coordinate space, and you have a line. Each point is specified by an enumerated (x, y) pair.

```
<svg xmlns="http://www.w3.org/2000/svg" version="1.1" width="1000"
height="1000">
  <line
    x1="50"
    y1="50"
    x2="300"
    y2="500"
    stroke-width="50"
    stroke="#c00" />
</svg>
```

Next we'll cover the polyline, which is an extension of a regular line. The difference between a line and a polyline is that, as the name implies, a polyline is a collection of lines. While a regular line only takes in two coordinate points, a polyline takes two or more points, with a line connecting them in order. Also, if we specify a fill color for the polyline, the last point will be connected to the first, and the shape formed by that enclosed area will have the fill applied to it. Obviously, if no fill is specified, the polyline is rendered as a simple shape made out of nothing but straight lines.

```
<svg xmlns="http://www.w3.org/2000/svg" version="1.1" width="1000"
height="1000">
  <polyline
    points="50, 10, 100, 50, 30, 100, 175, 300, 250, 10, 10, 400"
    fill="#fff"
    stroke="#c00"
    stroke-width="10"/>
</svg>
```

The next shape we'll look at is the polygon. Scarily similar to a polyline, the polygon is drawn exactly in the same way as a polyline, but with two very important distinctions. First, a polygon must have at least three points. Secondly, a polygon is always a closed shape. This means that the last point and the first point of the sequence are physically connected, whereas in a polyline, that connection is only made by the fill, if one is assigned to the polyline:

```
<svg xmlns="http://www.w3.org/2000/svg" version="1.1" width="1000"
height="1000">
    <polygon
        points="50, 10, 100, 50, 30, 100, 175, 300, 250, 10, 10, 400"
        fill="#fff"
        stroke="#c00"
        stroke-width="10"/>
</svg>
```

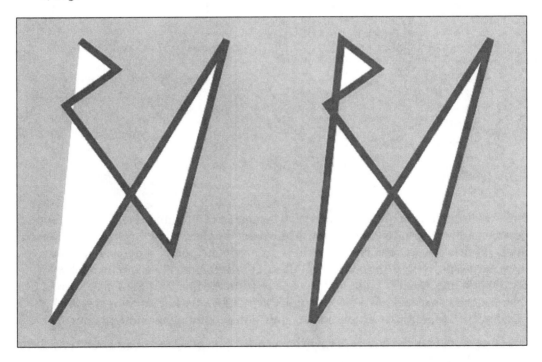

The polyline is shown on the left side of the preceding screenshot, while the shape on the right is a polygon that uses the exact same points to describe its position and orientation. The only difference between the two is that a polygon is forcefully closed. Of course, we can also simulate that behavior using a polyline by simply manually connecting the last point with the first.

SVG also allows us to draw very complex shapes with smooth curves, instead of the line-based shapes covered previously. To do so, we can use the path element, which might be a little complex at first, as it has several different attributes we can manipulate. One key feature of paths is that it allows us to either move the pointer to a location within the coordinate space, or to draw a line to a point.

All path attributes that describe the path are put inside the d attribute. These attributes are as follows:

- **M**: move to
- **L**: line to
- **H**: horizontal line to
- **V**: vertical line to
- **C**: curve to
- **S**: smooth curve to
- **Q**: quadratic Bezier curve
- **T**: smooth quadratic Bezier curve
- **A**: elliptical arc
- **Z**: close path

These attributes can be repeated as many times as needed, although it may be a good idea to break down the overall drawing into multiple smaller paths. Some reasons to separate a larger drawing into multiple paths are to make the figure more manageable, easier to troubleshoot, and easier to understand. The code for this is as follows:

```
<svg xmlns="http://www.w3.org/2000/svg" version="1.1" width="1000"
height="1000">
  <path
    d="M 100 100
    L 100 300
    M 250 100
    L 250 300
    M 400 100
    L 400 300"
    fill="transparent"
    stroke-width="45"
    stroke="#333" />
</svg>
```

Unless you practice and train yourself to look at path descriptions, it may be hard to just look at those codes and visualize the path. Take your time and look at each attribute individually. The preceding example first moves the pointer to point (100, 100), then a line is drawn from that point to another point (100, 300). This makes a vertical line from the last position where the pointer was, to the point specified by the line to attribute. Next, the cursor is changed from where it was to a new position (250, 100). Note that simply moving the cursor doesn't affect any previous drawing calls, nor does it do any drawing at that time. Finally, a second vertical line is drawn to point (250, 300). A third line is drawn at an equal distance from the first line. This can be seen in the following screenshot:

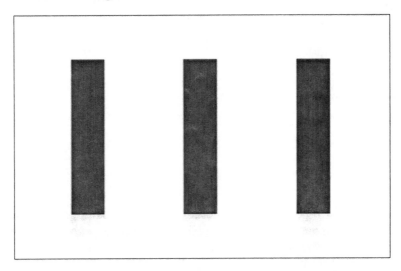

Note that whatever values we define for fill, stroke, stroke width, and so on, are applied to the entire path. The solution to the problem of wanting different fill and stroke values is to create additional paths.

Drawing curves is still a bit more complicated. A curve requires three values, namely two control points, and the final point to which the line is drawn. To illustrate how control points work, observe the following example:

```
<svg xmlns="http://www.w3.org/2000/svg" version="1.1" width="1000"
height="1000">
  <path
    d="M 250 100
    L 250 300
    M 400 100
    L 400 300"
    fill="transparent"
    stroke-width="45"
```

```
      stroke="#333" />
<path
   d="M 150 300
   C 200 500,
   450 500,
   500 300"

   fill="transparent"
   stroke-width="45"
   stroke="#333" />

<circle
   cx="150"
   cy="300"
   r="8"
   fill="#c00" />
<circle
   cx="200"
   cy="500"
   r="8"
   fill="#c00" />
<line
   x1="150"
   y1="300"
   x2="200"
   y2="500"
   stroke-width="5"
   stroke="#c00" />

<circle
   cx="450"
   cy="500"
   r="8"
   fill="#c00" />
<circle
   cx="500"
   cy="300"
   r="8"
   fill="#c00" />
<line
   x1="450"
   y1="500"
   x2="500"
```

```
          y2="300"
          stroke-width="5"
          stroke="#c00" />
   </svg>
```

While executing the preceding code as shown in the following screenshot, we can see the relationship between control points and the curvature of a line:

This is a cubic Bezier curve where the red lines show where the first and last curve points connect with the control points.

Drawing curves just the way you want is a rather complex problem to solve by hand. Different curve functions behave different from each other, so be sure to experiment with them all until you get a good feel for how they each work. Remember that although it is a good idea to have at least some understanding of how these curves and other drawing primitives work, it is highly recommended that you always use appropriate software to help you create your drawings. Ideally, we would use our creativity to create the drawing, and let the computer figure out how to represent that using SVG.

The description attributes for paths can be specified using either a lowercase or an uppercase letter. The difference is that an uppercase letter means that the point is absolute, and a lowercase letter means that the point is relative. This concept of relative and absolute points is not quite the same as in HTML, where a relative offset means that the destination point is relative to its own original location, and an absolute point is one that's completely relative to the element's parent.

In SVG world, an absolute point is relative to the canvas' origin, and a relative point is relative to the last point defined. For example, if you move the pointer to location (10, 10), then do a relative move with values of 10 15, the pointer will end up, not at location (10, 15), but 10 units away from the x position, and 15 units away from the y position. The new position of the pointer would then be location (20, 25).

Finally, SVG is capable of rendering text to the screen. Imagine how time consuming it would be to render each letter by hand using lines and paths. Thankfully, the SVG API specifies a very simple interface for text rendering.

```
<svg xmlns="http://www.w3.org/2000/svg" version="1.1" width="1000"
height="1000">
  <text
    x="100"
    y="300"
    fill="#c00"
    stroke="#333"
    stroke-width="2"
    style="font-size: 175px">I Love HTML5!</text>
</svg>
```

Now, the SVG standard does much more than simply define shapes, lines, paths, and colors. The specification also defines groups of elements, whereby one may literally group a collection of nodes, so that they can possibly all be treated together as a single unit. There are also transformations, animations, gradients, and even photo filters, all of which can be applied to the simple primitives that are described previously. Take a look at the following code:

```
<svg xmlns="http://www.w3.org/2000/svg" version="1.1" width="1000"
height="1000">
  <rect
    x="500"
    y="500"
    width="900"
    height="600"
```

```
      fill="#c00"
      stroke="#333"
      stroke-width="2"
      transform="translate(800, 50)
        rotate(55, 0, 0)
        scale(0.25)">

      <animate
        dur="1.5s"
        attributeName="x"
        values="-50; 100; -50"
        repeatCount="indefinite" />

      <animate
        dur="1.5s"
        attributeName="height"
        values="50; 300; 50"
        repeatCount="indefinite" />
   </rect>
</svg>
```

Drag-and-drop

Although creating drag-and-drop functionality manually is not a very challenging ordeal, HTML5 takes drag-and-drop to a whole new level. With the new API, we're given the ability to do so much more than just let the browser handle the dragging and dropping actions. The interface allows for customizing the exact way that things are dragged, how the dragging action looks, what data is carried with the draggable object, and so on. Plus, not having to worry about how the low level events are tracked in different platforms and devices is a nice, welcome touch.

For the curious reader, the way we could implement our own drag-and-drop behavior is really quite simple; first, we listen for a mouse down event on the element we want to drag. When that happens, we set a mouse down flag, which we unset once the mouse up event is fired, whether on the element we wish to drag or not. Next, we listen for a mouse movement event, where we check if the mouse is down. If the mouse is moving while the mouse down flag is set, we have a drag motion. One way to handle it is to update the position of the draggable element every time the mouse moves, then setting the element's position when the mouse up event is called. Of course, there are several small details that we'd need to keep track of, or at least be mindful of, such as how to detect where the draggable element was dropped, and how to move it back to its original position if needed.

The good news is that the drag-and-drop API provided by the browser is very flexible, and extremely efficient. Since this feature was first introduced, a lot of developers continued to use JavaScript implementations of it for various reasons, but mostly because a lot of people felt that the native HTML5 version was a bit hard to use, buggy, or not quite as practical as the version provided by whatever other library they chose to use. However, today the API is widely supported, fairly polished, and highly recommended.

How to use it

Now, the way that the drag-and-drop API works is very straight forward. First we need to mark one or more elements as draggable by setting the `draggable` attribute to true for those elements, as shown in the following code:

```
<ul>
  <li draggable="true" class="block"
    ondragstart="doOnDragStart(event)"
    data-name="Block 1">Block #1</li>
</ul>
```

Just this step alone will make those elements all draggable. Of course, that isn't of any use unless we have a place to drop those elements. Believe it or not, we actually can drop a dragged element anywhere. The problem is that we don't have any code in place to handle the event of something being dropped. We can register such events on any element, including the body tag, for example. This is shown in the following code:

```
document.body.ondragover = doOnDragOver;
document.body.ondragleave = doOnDragLeave;
document.body.ondrop = doOnDrop;

function doOnDragOver(event) {
  event.preventDefault();
  document.body.classList.add("dropme");
}

function doOnDragLeave(event) {
  event.preventDefault();
  document.body.classList.remove("dropme");
}

function doOnDrop(event) {
  event.preventDefault();
  document.body.classList.remove("dropme");
```

```
    var newItem = document.createElement("li");
    newItem.setAttribute("draggable", true);
    newItem.classList.add("block");

    document.querySelector("ul").appendChild(newItem);
}
```

In this example, we append a new list element to the unordered list every time a list element is dropped anywhere on the page, since every element on the page is a child of the body node. Also, whenever a draggable element hovers over the body element, we add a CSS class called dropme, which is meant to give the user a visual feedback letting them know that the drag event is taking place. When the draggable is dropped, we remove that class from the body element indicating the end of the drag action.

One thing we can do with the drag and drop API is transfer data between objects. This data can be a string, or any data type that can be converted into a string. We do this by setting the desired data to the dataTransfer object available to us during the drag action. The data must be set when the drag start function is fired by the system. The key associated with the dataTransfer data can be any string of our choosing as shown in the following code:

```
function doOnDragStart(event) {
    // First we set the data when the drag event first starts
    event.dataTransfer.setData("who-built-me", event.target.
getAttribute("data-name"));
}

function doOnDrop(event) {
    event.preventDefault();
    document.body.classList.remove("dropme");

    var num = document.querySelectorAll("li").length + 1;

    // Then we retrieve that data when the drop event is fired by the
browser
    var builtBy = event.dataTransfer.getData("who-built-me");

    var newItem = document.createElement("li");
    newItem.ondragstart = doOnDragStart;
    newItem.setAttribute("draggable", true);
    newItem.setAttribute("data-name", "Block " + num);
    newItem.innerText = "Block #" + num + ", built by " + builtBy;

    newItem.classList.add("block");

    document.querySelector("ul").appendChild(newItem);
}
```

Summary

This chapter touched on the very important topic of browser support and code portability. As productive and efficient developers, we should always strive to create maintainable code. Thus, the more browsers we can support with the same code base, the more efficient we are. In order to help us achieve this goal, we can create abstractions that encapsulate code that varies from browser to browser, as well as from device to device. Another alternative is to use existing polyfills that other people have written, and thus accomplish the same thing, but with possibly less effort and more reliability.

The game we built in this chapter makes use of three HTML5 APIs, namely drag-and-drop, web audio, and SVG. Native drag-and-drop provided in HTML5 is a lot more than simply dragging DOM elements around the screen. With it we can customize a lot of the visual elements related to the drag-and-drop action, as well as specify data that is carried through the draggable element and the target where it is dropped.

Web audio allows us to manage multiple audio entities. Although most modern browsers support more than one audio format, there is not yet a single audio format that is supported by all of these modern web browsers. Because of that, it is recommended that we link at least two different versions of each audio file we wish to play through the API, so that all modern browsers are capable of playing that file. Although we can specify multiple sources for each audio element (where each source is a different version of the same file, but encoded in a different format), the browser is smart enough to only download the one file that it supports and knows how to play, or the one file that is most appropriate for it to playback. This makes load time shorter, and saves both the user and your server quite a bit of bandwidth.

Scalable Vector Graphics is an XML-based description language for two dimensional graphics, which can be embedded in a web page in a variety of ways. Since all of the graphical elements are nothing more than XML nodes rendered by the browser onto an SVG canvas, each of these graphical elements are managed by the browser, and can, therefore, be styled through CSS, and have user input events linked to them. We can also register callback functions with each SVG primitive for events generated by the browser, such as when the element is loaded, focused, blurred, and so on.

Finally, we saw how none of the timer functions provided by JavaScript are at all appropriate for fast games. Thankfully, there is a new rendering API that we'll cover in the next chapter that can be used to overcome the deficiencies of JavaScript timers. Using the request animation frame interface allows us to render our games much more efficiently because the browser itself manages the timer that is used, as well as allows our games to be more CPU-friendly by not rendering a screen that is not visible (such as when the browser is minimized, or a different tab is focused).

In the next chapter, we will write a traditional snake game, with the main focus points being rendering the entire game scene using the canvas API (as opposed to using raw DOM elements), application cache for offline game play, web workers, and the new and powerful JavaScript typed arrays. As alluded earlier in this chapter, we will also take a look at the new way to render very dynamic graphics in HTML5 apps, using requestAnimationFrame to access the browser's very own rendering pipeline.

4
Using HTML5 to Catch a Snake

This chapter is the first part of a two-part series, where we'll build the first version of a game, and then spice it up with more HTML5 APIs in the next chapter. Both versions will be complete and playable, but since covering all of the APIs in the same game within one chapter would make for a very large chapter, we'll break things up into smaller chunks, and write two separate games.

The first version of the game will cover five new concepts, namely, **HTML5's 2D canvas API**, **offline application cache**, **web workers**, **typed arrays**, and **requestAnimationFrame**. The canvas element allows us to draw 2D as well as 3D graphics, and manipulate image data at a very low level, gaining access to individual pixel information. Offline application cache, also known as app cache, allows us to cache specific assets from a server into the user's browser, so that the application can work even when no internet access is available. Web workers is a thread-like mechanism that allows us to execute JavaScript code in a separate thread from the main UI thread. This way, the user interface is never blocked, and users don't see a **page not responsive** warning. Typed arrays is a new native JavaScript data type similar to arrays, but much more efficient, and specifically designed to handle binary data. Finally, requestAnimationFrame is an API offered by the browser to help us perform time-based animation. Instead of using a JavaScript timer (setTimeout or setInterval) multiple times a second in order to perform animations, we can let the browser do the heavy lifting, optimizing the animation beyond what we could achieve in JavaScript alone.

The game

You've certainly seen or played this game before. You control a snake in a 2D grid only moving up, down, left, or right. When you change the direction in which the snake's head is moving, each part of the snake's body gradually changes direction as well, following the head. If you run into a wall, or into the snake's own body, you lose. If you guide the snake's head over a fruit, the snake's body gets larger. The larger the snake gets, the more challenging the game becomes. Additionally, the speed at which the snake moves can be increased for an extra challenge. In order to stay true to the old school nature of this classic game, we opted for old school graphics and typefaces, as shown in following screenshot:

The image shows the look and feel of the game. When the game first starts, the snake has a total body length of zero—only the head is present. At first, the snake is randomly placed somewhere within the game grid, and is not given a starting direction to move towards. The player can control the snake with the arrow keys, and once the snake starts moving in a particular direction, the snake cannot be stopped. For example, if the snake is moving to the right, the player can move it up or down (but not backwards). If the player wishes to move the snake to the left (once it is currently moving to the right), the only possible ways are to first move the snake up, then to the left, or down, then left.

Whenever there are no fruits on the game grid, one is randomly added to the grid. That fruit stays there until the player eats it, at which point, a new fruit is added to the grid. For added difficulty, we could make a fruit disappear, if the snake can't get to it within so many seconds.

API usage

A general description and demonstration of each of the APIs used in the game are given as follows. For an explanation of how each of the functionality was incorporated into the final game, look at the following code section. For the complete source code for this game, check out the book's page at the Packt Publishing website.

Before `requestAnimationFrame` was introduced, the main method developers used to create animations in JavaScript was by using a timer to repeatedly call a function that gradually updated attributes of the element(s) being animated. While this is a straightforward method, what the browser provides through `requestAnimationFrame` has a couple of added benefits. First of all, the browser uses a single animation cycle to handle the rendering of a page, so any rendering we do using that same cycle will result in a smoother animation, since the browser can optimize the animation for us. Also, since the rendering would be done by the browser's internal rendering mechanism, our animation would not run when the browser tab running our animation is not shown. This way we don't waste battery life animating something that is not even visible.

How to use it

Using `requestAnimationFrame` is very simple, and similar to `setTimeout`. We call the `requestAnimationFrame` function on the global window object, passing a callback function that is executed whenever the browser is ready to run another animation cycle. When the callback is invoked, it is passed in a timestamp, which is normally used inside the animation function we register with `requestAnimationFrame`.

There are two common ways in which `requestAnimationFrame` is used, both of which achieve the same result. In the first method, you define your animation function with no references to `requestAnimationFrame`. Then, a second function calls that animation function, followed by a call to `requestAnimationFrame`.

```
function myAnimationLoop(time) {
    // 1. Perform the animation
    myAnimation(time);

    // 2. Register with request animation frame
    requestAnimationFrame(myAnimationLoop);
}

function myAnimation(time) {
    // Perform animation here
}
```

The second pattern that is commonly used is very similar, except that it only includes the main animation function. That function itself takes care of calling `requestAnimationFrame` when needed.

```
function myAnimation(time) {
    // 1. Perform the animation
    myAnimation(time);

    // 2. Register with request animation frame
    requestAnimationFrame(myAnimationLoop);
}
```

The reason that the time argument is useful is, because most of the time, you want the animation to run more or less at the same rate on different computers. `requestAnimationFrame` attempts to run as close to 60 times per second as possible. However, based on the code you execute inside it, that rate may drop significantly. Obviously, faster hardware would be able to execute your code much faster, and thus, display it to the screen more often than some slower hardware would. In order to make up for this possibility, we can use actual time to control how often the animation code runs. This way, we can specify a cap refresh rate, which, if a particular computer is able to run faster than this rate, can simply slowdown that computer, and all users experience about the same animation.

One possible implementation of this technique is shown in the following steps. Although it may seem like a lot of steps, the concept is really quite simple. The gist of it is this: we set two variables, one that keeps track of the cap speed that the animation will run (measured in **frames per second (fps)**), and the other keeps track of when the last time was, that a frame was rendered. Then, whenever the animation function executes, we take the current time, subtract the last time that a frame was rendered, and check if their difference is greater than, or equal to the ideal fps we have chosen. If it is less than our desired fps, we don't animate anything, but still register `requestAnimationFrame` to call us back in the future.

This we do until enough time has elapsed so that our frames per second rate can be achieved (in other words, so that the fastest frame rate we can possibly run would be our fps). If the system is running slower than that, there's nothing we can do about it. What this technique does is control the maximum speed.

Once `requestAnimationFrame` has called our animation function, and enough time has passed since the last time a frame was rendered, we update all the data we need to, for the animation, render the animation to the screen (or let the browser do it, if it can), and update the variable that keeps track of when a frame was last updated.

```
// 1. Create some element
var el = document.createElement("h1");
el.textContent = "I Love HTML5!";
el.style.position = "absolute";

// 2. Attach it to the document
document.body.appendChild(el);

// 3. Set some variables to control the animation
var loop = 0;
var lastFrame = 0;
var fps = 1000 / 60;

// 4. Perform the animation one frame at a time
function slideRight(time) {

    // 5. Control the animation to a set frames per second
    if (time - lastFrame >= fps) {

        var left = parseInt(el.style.left);
```

```
        // 6. Perform the animation while some condition is true
        if (left + el.offsetWidth < document.body.offsetWidth) {
            el.style.left = (left + loop) + "px";
            loop += 5;

            // 7. Perform the time control variable
            lastFrame = time;
        } else {

            // 8. If the animation is done, return from this function
            el.style.left = document.body.offsetWidth - el.offsetWidth;
            return true;
        }
    }

    // 9. If the animation is not done yet, do it again
    requestAnimationFrame(slideRight);
}

// 10. Register some event to begin the animation
el.addEventListener("click", function(){
    el.style.left = 0;
    loop = 0;
    slideRight(0);
});
```

This simple code snippet creates a **Document Object Model (DOM)** element, sets some text to it, and registers an onclick handler to it. When the click handler is called, we reset some styling properties of the element (namely, placing the element on the far left side of the screen), and get the animation routine started. The animation routine moves the element to the right a little bit every frame, until the element has reached the right side of the screen. If the element has not yet reached the right side of the screen, or in other words, if the animation is not yet completed, we perform the animation (move the element a few pixels), then register itself with requestAnimationFrame, thus continuing the cycle. Once the animation is complete, we simply stop calling requestAnimationFrame.

A key point to remember is that, one of the major optimizations that the browser does with requestAnimationFrame is to only call it when there is anything to render (in other words, when the tab holding the page is active relative to other tabs). Thus, if the user switches tabs while the animation is in progress, the animation will be paused until the tab is selected again.

In other words, what we ought to do is have `requestAnimationFrame` call the code that handles the rendering of the game, but not the code that updates the game state. This way, even if the browser is not rendering, the values related to the animation still get animated, but we don't waste CPU and GPU power, rendering something not visible. But as soon as the browser tab becomes active again, the latest data state will be rendered, as if it had been rendering the whole time.

This technique is especially useful for games, as we may not want the entire game to pause when a user switches browser tabs. Then again, we can always benefit from saving the user's battery, which we can achieve by not rendering data to the screen when we don't need to.

Keep in mind that `requestAnimationFrame` will, by definition, cap the frame rate of your animation loop to the refreshing rate of the monitor. Thus, `requestAnimationFrame` is not intended to replace native timer implementations, particularly in cases when we'd like the callback function to be invoked at a rate independent from, and possibly higher than a monitor's refresh rate.

Typed arrays

Over the years, JavaScript engines have become amazingly faster. However, simply being able to process data faster doesn't necessarily equate to being able to do more powerful things. Take WebGL, for example. Just because the browser now has the ability to understand OpenGL ES, it doesn't necessarily mean that it has all the tools we developers need to take advantage of that.

The good news is that the JavaScript language has also made some progress in order to satisfy this, and other needs that have come about. One such addition to JavaScript in recent years is a new data type: typed arrays. In general, typed arrays offer a structure similar to the array type already in JavaScript. However, these new arrays are much more efficient, and were designed with binary data in mind.

Why and how are typed arrays more efficient than regular arrays, you ask? Well, let's look at a trivial example, where all we do is traverse an array of integers the old way. Although most JavaScript engines don't particularly struggle to get this task done fairly fast, let us not overlook all the work the engine needs to do in order to do this.

```
var nums = [1, 2, 3, 4, 5];
for (var i = 0, len = nums.length; i < len; i++) {
    // ...
}
```

Since JavaScript is not strongly typed, the array `nums` is not restricted to holding data of any particular type. Furthermore, the `nums` array can store a different data type for each element in it. While this can sometimes be convenient for a programmer, the JavaScript engine needs to figure out where each element is stored, and what data type is being stored at said location. Contrary to what you may think, those five elements in the `nums` array may not be stored in a contiguous piece of memory, because, well, that's how JavaScript does it.

With typed arrays, on the other hand, each element in the array can only be an `integer` or a `float`. Based on the type of array we choose, we can have a different type of `integer` or `float` (`signed`, `unsigned`, 8, 16, or 32 bits), but every element in the array is always the same data type we decide to use (integer or float). This way, the browser knows precisely and instantly, where in memory element `nums[3]` is found which is at memory address `nums + 3`. This can be done because typed arrays are stored in a continuous chunk of memory, much like it does in array structures in C and C++ (which, by the way, is the language used to implement most, if not all JavaScript engines).

The major use case for typed arrays is, as hinted earlier, WebGL (which we'll cover in *Chapter 6, Adding Features to Your Game*). In WebGL, where we can perform 3D rendering right from JavaScript, we may need to process `integer` buffers, over a million elements long. These buffers can be used to represent a 3D model that we wish to draw to the screen. Now, imagine how long it would take for the browser to iterate through one such array. For each and every element, it would have to follow a memory location, check the value at that location, make sure the value is a number, attempt to convert the value into a number, and then finally use that value. Sounds like a lot of work? Well, that's because it is. With typed arrays, it can just run through that array as fast as it can, knowing that each element is indeed a number, and knowing exactly how much memory each element takes, so that jumping to the next memory address is a consistent and predictable process.

Typed arrays are also used in the 2D canvas context. As we'll see in the canvas API section later in the chapter, there is a way that we can get the pixel data from whatever is drawn into a canvas. All that this pixel data is, is a long array of 8bits clamped `unsigned integers`. What that means is that each element in this array can only be an `integer` value between 0 and 255, which is precisely what the acceptable values are for a pixel.

How to use it

Using typed arrays is really simple. It may be easier to understand how they work if you have at least some experience with C or C++. The easiest way to create a typed array is to declare our array variable, and assign it an instance of a particular typed array type.

```
var typedArr = new Int32Array(10);
```

In the example, we have created an instance of an `integer` array, where each element can be either positive or negative (`signed`). Each element will be stored as a 32 bits number. The `integer` argument that we pass in, indicates the size of the array. Once this array is created, its size cannot be changed. Any values assigned to it outside its bounds are silently ignored by the browser, as well as any illegal values.

Other than the restrictions on what can be stored in this special array, it all may seem just as an ordinary JavaScript array to the untrained eye. But if we look a bit deeper into it, we'll notice a couple more distinctions between an array and a typed array.

```
typedArr instanceof Int32Array; // True
typedArr.length == 10; // True

typedArr.push(23); // TypeError: <Int32Array> has no method 'push'
typedArr.pop(); // TypeError: <Int32Array> has no method 'pop'
typedArr.sort(); // TypeError; <Int32Array> has no method 'sort'

typedArr.buffer instanceof ArrayBuffer; // True
typedArr.buffer.byteLength == 40; //True

typedArr instanceof Array; // False
```

The first thing we notice is that the array is indeed an `Int32Array`, and not an Array. Next, we're happy to know that the length property is still there. So far so good. Then, things start to separate, as simple methods associated with regular arrays are no longer present. Not only that, but there's also a new attribute in the typed array object named `buffer`. This buffer object is of type `ArrayBuffer`, which has a `byteLength` property. In this case, we can see that the buffer's length is 40. It's easy to see where this 40 came from: `buffer` holds 10 elements (`typedArr.length`), and each element is 32 bits long (4 bytes), for a total of 40 bytes in the `ArrayBuffer` (hence the property name of `byteLength`).

Since typed arrays don't come with helper functions such as regular JavaScript arrays do, we read and write data to them using the old array notation, where we index into the array in order to read or write a value.

```
var typedArr = new Uint32Array(3);

typedArr[] = 0; // SyntaxError

typedArr[0] = 3;
typedArr[1] = 4;
typedArr[2] = 9;

for (var i = 0, len = typedArr.length; i < len; i++) {
    typedArr[i] >= 0; // True
}
```

Again, just to reinforce the fact that no helper functions or shortcuts related to ordinary JavaScript arrays work with typed arrays, notice that an attempt to access an element without providing an index will provide an exception being thrown by the browser.

ArrayBuffer and ArrayBufferView

Although, all the previous examples used a specific kind of typed array directly, the way that typed arrays work is slightly more involved than that. The implementation is broken down into two separate parts, namely, an array buffer and a view (or more specifically, an array buffer view). The array buffer is simply a chunk of memory that is allocated, so we can store our data there. The thing about this buffer is that it has no type associated with it, so we can't access that memory to store data to, or read data from it.

In order to be able to use the memory space allocated by the array buffer, we need a view. Although the base type for this view is `ArrayBufferView`, we actually need a subclass of `ArrayBufferView`, which defines a specific type to the data stored in the array buffer.

```
var buffer = new ArrayBuffer(32);
buffer.byteLengh == 32; // True

var i32View = new Int32Array(buffer);
i32View.length == 8; // True
```

Here's where things can get a bit confusing. The array buffer works in terms of bytes. As a refresher, a byte is made up of 8 bits. A bit is a single binary digit, which can have a value of either zero or one. This is how data is represented at its most basic format in computers.

Now, if a buffer works in terms of bytes, when we created our buffer in the example, we created a block of 32 bytes. The view that we create to hold and use the buffer can be one of nine possible types, each of which specifies a different data size (in terms of bits, not bytes). Thus, a view of type `Int32` represents a buffer where each element is an `integer`, 32 bits long. In other words, a 32 bits view can hold exactly 8 bytes (1 byte = 8 bits; 32 bits = 8 bytes), as illustrated in following screenshot:

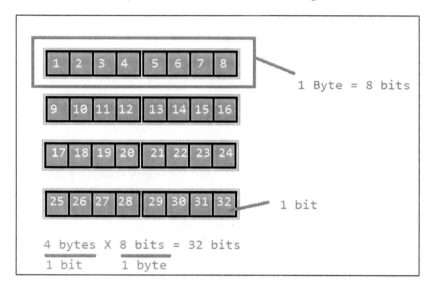

Array buffers work in terms of bytes. In the image, there are 4 bytes, although view types work in terms of bits. Thus, if we use a 32 bits view, it will result in an array that has a length of exactly one element. If the view uses a 16 bits data type, then the array will have 2 elements (4 bytes divided by 16 bits). Finally, if the view uses an 8 bits data type, the array stored in the 4 bytes buffer will have 4 elements.

> One important thing to always remember is that when you create an array buffer, the length you choose to make the buffer must divide perfectly into however large you make the array buffer view. If there is not enough room in the buffer to fit entire bytes, the JavaScript will throw an error of type `RangeError`.

In the following image, the buffer is only big enough for 8 bits, all of which must be occupied by whole bytes. Thus, a view is an 8 bits number which would fit exactly one whole element, which would be fine. A 16 bits element would only fit half of an element, which is not possible. A 32 bits element would likewise only fit a portion of it, which is also not allowed.

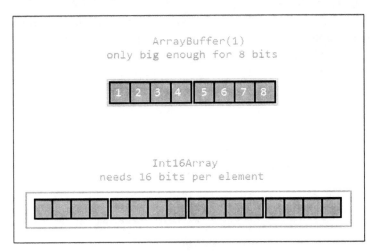

As you can see, as long as the array buffer has a bit length that is a multiple of the bit size of the data type used in the view, things work out fine. If the view is 8 bits long, then an array buffer of 8, 16, 24, 32, or 40, would work out fine. If the view is 32 bits long, then the buffer must be at least 4 bytes long (32 bits), 8 bytes (64 bits), 24 bytes (96 bits), and so on. Then, by dividing the amount of bytes in the buffer by the amount of bytes in the data type represented by the view, we can calculate the total number of elements that we can fit in said array.

```
// 96 bytes in the buffer
var buffer = new ArrayBuffer(96);

// Each element in the buffer is 32 bits long, or 4 bytes
var view = new Int32Array(buffer);

// 96 / 4 = 24 elements in this typed array
view.length == 24;
```

Typed array view types

As a summary, a plain old array buffer has no actual size. Although it wouldn't make sense to create an array buffer of a byte length of say 5 bytes, we are more than welcome to do so. Only after the array buffer is created can we create a view to hold the buffer. Based on the byte size of the buffer, we can determine how many elements the array buffer view can access by selecting an appropriate data type. Currently, there are nine data types that we can choose from for the array buffer view.

- **Int8Array**: It is a `signed integer`, 8 bits long, ranging from 32,768 to 32,767

- **Uint8Array**: It is an `unsigned integer`, 8 bits long, ranging from 0 to 65,535

- **Uint8ClampedArray**: It is an `unsigned integer`, 8 bits long, ranging from 0 to 255

- **Int16Array**: It is a `signed integer`, 16 bits long, ranging from 2,147,483,648 to 2,147,483,647

- **Uint16Array**: It is an `unsigned integer`, 16 bits long, ranging from 0 to 4,294,967,295

- **Int32Array**: It is a `signed integer`, 32 bits long, ranging from 9,223,372,036,854,775,808 to 9,223,372,036,854,775,807

- **Uint32Array**: It is an `unsigned integer`, 32 bits long, ranging from 0 to 18,446,744,073,709,551,615

- **Float32Array**: It is a `signed float`, 32 bits long, with a range of 3.4E +/- 38 (7 digits)

- **Float64Array**: It is a `signed float`, 64 bits long, with a range of 1.7E +/- 308 (15 digits)

It goes without saying that the larger the view type, the larger the buffer will need to be to hold the data. Obviously, it follows that the larger the buffer you create, the more memory the browser will need to set aside for you, whether or not you end up using that memory. Thus, we should always pay attention to how much memory we might actually need, and try to allocate no more than that. It would be an awesome waste of resources to allocate an array of 10,000 elements, each of which are 64 bits long, just to represent a snake in a game, such as the one that we're building in the chapter, where the maximum snake size might be no larger than 50 or so elements, and where each element needs not hold a value larger than say 10.

Given such constraints, we could calculate a rough, yet optimistic array size of 50, where each element only needs 8 bits (since we'll only need around 10 unique values). Thus, 50 elements times one byte each, gives us a total buffer size of 50 bytes. This should be more than enough for our purposes, while the memory consumption for this buffer alone should stay around 0.05 KB. Not bad.

Finally, you may have noticed, the first part of this section demonstrated typed array creation without using the `ArrayBuffer` construct explicitly.

```
// Create a typed array with 4 elements, each 32 bits long
var i32viewA = new Int32Array(4);

// Create the same typed array, but using an explicit ArrayBuffer
first
var buffer = new ArrayBuffer(16)
var i32viewB = new Int32Array(buffer)
```

While the two typed arrays above, refer to two separate and unique memory locations, they are identical at run time, and cannot be told apart (unless the actual arrays hold different values, of course); the point here being that an array buffer view constructor can take an `ArrayBuffer`, or simply an `integer`. If you use an `ArrayBuffer`, all of the restrictions just mentioned apply, and must be handled with care. If you only supply an `integer`, the browser will create an array buffer of the appropriate size for you automatically. In practice, there are rare occasions and reasons, where you'd want to manually create an array buffer separately. It is noteworthy, however, that it is totally legal to create multiple array buffer views for the same array buffer, even if each view is of a different data type. Remember that, since the buffer refers to a single memory location, so all views bound to the same buffer are sharing that memory space.

Canvas

Perhaps no other HTML5 feature is as powerful as the canvas API with regards to game development for the web platform. Although we may have every other feature currently in the specification, as well as any forthcoming feature that the browser can possibly support, it would be nearly impossible to produce a high quality, engaging, fun game using HTML and JavaScript. The canvas API allows us to create 2D, as well as 3D graphics right on the browser. It also lets us manipulate the graphical data stored in the canvas context, down to the individual pixel level.

One major difference between a canvas graphic and an SVG graphic, apart from the fact that SVG graphics are vector-based, and canvas graphics are always raster graphics, is that the canvas is a single HTML element, and everything drawn in it is, for all practical purposes, non-existent to the browser. Thus, any event handling on individual entities drawn on a canvas must be handled at the application level. There are generic events on the canvas that we can observe and respond to, such as clicks, move events, and keyboard events. Beyond that, we are free to do as we please.

Beyond the shape-based drawing that we can do on an HTML5 canvas, there are three major use cases for the API. We can create 2D, sprite-based games, full-blown 3D games (using WebGL with the help of the canvas), and manipulating photographs. The last use case mentioned: photo manipulation, is especially interesting. The API has a very handy function that allows us to not only export the data in the canvas as a PNG or JPG image, but it also supports various types of compression. That means, we can draw on a canvas, load graphics on it (for example photographs), manipulate that data at a pixel level (for example apply Photoshop-like filters to it), rotate, stretch, scale, and otherwise, play with the data. Then, the API allows us to export that data as a compressed file that can be saved to the file system.

For the purposes of this book, we'll focus on the aspects of the canvas API that we can best use for game development. Although WebGL is a very exciting aspect of the canvas element, but we will cover a very basic introduction to it in *Chapter 6, Adding Features to Your Game*. For other capabilities available on the canvas API, we will cover them briefly with a few examples in the following section.

How to use it

The first thing we need to understand about the canvas element is that there are two parts to it. One is the physical canvas element, and the other is the rendering context through which we can draw to the canvas. As of this writing, there are two rendering contexts that we can use in modern browsers, namely, `CanvasRenderingContext2D` and `WebGLRenderingContext`.

To obtain a reference to the rendering context of a canvas, we call a `factory` method on the canvas element itself.

```
var canvasA = document.createElement("canvas");
var ctx2d = canvas.getContext("2d");
ctx2d instanceof CanvasRenderingContext2D; // True

var canvasB = document.createElement("canvas");
var ctx3d = canvas.getContext("webgl") || canvas.
getContext("experimental-webgl");
ctx3d instanceof WebGLRenderingContext; // True
```

Note that the use of a fallback context is aimed at the prefixed `experimentalwebgl` context. As of this writing, most browsers that support WebGL will do so through the experimental tag.

The rest of the section will relate exclusively to the `CanvasRenderingContext2D` API. While it is technically possible to do everything that the 2D canvas context can, using the 3D canvas context of WebGL, the only thing that these two APIs have in common is their link to the HTML5 canvas element. WebGL is an entire programming language in and of itself, and a single chapter dedicated to it would not be enough to even scratch the surface.

Now, a very important aspect of the 2D rendering context is its coordinate space. Similar to most coordinate system in computers, the origin is located at the top left corner of the canvas. The horizontal axis increases to the right, while the vertical axis increases downwards. The size of the grid held in memory to represent the canvas is determined by the physical size of the canvas that generates the rendering context, and not the styled size of the canvas. This is a key principle that can't be emphasized enough. By default, a canvas is 300 x 150 pixels. Even if we resize the canvas through **Cascading Style Sheets (CSS)**, the rendering context that it generates will be that size (unless we physically resize the canvas, of course). Once the rendering context has been created, it cannot be resized.

```
<style>
canvas {
    border: 3px solid #ddd;
    width: 500px;
    height: 300px;
}
</style>

<script>
    var canvas = document.createElement("canvas");
    var ctx = canvas.getContext("2d");

    document.body.appendChild(canvas);

    alert(ctx.canvas.width);
</script>
```

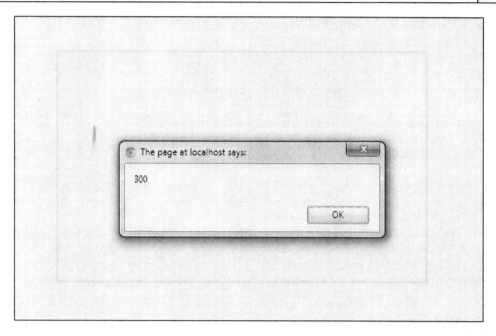

The border was added in order to make the canvas somewhat visible to us, as by default, the canvas is transparent.

You will observe that the CSS rule is indeed applied to the canvas element, even though the canvas' real size is still the default 300 x 150 pixels. If we were to draw a circle in the middle of that canvas, the circle would seem distorted, because the actual coordinate space where the circle is actually drawn, would be stretched by the styling applied to the canvas.

clearRect

The first drawing function we'll look at is `clearRect`. All that this function does is, clear a rectangular area of the canvas. This function is called on the context object, as do all drawing calls that we'll be making on the 2D canvas. The four parameters it takes, represent, in order, the x and y offset from the canvas' origin, plus a width and a height distance to clear. Keep in mind that unlike other popular drawing APIs in other programming languages, the last two parameters are not measured from the origin — they are displacement distances from the point specified by the first two parameters.

```
var canvas = document.querySelector("canvas");
var ctx = canvas.getContext("2d");

// Clear the entire canvas
ctx.clearRect(0, 0, canvas.width, canvas.height);

// Only clear the half inside area of the canvas
ctx.clearRect(canvas.width * 0.25, canvas.height * 0.25,
    canvas.width * 0.5, canvas.height * 0.5);

// Clear a square 100x100 at the lower right bottom of the canvas
ctx.clearRect(canvas.width - 100, canvas.height - 100, 100, 100);
```

Normally, when rendering many frames every second, we'd be calling this function to clear out the entire canvas before drawing the next frame. Luckily, in most JavaScript engines, this function performs fairly well; so that we don't need to worry too much about optimizing the precise area to clear out on a regular basis.

Fill and stroke

When drawing native objects such as lines, paths, text, and other shapes, we'll deal with the concept of strokes and fills; just as in SVG, a stroke refers to the outline of a primitive (such as a border or sorts), and the fill is the content that covers the inside of the shape.

The way we can change the color that is used to fill a shape, or the color used to stroke the shape, is by assigning any color to the fillStyle or strokeStyle properties. The color can be any string valid for a CSS color.

```
// Short hand hex colors are fine
ctx.fillStyle = "#c00";
ctx.fillRect(0, 0, canvas.width, canvas.height);

// Keyword colors are fine, though not as precise
ctx.strokeStyle = "white";

ctx.lineWidth = 10;
ctx.strokeRect(25, 25, 100, 100);
ctx.strokeRect(175, 25, 100, 100);

// Alpha transparency is also allowed
ctx.fillStyle = "rgba(100, 255, 100, 0.8)";

ctx.fillRect(5, 50, canvas.width - 10, 50);
```

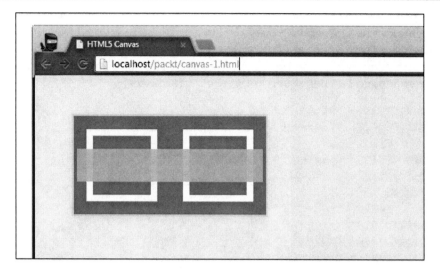

Any valid CSS color string can be assigned to color properties in the 2D rendering context, including colors with opacity.

Pay special attention to the fact that the rendering context acts much like a state machine. Once you set a fill or stroke style, as well as any other property, that property will maintain that value until you change it.

Also, note that each subsequent drawing call that you issue, draws on top of whatever is already on the canvas. Thus, we can layer shapes and images by carefully arranging the drawing calls in just the right order.

Lines

Drawing lines is as easy as calling the function `lineTo`, which only takes two parameters, indicating the point where the line is going to. Subsequent calls to `lineTo` will draw a line to the point specified by the function call, starting the line at the last point where the line was. More specifically, the line starts where the current drawing pointer is.

By default, the pointer is not defined anywhere, so drawing a line to some other point makes little sense. To help with that, we can make use of the function `moveTo`, which moves the drawing pointer without drawing anything.

Finally, any calls to `lineTo` only set the points in memory. In order to eventually draw the line, we need to make a quick call to the stroke function. Once this call is made, whatever attributes are currently set (such as line width and stroke style), will be drawn. Thus, changing line properties before actually stroking the line does little good, and can negatively influence performance.

```
ctx.fillStyle = "#fff";
ctx.fillRect(0, 0, canvas.width, canvas.height);

// This call is completely useless
ctx.strokeStyle = "#c0c";
ctx.lineWidth = 5;

ctx.moveTo(0, 0);
ctx.lineTo(100, 100);
ctx.lineTo(canvas.width, 0);

// This call is also useless because the line hasn't been drawn yet
ctx.strokeStyle = "#ca0";
ctx.moveTo(10, canvas.height - 10);
ctx.lineTo(canvas.width - 10, canvas.height * 0.5);

// This color is applied to every line drawn so far
ctx.strokeStyle = "#f5a";

// The line is finally drawn here
ctx.stroke();
```

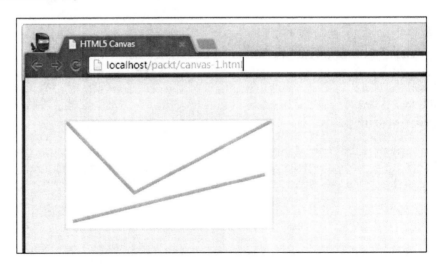

Shapes are only drawn after the call to stroke(), at which point the current style attributes are used.

Shapes

There are a couple of different shapes we can draw very effortlessly. These are rectangles and circles. While, there is no circle function as there is a `rect` function for drawing rectangles. There is, however, an `arc` function, from which we can draw circles.

The `rect` function takes four parameters, exactly as `fillRect`. `arc` takes an x and a y coordinate, followed by a radius, a starting angle (in radians, not degrees), an ending angle, and a Boolean, specifying, if the arc is to be drawn clockwise. To draw a circle, we can just draw an arc that goes from 0 to PI times 2, which is the same as 360 degrees.

```
ctx.fillStyle = "#fff";
ctx.strokeStyle = "#c0c";

ctx.fillRect(0, 0, canvas.width, canvas.height);

ctx.rect(10, 10, 50, 50);
ctx.rect(75, 50, 50, 50);

ctx.moveTo(180, 100);
ctx.arc(180, 100, 30, 1, 3, true);

ctx.moveTo(225, 40);
ctx.arc(225, 40, 20, 0, Math.PI * 2, false);

ctx.stroke();
```

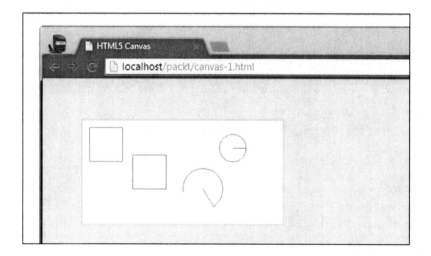

Arcs (including circles) are drawn from their center and not from some point on their outline.

Text

Drawing text on an HTML5 canvas is also pretty straightforward. The function `fillText` takes a string (the text to be drawn), and an x and y coordinate, where the text begins to draw. Additionally, we can style the text the same way that text can be styled through CSS. This can be done by setting the text style property string to the font attribute.

```
ctx.fillStyle = "#fff";
ctx.fillRect(0, 0, canvas.width, canvas.height);

ctx.fillStyle = "#f00";
ctx.font = "2.5em 'Times New Roman'";

ctx.fillText("I Love HTML5!", 20, 75);
```

Transformations

The canvas API also defines a few transformation functions that allow us to translate, scale, and rotate the context's coordinate system. After transforming the coordinate system, we can draw onto the canvas just as we normally would, and the transformations would apply.

```
ctx.fillStyle = "#fff";
ctx.fillRect(0, 0, canvas.width, canvas.height);

// Now the origin is at point 50x50
ctx.translate(50, 50);

ctx.fillStyle = "#f00";
ctx.fillRect(0, 0, 50, 50);
```

Rotation and scaling also works the same way. The `scale` function takes a value to scale the coordinate system by, on each axis. The `rotation` function takes a single parameter, which is the angle (in radian) to rotate the coordinate system by.

```
ctx.fillStyle = "#fff";
ctx.fillRect(0, 0, canvas.width, canvas.height);

// With transformations, order is very important
ctx.scale(2, 1);
ctx.translate(50, 50);
ctx.rotate(0.80);
ctx.translate(10, -20);

ctx.fillStyle = "#f00";
ctx.fillRect(0, 0, 50, 50);
```

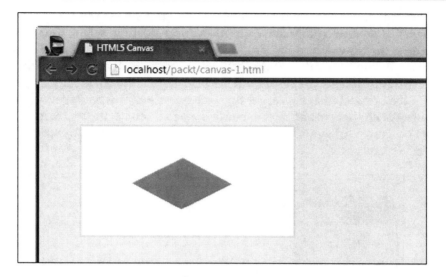

With transformations, order is very important.

Drawing images

Probably the most exciting and useful feature of the 2D canvas API from a game development perspective, is its ability to draw images onto it. Thankfully, for us, there are several ways to draw a regular JPG, GIF, or PNG image right on the canvas, including functions that handle scaling images from source to destination.

One other note that we need to make about the canvas element is that it follows the same origin policy. That means, in order for us to be able to draw an image onto a canvas context, the script attempting to draw the image must be served from the same domain (along with the same protocol and port number) as the image. Any attempt to load an image from a different domain into the canvas context and the browser will throw an exception.

```
ctx.fillStyle = "#fff";
ctx.fillRect(0, 0, canvas.width, canvas.height);

var img = new Image();
img.onload = function(){
    ctx.drawImage(img, 0, 0, this.width, this.height);
};

img.src = "img/html5-logo.png";
```

The simplest call to draw an image only takes five parameters. The first is a reference to an image. The next two parameters are the x and y position where that image will be drawn onto the canvas, and the last two parameters are the width and height to paint the image onto the canvas. If the last two parameters don't maintain the aspect ratio of the original image, the result will be distortion, rather than clipping. Also, note that, if the original image is larger than the canvas, or if the image is drawn from an offset such that part of the image runs off the canvas, that extra data will simply not be drawn (obviously), and the canvas will just ignore those pixels outside the viewable area:

The HTML5 logo drawn inside a canvas rendering context.

A very important observation is that if the browser has not yet finished downloading the image resource from the server by the time the call is made to `drawImage`, the canvas will simply not draw anything, since the image passed to be drawn onto it has not loaded yet. In the case where we draw the same image onto the canvas multiple times per second using a game loop of some sort, this is not really a problem, because whenever the image finally loads, the next pass through the game loop will successfully draw the image. However, in cases where the call to draw the image is only done once (as in the example above), we only get one chance to draw the image. Thus, it is very important that we don't make that call until the image is in fact loaded into memory, and ready to be drawn into the canvas.

In order to ensure that the call to draw the image into the canvas only happens after the image has been fully downloaded from the server, we can simply register a callback function on the load event of the image. This way, as soon as the image is done downloading, the browser can fire that callback, and the call can finally be made to draw the image. This way, we can be sure that the image will indeed be ready by the time we want to have it rendered in the canvas.

There is also another version of the same function, which takes into account, scaling from source to destination. In the case above, the source image is larger than the canvas. Instead of resizing the image using a photo editing software program, we can instead tell the canvas to draw the whole image into a smaller area of the canvas. The scaling is done by the canvas automatically. We could also draw the image into a larger area than the image itself, but doing so will result in pixilation depending on how much we scale the image.

The parameters for this function are the source image, the source x and y coordinates (in other words, where to start sampling the source image relative to the image itself), the source width and height (in other words, how much to sample the source image), and the destination x and y, followed by width and height.

```
ctx.fillStyle = "#fff";
ctx.fillRect(0, 0, canvas.width, canvas.height);

var img = new Image();
img.onload = function(){

    ctx.drawImage(img,
        // Sample part of the upper left corner of the source image
        35, 60, this.width / 2, this.height / 2,

        // And draw it onto the entire canvas, even if it distorts the
image
        0, 0, canvas.width, canvas.height);
};

img.src = "img/html5-logo.png";
```

Part of the HTML5 logo drawn inside a canvas rendering context, with some intentional stretching.

Manipulating pixels

Now that we know how to draw images into a canvas, let's take things to the next step, and work with the individual pixels drawn in the canvas. There are two functions that we can use in order to accomplish this. One function allows us to retrieve the pixel data from the canvas context, and the other lets us put a pixel buffer back into the canvas context. Additionally, there is a function that allows us to retrieve the pixel data as a data URL, meaning, that we can save the image data from the canvas right to the user's file system, just as we can with a regular image from an `<img />` tag.

```
ctx.fillStyle = "#fff";
ctx.fillRect(0, 0, canvas.width, canvas.height);

var img = new Image();
img.onload = function(){
    ctx.drawImage(img, 35, 60, this.width / 2, this.height / 2, 0, 0,
canvas.width, canvas.height);

    // Extract pixel data from canvas context
    var pixels = ctx.getImageData(0, 0, canvas.width, canvas.height);

    pixels instanceof ImageData; // True
    pixels.data instanceof Uint8ClampedArray; // True
    pixels.width == canvas.width; // True
    pixels.height == canvas.height; // True

    // Insert pixel data into canvas context
    ctx.putImageData(pixels, 0, 0);
};

img.src = "img/html5-logo.png";
```

To get the pixel data representing whatever is currently drawn in the canvas, we can use the function `getImageData`. The four parameters are the x and y offset on the source image, along with the width and height to be extracted. Note that the output from this function is an object of type `ImageData`, which has three attributes, namely, width, height, and a typed array with the actual pixel information. As mentioned earlier in the chapter, this typed array is of type `Uint8ClampedArray`, where each element can only be an `integer` with a value between 0 and 255 inclusive.

The pixel data is a buffer of length (`canvas.width x canvas.height x 4`). That is, each four elements represent one pixel, representing the red, green, blue, and alpha channels of the pixel in this order. Thus, in order to manipulate an image through this canvas API, we perform various calculations on this pixel buffer, which we can then put back in the canvas using the `putImageData` function.

The three parameters of `putImageData` are the `ImageData` object, along with the x and y offset on the destination canvas. From there, the canvas will render the image data as far as it can, clipping any extra data that would otherwise be drawn outside the canvas.

As an example of what we can do with an image, we'll take the HTML5 logo that we drew into the canvas, and apply a gray scale function to the pixel data representing it. If this sounds like a complex task, fear not. While there are several different formulas to turn a color image into gray scale, the easiest way to do this is to simply average the red, green, and blue values of each pixel.

```
ctx.fillStyle = "#fff";
ctx.fillRect(0, 0, canvas.width, canvas.height);

var img = new Image();
img.onload = function(){
   ctx.drawImage(img, 35, 60, this.width / 2, this.height / 2, 0, 0,
canvas.width, canvas.height);

   // Extract pixel data from canvas context
   var pixels = ctx.getImageData(0, 0, canvas.width, canvas.height);

   // Iterate over every four elements, which together represent a
single pixel
   for (var i = 0, len = pixels.data.length; i < len; i += 4) {
      var red = pixels.data[i];
      var green = pixels.data[i + 1];
      var blue = pixels.data[i + 2];
      var gray = (red + green + blue) / 3;

    // PS: Alpha channel can be accessed at pixels.data[i + 3]

      pixels.data[i] = gray;
      pixels.data[i + 1] = gray;
      pixels.data[i + 2] = gray;
   }
```

```
    // Insert pixel data into canvas context
    ctx.putImageData(pixels, 0, 0);
};

img.src = "img/html5-logo.png";
```

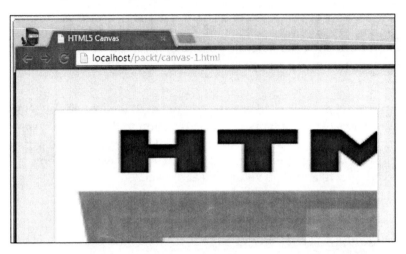

Manipulating an image is no more complex than performing various calculations
on each pixel of the pixel buffer that represents an image.

Finally, the way we can export the image from a canvas is as simple as calling the
toDataURL function. Make a special note that this function is called on the canvas
object, and not on the rendering context object. The toDataURL function of the canvas
object takes two optional parameters, namely, a string representing the MIME type
of the output image, and a float between 0.0 and 1.0, representing the quality of
the output image. If the output image type is anything other than "image/jpeg",
the quality parameter is ignored.

```
ctx.putImageData(pixels, 0, 0);

var imgUrl_LQ = canvas.toDataURL("image/jpeg", 0.0);
var out = new Image();
out.src = imgUrl_LQ;
document.body.appendChild(out);

var imgUrl_HQ = canvas.toDataURL("image/jpeg", 1.0);
var out = new Image();
out.src = imgUrl_HQ;
document.body.appendChild(out);

var imgUrl_raw = canvas.toDataURL("image/png");
var out = new Image();
out.src = imgUrl_raw;
document.body.appendChild(out);
```

Web workers

Web workers bring the ability to execute code outside the main UI thread. This thread-like behavior allows us to perform long lasting tasks without blocking the user interface. When a JavaScript task takes too long to complete, the browser displays an alert to the user, letting the user know that the page is not responsive. Using web workers, we can solve this problem.

There are a few restrictions with web workers that we need to keep in mind. First, workers run outside the DOM, so any functionality related to that is not available inside worker threads. Also, there is no concept of shared memory with workers—any data that is passed to and from a worker is copied into its own memory space. Finally, any objects passed to and from a worker can contain any data types, except for functions. If you attempt to pass a function to or from a worker (or an object holding a reference to a function), the browser will throw a **DataCloneError** (DOM Exception 25).

On the other hand, workers are completely capable of firing XHR requests (Ajax calls), starting other workers, and stopping other workers, including themselves. Once a worker is terminated, it can no longer be started, similar to other threading constructs available in other languages such as Java.

How to use it

In this section, we'll create a sample mini application that generates prime numbers in a worker thread. The user can input a number into the application, and the application will return a list of primes up to that number. Those prime numbers will then be passed back to the main application, which will then list the prime numbers back to the user.

To get started with web workers, we must first create a separate JavaScript file that will be run in the worker thread. The way this script will communicate with its parent thread is through messages. In order to receive messages from a parent thread, the worker needs to register a callback function that is called whenever a message is passed to it.

```
self.addEventListener("message", getPrimes);
```

The function is called when a message is received, both in the worker thread and in its parent thread, and a `MessageEvent` object is passed to the function. This object contains many attributes, including a timestamp, and most importantly, a data attribute, which contains any data passed into the worker.

To post a message to a worker or back to its parent, we simply call the function `postMessage` on the appropriate object (either the worker object, or on the self-object, if inside a worker), passing the data along with the function call. This data can be a single value, an array, or an object of any type, as long as no functions are included.

Finally, to create a `worker` object, we simply create an instance of the class `Worker`, passing the path to the worker script as a constructor parameter. This `worker` object will need to register callback functions for whatever events it wants to observe: `onMessage` or `onError`. To kill the worker thread, we can either call the `terminate` function directly on the worker object, or the `close` function on the worker script.

```
// index.html
var worker = new Worker("get-primes.worker.js");

worker.addEventListener("message", function(event){
    var primes = event.data.primes;
    var ul = document.createElement("ul");

    // Parse each prime returned from the worker
    for (var i = 0, len = primes.length; i < len; i++) {
        var li = document.createElement("li");
        li.textContent = primes[i];
        ul.appendChild(li);
    }

    // Clear any existing list items
    var uls = document.querySelectorAll("ul");
    for (var i = 0, len = uls.length; i < len; i++)
        uls[i].remove();

    // Display the results
    document.body.appendChild(ul);
});

var input = document.createElement("input");
input.addEventListener("keyup", function(event){
    var key = event.which;

    // Call the worker when the Enter key is pressed
    if (key == 13 /* Enter */) {
        var input = this.value;
```

```
    // Only use input that's a positive number
    if (!isNaN(input) && input > 0) {
       worker.postMessage({max: input});
    } else if (input == -1) {
       worker.terminate();
       this.remove();
    }
  }
});
```

```
input.setAttribute("autofocus", true);
document.body.appendChild(input);
```

In the above snippet, we set up two things: a worker and an input field. We then set up a `keydown` listener on the input field, which we use so the user can input a number to send to the worker. To send this number to the worker, the user must press the **Enter** key. When that happens, the number in the input field will be the highest possible prime number generated by the worker. If the user inputs the number `-1`, the worker is terminated, and the input field is removed from the DOM.

For simplicity, the worker thread will use the **Sieve of Eratosthenes** to find the primes. Keep in mind that this exercise is only a proof of concept to illustrate how web workers work, and not a lesson on advanced mathematics.

```
// get-primes.worker.js

// Register the onMessage callback
self.addEventListener("message", getPrimes);

// This function implements the Sieve of Eratosthenes to generate the
primes.
// Don't worry about the algorithm so much - focus on the Worker API
function getPrimes(event) {

   var max = event.data.max;
   var primes = [];
   var d = [];
```

```
for (var q = 2; q < max; q++) {
    if (d[q]) {
        for (var i = 0; i < d[q].length; i++) {
            var p = d[q][i];
            if (d[p + q])
                d[p + q].push(p);
            else
                d[p + q] = [p];
        }
        delete d[q];
    } else {
        primes.push(q);
        if (q * q < max)
            d[q * q] = [q];
    }
}

// Return the list of primes to the parent thread
self.postMessage({primes: primes});
}
```

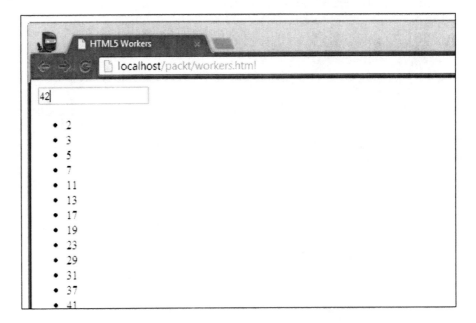

The worker can be invoked an infinite amount of times, as long as it is not terminated.
Once terminated, the worker can be deleted, as it serves no useful purpose from that point on.

Offline application cache

Offline application cache is a way to store assets on the browser for use when the user is not connected to the internet. This API further breaks down any barriers between a native application and a web application, since it does away with the major characteristic that sets a web application apart from a native one—the need for a connection to the World Wide Web. Although the user will obviously still need to be connected to the network at some point, so the application can be downloaded initially; after that, the application can run completely from the user's cache.

Probably the main use case for offline application cache is when the user's connection is not stable, consistent, or simply not on every time the application is used. This is especially true with games, as the user may choose to play a certain online game some of the time, but offline later on. Similarly, if the game needs to connect to a backend server, in order to perform whatever task (such as to retrieve new game data), this can be done whenever the user is connected, the resources can be again cached locally, and the new data can be used again, if and when the user's connectivity becomes unavailable.

How to use it

The backbone of the offline application cache API is the manifest file, which specifies to the browser which resources should be cached for offline use, which resources must never be cached, and what the browser should do when an attempt is made to connect to the server, but no connection is found.

The manifest file is served with the HTML file that the user requests, when loading your application. More specifically, the host HTML file specifies the path to the manifest file, which the browser then fetches and processes in parallel, with the download and processing of the main application. This is done with the `manifest` attribute in the root `html` tag.

```
<!doctype html>
<html manifest="manifest.appcache">
```

Observe that the above snippet specifies a manifest file named `manifest.appcache`, located in the same directory as the HTML file specifying the manifest. The name of the file, along with its extension, is completely arbitrary. By convention, many developers named the manifest simply `manifest.appcache`, `manifest` (without an extension), or `appcache.manifest`. However, this file could very well be named `manifest.php?id=2642`, `my-manifest-file.txt`, or `the_file.json`.

An important thing to remember is that the manifest file be served with the proper MIME type. If the browser attempts to fetch whatever file is listed in the `manifest` attribute of the root HTML tag, and the MIME type is not `text/cache-manifest`, then the browser will reject the manifest, and no offline application cache will take place.

There are many ways to set the MIME type to a file, but generally this is a server setting. If using an Apache server, such as the one we are using with WAMP, MAMP, or LAMP (see the online chapter, *Setting Up the Environment*), we can easily do this with a `.htaccess` file. For example, in the root directory of our project, we can create a file named `.htaccess` containing the following code:

```
AddType text/cache-manifest .appcache
```

This would tell the server to add the right MIME type to any file with an extension of `.appcache`. Of course, if you decide to tweak the `htaccess` file to serve the `cache-manifest` MIME type to other file extensions, you could possibly run into issues if the extension you choose is already associated with other MIME types (such as `.json`).

The first line of the manifest file must be the following string:

```
CACHE MANIFEST
```

If this line isn't present again, the entire API will take no effect. If there is as much as an extra white space before the string listed above, the browser will throw the following error, indicating that the file manifest is invalid, and nothing will be cached:

```
Application Cache Error event: Failed to parse manifest
```

 When using offline application cache on your games, make sure to keep an open eye on your browser's JavaScript console. If anything goes wrong at all, such as finding the manifest file, parsing the manifest, or loading any of the resources described in the manifest, the browser will let you know that something went wrong by raising an exception, but it will go on. Unlike most fatal JavaScript exceptions, a fatal offline application cache exception doesn't stop or influence the execution of the script that initiated the caching process. Thus, you may be getting app cache exceptions and not know it, so get acquainted with whatever developer tools your browser supports, and make good of it.

The rest of the manifest can be divided into three main categories, namely, assets to be cached, assets to never be cached, and the fallback asset. Comments can be placed anywhere within the file, and are denoted by a pound sign. The entire line following a pound sign is ignored by the manifest parser.

```
CACHE MANIFEST

# HTML5 Snake, Version 1.0.0

CACHE:
index.html
js/next-empty.worker.js
js/renderer.class.js
js/snake.class.js
img/block-green.png
img/fruit-01.png
fonts/geo.woff
fonts/vt323.woff
css/style.css

NETWORK:
*

FALLBACK:
fallback.html
```

By using the wild card under the network section, we indicate that any resource not specified under cache, qualified under the network section, meaning that those resources are not to be cached. Any attempt to load those resources when network access is not available will result in the fallback file being loaded instead. This is a good option to let the user know that network access is needed without needing to special case any extra code.

Once the manifest is parsed and all the resources are cached, all of the resources will remain cached, until the user deletes the offline application cache data (or all of the data cached by the browser), or the manifest is changed. Even if only a single character changes in the manifest file, the browser will consider it to be an update, thus, all of the resources are cached anew. Because of this, many developers write a comment line right at the top of the manifest file that, among other optional things, they include some sort of version number that identifies a unique version of the manifest. This way, if one or more assets changes, we can force the browser to re-cache those assets by simply changing the version number listed in the manifest file. Remember, the browser will only check the text in the manifest file in order to determine if it needs to download new assets. If assets change (say, you update JavaScript code listed in the manifest, or some graphics, or any other resource), but the manifest text doesn't, those resources will not be pulled from the server, and the user will continue to use an outdated asset in his or her application, since the assets are loaded only from the cache.

The code

The way this game was laid out is actually quite simple. The HTML has only three widgets: the title of the game, a score board for the player's current score, and a score board for the overall high score across multiple games. This last score board is not used in this version of the game, and we'll get more into it in the next game (see *Chapter 5, Improving the Snake Game*).

```
<h1>HTML5 Snake</h1>

<section id="scores">
    <h3>Score: <span>0</span></h3>
    <h3>High Score: <span>0</span></h3>
</section>

<section id="gameMenu" class="hide">
    <h3>Ready!</h3>
    <button>Play</button>
</section>
```

In order to separate the various responsibilities from all the different components in the game, we abstracted out all the rendering for the entire game into a single `Renderer` class. This class is in charge of drawing data to a `canvas` reference that is given to it. The data that it draws, be it a snake or any other objects, is passed in to it as a typed array, representing the coordinates where the entity is to be drawn, along with the image resource that is drawn at the location specified by the typed array. The `Renderer` class also includes a few helper functions to help us easily clear the canvas, and convert an x and y point into an index used to traverse the flat array representing a 2D one.

```
var Renderer = function(canvas) {

    var canvas = canvas;
    var ctx = canvas.getContext("2d");
    var width = canvas.width;
    var height = canvas.height;

    var getIndex = function(x, y) {
        return width * y + x;
    };
```

```
    var getPosition = function(index) {
        return {
            x: index % width,
            y: parseInt(index / width)
        };
    };

    this.clear = function() {
        ctx.clearRect(0, 0, canvas.width, canvas.height);
    };

    this.draw = function(points, img) {
        for (var i = 0, len = points.length; i < len; i += 2) {
            ctx.drawImage(img, points[i] * img.width, points[i + 1] *
img.height, img.width, img.height);
        }
    };
};
```

Next, we create a `Snake` class that encapsulates all of the data and behavior associated with the snake. The data that this class stores is the current position of the snake's head, the current length of the snake's body, the image that is to be drawn representing the snake, and whether the snake is alive or not. The behavior that it handles includes the moving of the snake and the handling of user input (which is included in this class for simplicity and brevity). There are a few helper functions that allow us to delegate other behaviors to the client. For example, through the API exposed, the client can check at each frame whether the snake has gone outside the world grid, if it has eaten a fruit, or if the snake ran into its own body. The client can also use the API provided, to take action on the snake, such as setting its life attribute (dead or alive), as well as reset the image used to draw the snake, or any other attribute of it.

```
var Snake = function(x, y, width, height, maxSize) {
    var isAlive = true;
    var size = 0;
    var body = new Int8Array(maxSize * 2);
    for (var i = 0, len = body.length; i < len; i++)
        body[i] = -1;
    body[0] = x, body[1] = y;
    var worldWidth = width;
    var worldHeight = height;
    var skin;
```

```
var dir = { 38: false, 40: false, 37: false, 39: false };
var keys = { UP: 38, DOWN: 40, LEFT: 37, RIGHT: 39 };
// To move the snake, we first move each body part to where the
// part before it used to be, starting at the tail and moving
// towards the head. Lastly, we update the head's position
var move = function() {
    // Traverse the snake backwards and shift each piece one spot
    for (var i = size * 2 + 1; i > 1; i -= 2) {
        body[i] = body[i - 2];
        body[i - 1] = body[i - 3];
    }
    if (dir[keys.UP]) {
        body[1]--;
    } else if (dir[keys.DOWN]) {
        body[1]++;
    } else if (dir[keys.LEFT]) {
        body[0]--;
    } else if (dir[keys.RIGHT]) {
        body[0]++;
    }
};
// Update the snake's position vectors on key presses
this.doOnKeyDown = function(event) {
    var key = event.which;
    // Don't process a key that's already down
    if (dir[key])
        return;
    dir[keys.UP] = false;
    dir[keys.DOWN] = false;
    dir[keys.LEFT] = false;
    dir[keys.RIGHT] = false;
    if (key == keys.UP && !dir[keys.DOWN]) {
        return dir[keys.UP] = true;
    } else if (key === keys.DOWN && !dir[keys.UP]) {
        return dir[keys.DOWN] = true;
    } else if (key === keys.LEFT && !dir[keys.RIGHT]) {
        return dir[keys.LEFT] = true;
    } else if (key === keys.RIGHT && !dir[keys.LEFT]) {
        return dir[keys.RIGHT] = true;
    }
};
```

```
   // This allows us to use different images to represent the snake
   this.setSkin = function(img) {
      skin = new Image();
      skin.onload = function() {
         skin.width = this.width;
         skin.height = this.height;
      };
      skin.src = img;
   };
      this.move = move;
   this.getSkin = function() { return skin; };
   this.setDead = function(isDead) { isAlive = !isDead; };
   this.isAlive = function() { return isAlive; };
   this.getBody = function() { return body; };
   this.getHead = function() { return {x: body[0], y: body[1]}; };
   this.grow = function() { if (size * 2 < body.length) return size++;
};
   // Check if the snake is at a certain position on the grid
   this.isAt = function(x, y, includeHead) {
      var offset = includeHead ? 0 : 2;
      for (var i = 2, len = body.length; i < len; i += 2) {
         if (body[i] == x && body[i + 1] == y)
            return true;
      }
      return false;
   };
   this.reset = function(x, y) {
      for (var i = 0, len = body.length; i < len; i++)
         body[i] = -1;
      body[0] = x;
      body[1] = y;
      size = 0;
      isAlive = true;
      dir[keys.UP] = false;
      dir[keys.DOWN] = false;
      dir[keys.LEFT] = false;
      dir[keys.RIGHT] = false;
   };
};
```

Similar to the `snake` class, we also create a class to encapsulate the fruit that the snake will eat. The only difference between the `snake` class and the `fruit` class is that the `fruit` class will not do anything other than show up in the map. For all practical purposes, the `fruit` class shares a common entity interface with the `snake` class, which allows them to be reset to a default state, set their position, and check for collision.

```
var fruit = {
    position: new Int8Array(2),
    reset: function() {
        this.position[0] = -1;
        this.position[1] = -1;
    },
    isAt: function(x, y) {
        return this.position[0] == x && this.position[1] == y;
    },
    img: null
};
```

Finally, in the main code, we perform the following setup task:

- Create a canvas element and attach it to the DOM.
- Instantiate the `renderer`, `snake`, and `fruit` objects.
- Create a game loop that places a fruit on the grid when one is not present, update the snake's position, check where the snake is, and render the game state to the canvas.

We also use the game loop to hook into the score board widgets, to add to the user experience. The complete source code for the game available at the book's page on the website of Packt Publishing also includes extra menus, but these have been left out of the code snippets shown here for brevity.

The other thing we take advantage of in this game loop is the `requestAnimationFrame` API. In order to assure that different CPUs and GPUs, all render the game at the same pace, we added a simple frame rate controller inside the game loop. The frame rate is controlled by a variable that specified how many fps the game should attempt to run.

```
function gameLoop() {
    // Only do anything here if the snake is not dead
    if (snake.isAlive()) {

        // Make the frame rate no faster than what we determine (30 fps)
        renderTime.now = Date.now();
        if (renderTime.now - renderTime.last >= renderTime.fps) {
```

```
            // If there is no fruit on the grid, place one somewhere.
Here we
            // use a web worker to calculate an empty square on the map
            if (fruit.position[0] < 0) {
                cellGen.postMessage({
                    points: snake.getBody(),
                    width: worldWidth,
                    height: worldHeight
                });
            } else {

                snake.move();
                head = snake.getHead();

                // Check if the snake has ran into itself, or gone outside
the grid
                if (snake.isAt(head.x, head.y, false) ||
                        head.x < 0 || head.y < 0 ||
                        head.x >= worldWidth || head.y >= worldHeight) {
                    snake.setDead(true);
                }

                // Check if the snake has eaten a fruit
                if (fruit.isAt(head.x, head.y)) {
                    fruit.reset();
                    snake.grow();
                    score.up();
                }

                renderTime.last = renderTime.now;
            }
        }

        // Render everything: clear the screen, draw the fruit, draw the
snake,
        // and register the callback with rAF
        renderer.clear();
        renderer.draw(fruit.position, fruit.img);
        renderer.draw(snake.getBody(), snake.getSkin());
        requestAnimationFrame(gameLoop);
    }

    // If the snake is dead, stop rendering and disable
    // the key handlers that controlled the snake
    else {
        document.body.removeEventListener("keydown", snake.doOnKeyDown);
    }
}
```

Summary

In the chapter we got started with 2D rendering using the long-awaited canvas API. We looked at the various drawing functions available to us through the canvas rendering context, which includes drawing simple lines and shapes, drawing images from an external image source, pixel manipulation, and image extraction, which allows us to save the image from the canvas back to the user's file system.

We also looked at the new threading system available to us through the web worker interface. This allows us to free up the user interface thread, while we perform long lasting tasks that would otherwise lock up the interface, and cause the browser to display a non-responsive page alert. Unfortunately, there are a few limitations to web workers, since there is no shared memory between workers, and no DOM associated with, or allowed in a worker thread. Still, much can be done with this magnificent new feature of HTML5.

The other HTML5 specific API that we covered in the chapter was the offline application cache. Through this mechanism, we can save specific assets from a web server, storing it as a fast, highly available cache, powered by the user's browser. The specific assets that are saved by the browser are specified by a manifest file, while it is a simple text-based file, and must be served by the server with the `text/cache-manifest` MIME type.

Finally, we looked at two new additions to the JavaScript language that make game development more efficient and exciting. The first of these two features is `requestAnimationFrame`, which allows us to render all of our content in a single, synchronized call, managed by the browser itself. This is often the best way possible to render all of our graphics, since the browser can highly optimize the rendering process. The second feature is the typed array data type, which allows for much efficient data storage and access. This is especially attractive to game development because of the extra boost in performance we can get, just by using this new data type, even though it looks and behaves almost 100% the same as regular arrays. Thus, writing new code using typed arrays should include no learning curve whatsoever, as porting existing code that uses arrays is a real treat.

In the next chapter we continue working on the Snake game, making it more robust and feature rich. We'll learn about four more HTML5 APIs, namely sessionStorage, localStorage, IndexedDB, and web messaging.

5
Improving the Snake Game

This chapter is the second and final part of the series where we're building a more robust snake game. In this chapter, we'll take what we already had from *Chapter 3, Understanding the Gravity of HTML5*, and add more HTML5 APIs to it, so as to make the game more feature rich, providing an even more engaging user experience.

The first version of the game used five HTML5 concepts, namely 2D canvas rendering, offline application cache, web workers, typed arrays, and requestAnimationFrame. In this version, we'll include two features from the new web storage API, namely local storage and session storage. We'll also look at a third API that is part of web storage, IndexedDB, as well as the web messaging feature, which includes cross-domain messaging.

Local storage and session storage are two mechanisms that allow us to save data on the user's browser using a key-value strategy. This is similar to a cookie, where every value must be a string. The difference between these two storage options and a cookie, first and foremost, is that a cookie is always sent back to the server through HTTP requests. This can be especially undesirable when we have larger amounts of data that we would like to store, since that data would be traveling around consuming extra bandwidth, and there is nothing that we can do about it. With HTML5's web storage, we can save more data locally, and that data never leaves the user's machine, though HTTP components like cookies do.

IndexedDB, also part of web storage, is similar to local and session storage, where data is stored in a key-value manner, but instead of values being limited to strings only, IndexedDB is more of an object store, where we can store entire JavaScript objects. Of course, IndexedDB is much more than a mere hash map that holds objects for us. As the name implies, this new API allows us to index these stored objects with the purpose of being able to search for them through a query system. In summary, IndexedDB is a NoSQL database accessed through an asynchronous programming interface.

Finally, the web messaging API provides an interface through which an HTML document can communicate with other HTML contexts. These documents can be related by iframes, in separate windows, and even in different domains.

The game

Two new features were added to this second version of the game. First, we now keep track of the highest score achieved by a player, saving it through local storage. Even if the player closes the browser application, or turns off the computer, that value will still be safely stored in the player's hard drive, and will be loaded when the game starts again. Second, we use session storage to save the game state every time the player eats a fruit in the game, and whenever the player kills the snake. This is used as an extra touch of awesomeness, where after the player loses, we display a snapshot of all the individual level ups the player achieved in that game, as well as a snapshot of when the player hit a wall or run the snake into itself, as shown in the following screenshot:

At the end of each game, an image is shown of each moment when the player acquired a level up, as well as a snapshot of when the player eventually died. This images are created through the canvas API (calling the toDataURL function), and the data that composes each image is saved throughout the game, and stored using the web storage API.

With a feature such as this in place, we make the game much more fun, and potentially much more social. Imagine how powerful it would be if the player could post, not only his or her high score to their favorite social network website, but also pictures of their game at key moments. Of course, only the foundation of this feature is implemented in this chapter (in other words, we only take the snapshots of these critical moments in the game). Adding the actual functionality to send that data to a real social network application is left as an exercise for the reader.

API usage

A general description and demonstration of each of the APIs used in the game are given in the following sections. For an explanation of how each piece of functionality was incorporated into the final game, look at the code section. For the complete source code for this game, check out the book's page from Packt Publishing's website.

Web messaging

Web messaging allows us to communicate with other HTML document instances, even if they're not in the same domain. For example, suppose our snake game, hosted at `http://snake.fun-html5-games.com`, is embedded into a social website through `iframe` (let's say this social website is hosted at `http://www.awesome-html5-games.net`). When the player achieves a new high score, we want to post that data from the snake game directly into the host page (the page with `iframe` from which the game is loaded). With the web messaging API, this can be done natively, without the need for any server-side scripting whatsoever.

Before web messaging, documents were not allowed to communicate with documents in other domains mostly because of security. Of course, web applications can still be vulnerable to malicious external applications if we just blindly take messages from any application. However, the web messaging API provides some solid security measures to protect the page receiving the message. For example, we can specify the domains that the message is going to, so that other domains cannot intercept the message. On the receiving end, we can also check the origin from whence the message came, thus ignoring messages from any untrusted domains. Finally, the DOM is never directly exposed through this API, providing yet another layer of security.

How to use it

Similar to web workers, the way in which two or more HTML contexts can communicate through the web messaging API is by registering an event handler for the on-message event, and sending messages out by using the `postMessage` function:

```
// --------------------------------
// Host document: web-messaging.html
// --------------------------------
var doc = document.querySelector("iframe").contentWindow;
// alternatively:
// var doc = window.open("web-messaging-rec.html", "",
"width=800,height=600");
// Post a message to the child document
```

```
doc.postMessage({msg: "Hello!"}, "http://localhost");
// -----------------------------------
// Child document: web-messaging-rec.html
// -----------------------------------
window.addEventListener("message", function(event) {
    var data = event.data;
    // Post a message back to the parent document
    event.source.postMessage({msg: "Thanks for saying " + data.msg},
"*");
});
```

The first step to using the web messaging API is to get a reference to some document with whom we wish to communicate. This can be done by getting the `contentWindow` property of an `iframe` reference, or by opening a new window and holding on to that reference. The document that holds this reference is called the parent document, since this is where the communication is initiated. Although a child window can communicate with its parent, this can only happen when and for as long as this relationship holds true. In other words, a window cannot communicate with just any window; it needs a reference to it, either through a parent-child relationship, or through a child-parent relationship.

Once the child window has been referenced, the parent can fire messages to its children through the `postMessage` function. Of course, if the child window hasn't defined a callback function to capture and process the incoming messages, there is little purpose in sending those messages in the first place. Still, the parent has no way of knowing if a child window has defined a callback to process incoming messages, so the best we can do is assume (and hope) that the child window is ready to receive our messages.

The parameters used in the `postMessage` function are fairly similar to the version used in web workers. That is, any JavaScript value can be sent (numbers, strings, Boolean values, object literals, and arrays, including typed arrays). If a function is sent as the first parameter of `postMessage` (either directly, or as part of an object), the browser will raise a `DATA_CLONE_ERR: DOM Exception 25` error. The second parameter is a string, and represents the domain that we allow our message to be received by. This can be an absolute domain, a forward slash (representing the same origin domain as the document sending the message), or a wild card character (*), representing any domain. If the message is received by a domain that doesn't match the second parameter in `postMessage`, the entire message fails.

When receiving the message, the child window first registers a callback on the message event. This function is passed a `MessageEvent` object, which contains the following attributes:

- `event.data`: It returns the data of the message
- `event.origin`: It returns the origin of the message, for server-sent events and cross-document messaging
- `event.lastEventId`: It returns the last event ID string, for server-sent events
- `event.sourceReturns`: It is the WindowProxy of the source window, for cross-document messaging
- `event.portsReturns`: It is the MessagePort array sent with the message, for cross-document messaging and channel messaging

 Source: `http://www.w3.org/TR/webmessaging/#messageevent`

As an example of the sort of things we could use this feature for in the real world, and in terms of game development, imagine being able to play our snake game, but where the snake moves through a couple of windows. How creative is that?! Of course, in terms of being practical, this may not be the best way to play a game, but I find it hard to argue with the fact that this would indeed be a very unique and engaging presentation of an otherwise common game.

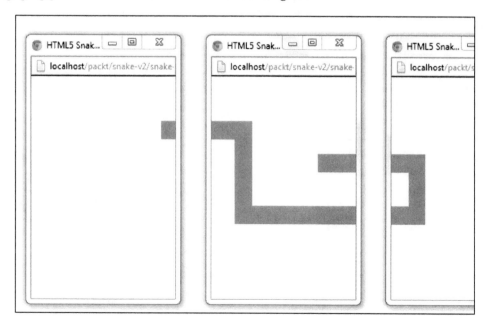

With the help of the web messaging API, we can set up a snake, where the snake is not constrained to a single window. Imagine the possibilities when we combine this clever API with another very powerful HTML5 feature, which just happens to lend itself incredibly well to games – web sockets. By combining web messaging with web sockets, we could play a game of snake, not only across multiple windows, but also with multiple players at the same time. Perhaps each player would control the snake when it got inside a given window, and all players could see all windows at the same time, even though they are each using a separate computer. The possibilities are endless, really.

Surprisingly, the code used to set up a multi-window port of snake is incredibly simple. The basic setup is the same, we have a snake that only moves in one direction at a time. We also have one or more windows where the snake can go. If we store each window in an array, we can calculate which screen the snake needs to be rendered in, given its current position. Finding out which screen the snake is supposed to be in, given its world position, is the trickiest part.

For example, imagine that each window is 200 pixels wide. Now, suppose there are three windows opened. Each window's canvas is only 200 pixels wide as well, so when the snake is at position 350, it would be printed too far to the right in all of the canvases. So what we need to do is first determine the total world width (canvas width multiplied by the total number of canvases), calculate which window the snake is at (position/canvas width), then convert the position from world space down to canvas space, given the canvas the snake is in.

First, lets define our structures in the parent document. The code for this is as follows:

```
// 1. Create an array to hold each frame (aka. window)
var frames = new Array();
// 2. Let's keep track of some settings for these frames
frames.max = 3;
frames.width = 200;
frames.height = 300;
frames.margin = 50;
// 3. Finally, we'll need a snake to move around
var snake = {
  max: 3,
  pos: {
    x: 0,
    y: 0
  },
```

```
  w: 25,
  h: 25,
  speed: 3,
  dir: {
    x: 1,
    y: 0
  },
  color: "#0a0"
};
```

When this script loads, we'll need a way to create new windows, where the snake will be able to move about. This can easily be done with a button that spawns a new window when clicked, then adding that window to our array of frames, so that we can iterate through that array, and tell every window where the snake is. The code for this is as follows:

```
// Define a few global variables in order to keep the code shorter
and simpler
var isPaused = true;
var timer;
var dirChange = 100;
var btn = document.createElement("button");
btn.textContent = "Add Window";
btn.addEventListener("click", function(event){
  var left = frames.length * frames.width + frames.margin * frames.
length;
  frames[frames.length] = window.open("/packt/snake-v2/snake-panels.
html", "",
    "width=" + frames.width + "," +
    "height=" + frames.height + "," +
    "top=100, left=" + left);
  isPaused = false;
  clearTimeout(timer);
  play();
}, false);
document.body.appendChild(btn);
// We'll close all the windows we have opened to save us the
// trouble of clicking each window when we want them closed
function closeAll() {
  for (var i = 0, len = frames.length; i < len; i++) {
    frames[i].close();
  }
}
window.onunload = closeAll;
```

Now, the real magic happens in the following method. All that we'll do is update the snake's position, then tell each window where the snake is. This will be done by converting the snake's position from world coordinates to canvas coordinates (since every canvas has the same width, this is easy to do for every canvas), then telling every window where the snake should be rendered within a canvas. Since that position is valid for every window, we also tell each window individually whether or not they should render the information we're sending them. Only the window that we calculate the snake is in, is told to go ahead and render.

```
function play() {
  // This is used to change the snake's position randomly
  // from time to time. The reason for this is so we don't
  // need to implement any event handling to handle user input,
  // since this is just a simple demonstration.
  if (dirChange-- < 0) {
    dirChange = 100;
    var rand = parseInt(Math.random() * 1000) % 4;
    // Make the snake move to the right
    if (rand == 0) {
      snake.dir.x = 1;
      snake.dir.y = 0;
    // Make the snake move to the left
    } else if (rand == 1) {
      snake.dir.x = -1;
      snake.dir.y = 0;
    // Make the snake move down
    } else if (rand == 2) {
      snake.dir.x = 0;
      snake.dir.y = 1;
      // Make the snake move up
    } else if (rand == 3) {
      snake.dir.x = 0;
      snake.dir.y = -1;
    }
  };
  // Update the snake's position, making sure to wrap the snake
  // around each window. If it goes too far to the right, and
  // wanders off one window, it needs to wrap to the left side
  // of the next window.
  snake.pos.x += snake.dir.x * snake.speed;
  snake.pos.x %= frames.width * frames.length;
  snake.pos.y += snake.speed * snake.dir.y;
```

```
  if (snake.pos.y < 0)
    snake.pos.y = frames.height - snake.h;
  if (snake.pos.y + snake.h > frames.height)
    snake.pos.y = 0;
  if (snake.pos.x < 0)
    snake.pos.x = (frames.width - snake.w) * frames.width * frames.
length;
  var shouldDraw;
  for (var i = 0, len = frames.length; i < len; i++) {
    // Determine which window the snake is in, and tell only that
    // window that it needs to render the snake
    shouldDraw = snake.pos.x + snake.w <= frames.width * (i + 1) &&
        snake.pos.x >= frames.width * i ||
        snake.pos.x <= frames.width * (i + 1) &&
        snake.pos.x >= frames.width * i;
    // Lastly, we pass all this information to each window in canvas
coordinates.
    frames[i].postMessage({
      x: snake.pos.x % frames.width,
      y: snake.pos.y,
      w: snake.w,
      h: snake.h,
      shouldDraw: shouldDraw,
      color: snake.color
    }, "*");
  }
}
```

That's really all there is to it. The code that makes up all the other windows is the same for all of them. In fact, we only open a bunch of windows pointing to the exact same script. As far as each window is concerned, they are the only window opened. All they do is take a bunch of data through the messaging API, then render that data if the `shouldDraw` flag is set. Otherwise, they just clear their canvas, and sit tight waiting for further instructions from their parent window.

```
// 1. Create a canvas
var canvas = document.createElement("canvas");
canvas.width = 400;
canvas.height = 300;
// 2. Attach the canvas to the DOM
document.body.appendChild(canvas);
// 3. Get a reference to the canvas' context
var ctx = canvas.getContext("2d");
```

```
  // 4. Set up the callback to receive messages from some parent window
  function doOnMessage(event) {
    // 5. For security, make sure we only process input from a trusted
  window
    if (event.origin == "http://localhost") {
      var data = event.data;
      ctx.clearRect(0, 0, canvas.width, canvas.height);
      // 6. And here's where the magic happens for this window. If told
  to
      // draw something through the message received, go ahead and do
  so.
      if (data.shouldDraw) {
        ctx.fillStyle = data.color;
        ctx.fillRect(data.x, data.y, data.w, data.h);
      }
    }
  }
  window.addEventListener("message", doOnMessage, false);
```

Web storage

Before HTML5 came along, the only way web developers had to store data on the client was through cookies. While limited in scope, cookies did what they were meant to, although they had several limitations. For one thing, whenever a cookie was saved to the client, every HTTP request after that included the data for that cookie. This meant that the data was always explicitly exposed, and each of those HTTP requests were heavily laden with extra data that didn't belong there. This is especially inefficient when considering web applications that may need to store relatively large amounts of data.

With the new web storage API, these issues have been addressed and satisfied. There are now three different options for client storage, all of which solve a different problem. Keep in mind, however, that any and all data stored in the client is still exposed to the client in plain text, and is therefore not meant for a secure storage solution.

These three storage solutions are session storage, local storage, and the IndexedDB NoSQL data store. Session storage allows us to store key-value data pairs that persist until the browser is closed (in other words, until the session finishes). Local storage is similar to session storage in every way, except that the duration that the data persists is longer.

Even when a session is closed, data stored in a local storage still persists. That data in local storage is only cleared when the user specifically tells the browser to do so, or when the application itself deletes data from the storage. Finally, IndexedDB is a robust data store that allows us to store custom objects (not including objects that contains functions), then query the database for those objects. Of course, with much robustness comes great complexity. Although having a dedicated NoSQL database built in right into the browser may sound exciting, but don't be fooled. While using IndexedDB can be a fascinating addition to the world of HTML, it is also by no means a trivial task for beginners. Compared to local storage and session storage, IndexedDB has somewhat of a steep learning curve, since it involves mastering some complex database concepts.

As mentioned earlier, the only real difference between local storage and session storage is the fact that session storage clears itself whenever the browser closes down. Besides that, everything about the two is exactly the same. Thus, learning how to use both will be a simple experience, since learning one also means learning the other. However, knowing when to use one over the other might take a bit more thinking on your part. For best results, try to focus on the unique characteristics and needs of your own application before deciding which one to use. More importantly, realize that it is perfectly legal to use both storage systems in the same application. The key is to focus on a unique feature, and decide what storage API best suits those specific needs.

Both the local storage and session storage objects are instances of the class `Storage`. The interface defined by the `storage` class, through which we can interact with these storage objects, is defined as follows (source: Web Storage W3C Candidate Recommendation, December 08, 2011, `http://www.w3.org/TR/webstorage/`):

- `getItem(key)`: It returns the current value associated with the given key. If the given key does not exist in the list associated with the object then this method must return null.

- `setItem(key, value)`: It first checks if a key/value pair with the given key already exists in the list associated with the object. If it does not, then a new key/value pair must be added to the list, with the given key and with its value set to `value`. If the given key does exist in the list, then it must have its value updated to `value`. If it couldn't set the new value, the method must throw a `QuotaExceededError` exception. (Setting could fail if, for example, the user has disabled storage for the site, or if the quota has been exceeded.)

- `removeItem(key)`: It causes the key/value pair with the given key to be removed from the list associated with the object, if it exists. If no item with that key exists, the method must do nothing.

- `clear()`: It automatically causes the list associated with the object to be emptied of all key/value pairs, if there are any. If there are none, then the method must do nothing.

- `key(n)`: It returns the name of the nth key in the list. The order of keys is user-agent defined, but must be consistent within an object so long as the number of keys doesn't change. (Thus, adding or removing a key may change the order of the keys, but merely changing the value of an existing key must not.) If n is greater than or equal to the number of key/value pairs in the object, then this method must return null. The supported property names on a Storage object are the keys of each key/value pair currently present in the list associated with the object.

- `length`: It returns the number of key/value pairs currently present in the list associated with the object.

Local storage

The local storage mechanism is accessed through a property of the global object, which on browsers is the `window` object. Thus, we can access the storage property explicitly through `window.localStorage`, or implicitly as simply `localStorage`.

```
window.localStorage.clear();

localStorage.length == 0; // True
```

Since only DOMString values are allowed to be stored in localStorage, any other values other than strings are converted into a string before being stored in localStorage. That is, we can't store arrays, objects, functions, and so on in `localStorage`. Only plain JavaScript strings are allowed.

```
var typedArray = new Uint32Array(100);
localStorage.setItem("my-array", typedArray);
var myArray = localStorage.getItem("my-array");
myArray == "[object Uint32Array]"; // True
```

Now, while this might seem like a limitation to the storage API, this is in fact done by design. If your goal is to store complex data types for later use, localStorage wasn't necessarily designed to solve this problem. In those situations, we have a much more powerful and convenient storage solution, which we'll look at soon (that is, IndexedDB). However, there is a way to store complex data (including arrays, typed arrays, objects, and so on) in localStorage.

The key lies in the wonderful JSON data format. Modern browsers have the very handy JSON object available in the global scope, where we can access two important functions, namely JSON.stringify and JSON.parse. With these two methods, we can serialize complex data, store that in localStorage, then unserialize the data retrieved from the storage, and continue using it in the application.

```
// 1. Define some class
var Person = function(name) {
  this.name = name;
};
// 2. Add functions to the class
Person.prototype.greet = function(){
  return "Hello, " + this.name;
};
// 3. Create an array of objects of that class
var people = new Array();
people.push(new Person("Rodrigo"));
people.push(new Person("Silveira"));
// 4. Stringify the complex array, and store it away
var json = JSON.stringify(people);
localStorage.setItem("people", json);
// 5. Retrieve that serialized data, and parse it back into what it
was
people = JSON.parse(localStorage.getItem("people"));
people[0].name == "Rodrigo"; // True
people[0] instanceof Person; // False
people[0].greet(); // TypeError: Object has no method 'greet'
```

While this is a nice little trick, you will notice what can be a major limitation: JSON stringify does not serialize functions. Also, if you pay close attention to the way that JSON.stringify works, you will realize that class instances lose all of their "identity", and only the hard data is maintained. In other words, after we serialize and unserialize an instance of Person, the result will be a simple object literal with no constructor or prototype information. Still, given that localStorage was never intended to fill the role of object persistence (but rather, simple key-value string pairs), this should be seen as nothing more than a limited, yet very neat trick.

Session storage

Since the sessionStorage interface is identical to that of localStorage, there is no reason to repeat all of the information just described. For a more in-depth discussion about sessionStorage, look at the two previous sections, and replace the word "local" with "session". Everything mentioned above that applies to local storage is also true for session storage. Again, the only difference between the two is that any data saved on `sessionStorage` is erased when the session with the client ends (that is, whenever the browser is shut down).

Some examples of how to use sessionStorage will be shown below. In the example, we will attempt to store a value in the sessionStorage if that value doesn't already exist. Remember, when we set a key-value pair to the storage, if that key already exists in the storage, then whatever value was associated with that key will be overwritten. If the key doesn't exist, it gets created automatically.

```
var name = sessionStorage.getItem("coolestPerson");
// Only set a new value if the key exists,
// and the value is not what we want
if (name != null && name != "Rodrigo") {
  sessionStorage.setItem("coolestPerson", "Rodrigo");
}
```

Note that we can also query the sessionStorage object for a specific key using the `in` operator, which returns a Boolean value shown as follows:

```
if ("coolestPerson" in sessionStorage) {
  // ...
}
```

Finally, although we can check the total amount of keys in the storage through `sessionStorage.length`, that by itself may not be very useful if we don't know what all the different keys are. Thankfully, the `sessionStorage.key` function allows us to get a specific key, through which we can then get a hold of the value stored with that key.

```
sessionStorage.clear();
sessionStorage.length == 0; // True
sessionStorage.setItem("name", "Rodrigo");
sessionStorage.setItem("book", "Learn HTML5");
sessionStorage.setItem("publisher", "Packt Pub");
sessionStorage.setItem("isColor", true);
sessionStorage.setItem("rating", 5);
```

```
var values = new Array();
for (var i = 0, len = sessionStorage.length; i < len; i++) {
    var key = sessionStorage.key(i);
    var value = sessionStorage.getItem(key);
    values.push({key: key, value: value});
}
values.length == sessionStorage.length; // True
values[0].key == "book"; // True*
values[0].value == "Learn HTML5"; // True*
```

Thus, we can query `sessionStorage` for a key at a given position, and receive the string key representing that key. Then, with the key we can get a hold of the value stored with that key. Note, however, that the order in which items are stored within the `sessionStorage` object is totally arbitrary. While some browsers may keep the list of stored items sorted alphabetically by key value, this is clearly specified in the HTML5 spec as a decision to be left up to browser makers.

IndexedDB

As exciting as the web storage API might seem so far, there are cases when our needs might be such that serializing and unserializing data, as we use local or session storage, might not be quite sufficient. For example, imagine we have a few hundred (or perhaps, several thousand) similar records stored in local storage (say we're storing enemy description cards that are part of an RPG game). Think about how you would do the following using local storage:

- Retrieve, in alphabetical order, the first five records stored
- Delete all records stored that contain a particular characteristic (such as an enemy that doesn't survive in water, for example)
- Retrieve up to three records stored that contain a particular characteristic (for example, the enemy has a Hit Point score of 42,000 or more)

The point is this: any querying that we may want to make against the data stored in local storage or session storage, must be handled by our own code. In other words, we'd be spending a lot of time and effort writing code just to help us get to some data. Let alone the fact that any complex data stored in local or session storage is converted to literal objects, and any and all functions that were once part of those objects are now gone, unless we write even more code to handle some sort of custom unserializing.

In case you have not guessed it by now, IndexedDB solves these and other problems very beautifully. At its heart, IndexedDB is a NoSQL database engine that allows us to store whole objects and index them for fast insertions, deletions, and retrievals. The database system also provides us with a powerful querying engine, so that we can perform very advanced computations on the data that we have persisted.

The following figure shows some of the similarities between IndexedDB and a traditional relational database. In relational databases, data is stored as a group of rows within a specific table structure. In IndexedDB, on the other hand, data is grouped in broadly-defined buckets known as data stores.

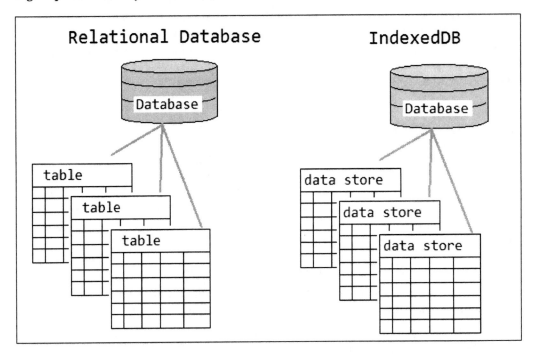

The architecture of IndexedDB is somewhat similar to the popular relational database systems used in most web development projects today. One core difference is that, whereas relational databases store data in a database, which is a collection of related tables, an IndexedDB system groups data in databases, which is a collection of data stores. While conceptually similar, in practice these two architectures are actually quite different.

If you come from a relational database background, and the concept of databases, tables, columns, and rows makes sense to you, then you're well on your way to becoming an IndexedDB expert. As you'll see, there are some significant distinctions between both systems and methodologies. While you might be tempted to simply replace the words data store with tables, know that the difference between the two concepts extends beyond a name difference.

One key feature of data stores is that they don't have any specific schema associated with them. In relational databases, a table is defined by its very particular structure. Each column is specified ahead of time, when the table is first created. Then, every record saved in such a table follows the exact same format. In NoSQL databases (which IndexedDB is a type of), a data store can hold any object, with whatever format they may have. Essentially, this concept would be the same as having a relational database table that has a different schema for each record in it.

IDBFactory

To get started with IndexedDB, we first need to create a database. This is done through an implementation of IDBFactory, which in the browser, is the `window.indexedDB` object. Deleting a database is also done through the indexedDB object, as we'll see soon.

In order to open a database (or create one if it doesn't exist yet), we simply call the `indexedDB.open` method, passing in a database name, along with a version number. If no version number is supplied, the default version number of one will be used as shown in the following code snippet:

```
var dbName = "myDatabase";
var dbVersion = 1;
var request = indexedDB.open(dbName, dbVersion);
```

As you'll soon notice, every method for asynchronous requests in IndexedDB (such as `indexedDB.open`, for example), will return a request object of type IDBRequest, or an implementation of it. Once we have that request object, we can set up callback functions on its properties, which get executed as the various events related to them are fired, as shown in the following code snippet:

```
var dbName = "myDatabase";
var dbVersion = 1;
```

```
var db = null;
var request = indexedDB.open(dbName, dbVersion);
request.onerror = function(event) {
    console.log("Error:", event);
};
request.onsuccess = function(event) {
    db = event.target.result;
};
```

IDBOpenDBRequest

As mentioned in the previous section, once we make an asynchronous request to the IndexedDB API, the immediately returned object will be of type IDBRequest. In the particular case of an open request, the object that is returned to us is of type IDBOpenDBRequest. Two events that we might want to listen to on this object were shown in the preceding code snippet (onerror and onsuccess). There is also a very important event, wherein we can create an object store, which is the foundation of this storage system. This event is the onupgradeneeded (that is, on upgrade needed) event. This will be fired when the database is first created and, as you might expect, whenever the version number used to open the database is higher than the last value used when the database was opened, as shown in the following code:

```
var dbName = "myDatabase";
var dbVersion = 1;
var db = null;
var store = null;
var request = indexedDB.open(dbName, dbVersion);
request.onupgradeneeded = function(event) {
    db = event.target.result;
    store = db.createObjectStore("myDataStore", {keyPath: "myKey"});
};
```

The call to createObjectStore made on the database object takes two parameters. The first is a string representing the name of the object store. This store can be thought of as a table in the world of relational databases. Of course, instead of inserting records into columns from a table, we insert whole objects into the data store. The second parameter is an object defining properties of the data store. One important attribute that this object must define is the keyPath object, which is what makes each object we store unique. The value assigned to this property can be anything we choose.

Now, any objects that we persist in this data store must have an attribute with the same name as the one assigned to keyPath. In this example, our objects will need to have an attribute of myKey. If a new object is persisted, it will be indexed by the value of this property.

Any additional objects stored that have the same value for myKey will replace any old objects with that same key. Thus, we must provide a unique value for this object every time we want a unique object persisted.

Alternatively, we can let the browser provide a unique value for this key for us. Again, comparing this concept to a relational database, we can think of the keyPath object as being the same thing as a unique ID for a particular element. Just as most relational database systems will support some sort of auto increment, so does IndexedDB. To specify that we want auto-incremented values, we simply add the flag to the object store properties object when the data store is first created (or upgraded) as shown in the following code snippet:

```
request.onupgradeneeded = function(event) {
  var settings = {
    keyPath: "myKey",
    autoIncrement: true
  };
  db = event.target.result;
  store = db.createObjectStore("myDataStore", settings);
};
```

Now we can persist an object without having to provide a unique value for the property myKey. As a matter of fact, we don't even need to provide this attribute at all as part of any objects we store here. IndexedDB will handle that for us. Take a look at the following diagram:

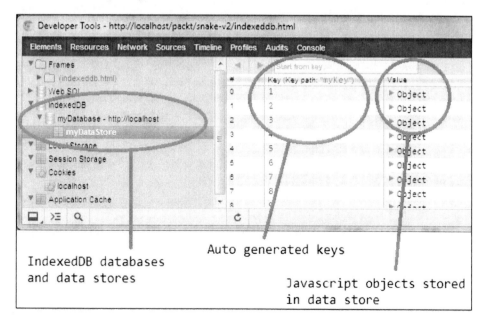

Using Google Chrome's developer tools, we can see all of the databases and data stores we have created for our domain. Note that the primary object key, which has whatever name we give it during the creation of our data store, has IndexedDB-generated values, which, as we have specified, are incremented over the last value.

With this simple, yet verbose boilerplate code in place, we can now start using our databases and data stores. From this point on, the actions we take on the database will be done on the individual data store objects, which are accessed through the database objects that created them.

IDBTransaction

The last general thing we need to remember when dealing with IndexDB, is that every interaction we have with the data store is done inside transactions. If something goes wrong during a transaction, the entire transaction is rolled back, and nothing takes effect. Similarly, if the transaction is successful, IndexedDB will automatically commit the transaction for us, which is a pretty handy bonus.

To use transaction, we need to get a reference to our database, then request a transaction for a particular data store. Once we have a reference to a data store, we can perform the various functions related to the data store, such as putting data into it, reading data from it, updating data, and finally, deleting data from a data store.

```
var TodoItem = function(task) {
  this.task = task;
  this.completed = false;
};
try {
  var trans = db.transaction(storeName, "readwrite");
  var store = trans.objectStore(storeName);
  var task1 = new TodoItem("Buy more pizza");
  var task2 = new TodoItem("Finish writing the book");
  var task3 = new TodoItem("Shave before going to work");
  var request = store.put(task1);
  // We can reuse this request object to store multiple objects
  request = store.put(task2);
  request = store.put(task3);
  request.onsuccess = function(e) {
    log("Success!" + value.key);
  };
  request.onerror = function(e) {
    log(e.stack);
```

```
    };
  } catch (e) {
    log(e.stack);
  }
```

To store an item in our data store we need to follow a couple of steps. Note that if anything goes wrong during this transaction, we simply catch whatever error is thrown by the browser, and execution continues uninterrupted because of the try/catch block.

The first step to persisting objects in IndexedDB is to start a transaction. This is done by requesting a transaction object from the database we have opened earlier. A transaction is always related to a particular data store. Also, when requesting a transaction, we can specify what type of transaction we'd like to start. The possible types of transactions in IndexedDB are as follows:

readwrite

This transaction mode allows for objects to be stored into the data store, retrieved from it, updated, and deleted. In other words, readwrite mode allows for full CRUD functionality.

readonly

This transaction mode is similar to readwrite, but clearly restricts the interactions with the data store to only reading. Anything that would modify the data store is not allowed, so any attempt to create a new record (in other words, persisting a new object into the data store), update an existing object (in other words, trying to save an object that was already in the data store), or delete an object from the data store will result in the transaction failing, and an exception being raised.

versionchange

This transaction mode allows us to create or modify an object store or indexes used in the data store. Within a transaction of this mode, we can perform any action or operation, including modifying the structure of the database.

Getting elements

Simply storing data into a black box is not at all useful if we're not able to retrieve that data at a later point in time. With IndexedDB, this can be done in several different ways. More commonly, the data store where we persist the data is set up with one or more indexes, which keep the objects organized by a particular field. Again, for those accustomed to relational databases, this would be similar to indexing/applying a key to a particular table column. If we want to get to an object, we can query it by its unique ID, or we can search the data store for objects that fit particular characteristics, which we can do through indexed values of that object.

To create an index on a data store, we must specify our intentions during the creation of the data store (inside the onupgradeneeded callback when the store is first created, or inside a transaction mode versionchange). The code for this is as follows:

```
request.onupgradeneeded = function(event) {
  var settings = {
    keyPath: "myKey",
    autoIncrement: true
  };
  db = event.target.result;
  store = db.createObjectStore("myDataStore", settings);
  var indexSettings = {
    unique: true
  };
  store.createIndex("taskIndex", "task", indexSettings);
};
```

In the preceding example, we create an index for the task attribute of our objects. The name of this index can be anything we want, and commonly is the same name as the object property to which it applies. In our case, we simply named it taskIndex. The possible settings we can configure are as follows:

- unique – if true, an object being stored with a duplicate value for the same attribute is rejected

- multiEntry – if true, and the indexed attribute is an array, each element will be indexed

Note that zero or more indexes can be created for a data store. Just like any other database system, indexing your database/data store can really boost the performance of the storage container. However, just adding indexes for the fun it provides is not a good idea, as the size of your data store will grow accordingly. A good data store design is one where the specific context of the data store with respect to the application is taken into account, and each indexed field is carefully considered. The phrase to keep in mind when designing your data stores is the following: measure it twice, cut it once.

Although any object can be saved in a data store (as opposed to a relational database, where the data stored must carefully follow the table structure, as defined by the table's schema), in order to optimize the performance of your application, try to build your data stores with the data that it will store in mind. It is true that any data can be smacked into any data store, but a wise developer considers the data being stored very carefully before committing it to a database.

Once the data store is set up, and we have at least one meaningful index, we can start to pull data out of the data store. The easiest way to retrieve objects from a data store is to use an index, and query for a specific object, as shown in the following code:

```
var TodoItem = function(task) {
  this.task = task;
  this.completed = false;
};
function getTask(taskName, callback) {
  // 1. Open a transaction. Since we don't need to write anything to
  // the data store, a simple readonly transaction will sufice.
  var trans = db.transaction(storeName, "readonly");
  var store = trans.objectStore(storeName);
  // 2. specify an index to use, and the data to get from it
  var req = store.index("taskIndex").get(taskName);
  req.onsuccess = function(e) {
    var todoItem = e.target.result;
    // todoItem.task => "Buy more pizza"
    // todoItem.completed => false
    callback(todoItem);
  };
  req.onerror = function(e) {
    // Handle error
  };
};
```

```
// Search for a TodoItem object with a task property of "Buy more
pizza"
getTask("Buy more pizza", function(taskItem) {
  console.log("TaskItem object: " + taskItem.task);
});
```

The preceding function attempts to retrieve a single saved object from our data store. The search is made for an object with its task property that matches the task name supplied to the function. If one is found, it will be retrieved from the data store, and passed to the store object's request through the event object passed in to the callback function. If an error occurs in the process (for example, if the index supplied doesn't exist), the onerror event is triggered. Finally, if no objects in the data store match the search criteria, the resulting property passed in through the request parameter object will be null.

Now, to search for multiple items, we can take a similar approach, but instead we request an IndexedDBCursor object. A cursor is basically a pointer to a particular result from a result set of zero or more objects. We can use the cursor to iterate through every object in the result set, until the current cursor points at no object (null), indicating that there are no more objects in the result set.

```
var TodoItem = function(task) {
  this.task = task;
  this.completed = false;
};
function getTask(taskName, callback) {
  // 1. Open a transaction. Since we don't need to write anything to
  // the data store, a simple readonly transaction will sufice.
  var trans = db.transaction(storeName, "readonly");
  var store = trans.objectStore(storeName);
  // 2. specify the range in the data store to request data from
  var keyRange = IDBKeyRange.lowerBound(0);
  var req = store.openCursor(keyRange);
  req.onsuccess = function(e) {
    // cursor IDBCursorWithValue
    //    key : int
    //    primaryKey : int
    //    source : IDBObjectStore
    //    value : Object
    //
    var cursor = e.target.result;
    // Before we continue, we need to make sure that we
    // haven't hit the end of the result set
```

```
      if (!cursor) {
        callback();
      }
      // If there are still results, let's process them
      //    cursor.value === todoItem
      //    cursor.value.task => "Buy more pizza"
      //    cursor.value.completed => false
      // Since results are plain, typeless object literals, we need to
rebuild
      // each object from scratch.
      var todoItem = new TodoItem(cursor.value.task);
      todoItem.myKey = cursor.value.myKey;
      todoItem.completed = cursor.value.completed;
      todoItems.push(todoItem);
        // Tell the cursor to fetch the next result
        cursor.continue();
    };
    req.onerror = function(e) {
      // Handle error
    };
  };
  // Retrieve every TodoItem in the data store
  var todoItems = new Array();
  getTask("Buy more pizza", function() {
    for (var i = 0; i < todoItems.length; i++) {
      console.log("TaskItem object: " + todoItems[i].task);
    }
  })
```

You will note a few things with the above code snippet. First, any object that goes into our IndexedDB data store is stripped of its DNA, and only a simple hash is stored in its stead. Thus, if the prototype information of each object we retrieve from the data store is important to the application, we will need to manually reconstruct each object from the data that we get back from the data store.

Second, observe that we can filter the subset of the data store that we would like to take out of it. This is done with an IndexedDB Key Range object, which specifies the offset from which to start fetching data. In our case, we specified a lower bound of zero, meaning that the lowest primary key value we want is zero. In other words, this particular query requests all of the records in the data store.

Finally, remember that the result from the request is not a single result or an array of results. Instead, all of the results are returned one at a time in the form of a cursor. We can check for the presence of a cursor altogether, then use the cursor if one is indeed present. Then, the way we request the next cursor is by calling the `continue()` function on the cursor itself.

Another way to think of cursors is by imagining a spreadsheet application. Pretend that the 10 objects returned from our request each represent a row in this spreadsheet. So IndexedDB will fetch all 10 of those objects to memory, and send a pointer to the first result through the `event.target.result` property in the `onsuccess` callback. By calling `cursor.continue()`, we simply tell IndexedDB to now give us a reference to the next object in the result set (or, in other words, we ask for the next row in the spreadsheet). This goes on until the tenth object, after which no more objects exist in the result set (again, to go along with the spreadsheet metaphor, after we fetch the last row, the next row after that is null – it doesn't exist). As a result, the data store will call the `onsuccess` callback, and pass in a null object. If we attempt to read properties in this null reference, as though we were working with a real object returned from the cursor, the browser will throw a null pointer exception.

Instead of trying to reconstruct an object from a cursor one property at a time, we could abstract this functionality away in a generic form. Since objects being persisted into the object store can't have any functions, we're not allowed to keep such functionality inside the object itself. However, thanks to JavaScript's ability to build an object from a reference to a constructor function, we can create a very generic object builder function as follows:

```
var TodoItem = function(task) {
  this.task = task;
  this.completed = false;
  this.toHTML = function() {
    var el = document.createElement("li");
    el.textContent = this.task;
    if (this.completed) {
      el.style.textDecoration = "line-through";
    }
    return el;
  };
};
function inflatObject(class, object) {
  // 1. Create an instance of whatever class we reference
  var obj = new class();
  // 2. Copy every property from the object returned by the cursor
```

```
    // into the newly created object
    for (var property in object) {
      obj[property] = object[property];
    }
    // 3. Return the inflated object
    return obj;
  }
  // …
  var req = store.openCursor(keyRange);
  req.onsuccess = function(e) {
    var cursor = e.target.result;
    // Before we continue, we need to make sure that we
    // haven't hit the end of the result set
    if (!cursor) {
      callback();
    }
    var todoItem = inflatObject(TodoItem, cursor.value);
    // We could even call methods on the new inflated object
    var itemElement = todoItem.toHTML();
    document.body.appendChild(itemElement);
    todoItem.myKey == cursor.myKey; // True
    todoItem.task == cursor.task; // True
    todoItem.completed == cursor.completed; // True
    todoItems.push(todoItem);
    // Tell the cursor to fetch the next result
    cursor.continue();
  };
```

Deleting elements

To remove specific elements from a data store, the same principles involved in retrieving data apply. In fact, the entire process looks fairly identical to retrieving data, only we call the delete function on the object store object. Needless to say, the transaction used in this action must be readwrite, since readonly limits the object so that no changes can be done to it (including deletion).

The first way to delete an object is by passing the object's primary key to the delete function. This is shown as follows:

```
function deleteTask(taskId, callback) {
  // 1. Open a transaction. Since we definitely need to change the
object
```

```
     // in the data store, we need proper access and benefits
     var trans = db.transaction(storeName, "readwrite");
     var store = trans.objectStore(storeName);
     // 2. specify an index to use, and the data to get from it
     var req = store.delete(taskId);
     req.onsuccess = function(e) {
       // Do something, then call callback
     };
     req.onerror = function(e) {
       // Handle error
     };
   };
```

The difficulty with this first approach is that we need to know the ID of the object. In some cases, this would involve a prior transaction request where we'd retrieve the object based on some easier to get data. For example, if we want to delete all tasks with the attribute of complete set to true, we'd need to query the data store for those objects first, then use the IDs associated with each result, and use those values in the transaction where the objects are deleted.

A second way to remove data from the data store is to simply call `clear()` on the object store object. Again, the transaction must be set to readwrite. Doing this will obliterate every last object in the data store, even if they're all of different types as shown in the following code snippet:

```
   var trans = db.transaction(storeName, "readwrite");
   var store = trans.objectStore(storeName);
   var req = store.clear();
   req.onsuccess = function(e) {
     // Do something, then call callback
   };
   req.onerror = function(e) {
     // Handle error
   };
```

Finally, we can delete multiple records using a cursor. This is similar to the way we retrieve objects. As we iterate through the result set using the cursor, we can simply delete the object at whatever position the cursor is currently on. Upon deletion, the reference from the cursor object is set to null as shown in the following code snippet:

```
   // 1. Be sure to set the transaction to readwrite. Else, there will
   be a nice
   // exception raised if we try to delete readonly data.
   var trans = db.transaction(storeName, "readwrite");
```

```
var store = trans.objectStore(storeName);
// 2. specify the range in the data store to request data from
var keyRange = IDBKeyRange.lowerBound(0);
var req = store.openCursor(keyRange);
req.onsuccess = function(e) {
  var cursor = e.target.result;
  // Before we continue, we need to make sure that we
  // haven't hit the end of the result set
  if (!cursor) {
    callback();
  }
  // Here, we could have accessed the object's primary ID through
  // the cursor object in cursor.value.myKey. However, accessing
  // cursor.primaryKey maps to the specific property name that holds
  // the value of the primary key.
  store.delete(cursor.primaryKey);
  // Tell the cursor to fetch the next result
  cursor.continue();
};
```

This is pretty much the same routine as fetching data. The only detail is that we absolutely need to supply an object's key. The key is the value stored in the object's `keyPath` attribute, which can be user-provided, or auto-generated. Fortunately for us, the cursor object returns at least two references to this key through the `cursor.primaryKey` property, as well as through the object's own property that references that value (in our case, we chose the `keyPath` attribute to be named `myKey`).

The code

The two upgrades we added to this second version of the game are simple, yet they add a lot of value to the game. We added a persistent high score engine, so users can actually keep track of their latest record, and have a sticky record of past successes. We also added a pretty nifty feature that takes a snapshot of the game board each time the player scores, as well as whenever the player ultimately dies out. Once the player dies, we display all of the snapshots we had collected throughout the game, allowing the player to save those images, and possibly share it with his or her friends.

Saving the high score

The first thing you probably noticed about the previous version of this game was that we had a placeholder for a high score, but that number never changed. Now that we know how to persist data, we can very easily take advantage of this, and persist a player's high score through various games. In a more realistic scenario, we'd probably send the high score data to a backend server, where every time the game is served, we can keep track of the overall high score, and every user playing the game would know about this global score. However, in our situation, the high score is local to a browser only, since none of the persistence APIs (local and session storage, as well as IndexedDB) share data across other browsers, or natively to a remote server.

Since we want the high score to still exist in a player's browser even a month from now, after the computer has been powered off (along with the browser, of course) multiple times, storing this high score data on sessionStorage would be silly. We could store this single number either in IndexedDB or in localStorage. Since we don't care about any other information associated with this score (such as the date when the score was achieved, and so on), all we're storing really is just the one number. For this reason, I think localStorage is a much better choice, because it can all be done in as few as 5 lines of code. Using IndexedDB would work, but would be like using a cannon to kill a mosquito:

```
function setHighScore(newScore, el) {
  var element = document.querySelector(el);
  // Multiply by 1 to cast the value from a string to a number
  var score = localStorage.getItem("high-score") * 1;
  // Check if there is a numerical score saved
  if (score && !isNaN(score)) {
    // Check if new score is higher than current high score
    if (newScore > element.textContent * 1) {
      localStorage.setItem("high-score", newScore);
      element.textContent = newScore;
    } else {
        element.textContent = score;
    }
  } else {
    localStorage.setItem("high-score", newScore);
    element.textContent = newScore;
  }
}
```

This function is pretty straight forward. The two values we pass it are the actual score to set as the new high score (this value will be both saved to localStorage, as well as displayed to the user), and the HTML element where the value will be shown.

First, we retrieve the existing value saved under the key high-score, and convert it to a number. We could have used the function `parseInt()`, but multiplying a string by a number does the same thing, but with a slightly faster execution.

Next, we check if that value evaluated to something real. In other words, if there was no high-score value saved in local storage, then the variable score would have been evaluated to undefined multiplied by one, which is not a number. If there is a value saved with the key high-score, but that value is not something that can be converted into a number (such as a string of letters and such), we know that it is not a valid value. In this case, we set the incoming score as the new high score. This would work out in the case where the current persisted value is invalid, or not there (which would be the case the very first time the game loads).

Next, once we have a valid score retried from local storage, we check if the new value is higher than the old, persisted value. If we have a higher score, we persist that value, and display it to the screen. If the new value is not higher than the existing value, we don't persist anything, but display the saved value, since that is the real high score at the time.

Taking screenshots of the game

This feature is not as trivial as saving the user's high score, but is nonetheless very straightforward to implement. Since we don't care about snapshots that we captured more than one game ago, we'll use `sessionStorage` to save data from the game, in real time as the player progresses.

Behind the scenes, all we do to take these snapshots is save the game state into `sessionStorage`, then at the end of the game we retrieve all of the pieces that we'd been saving, and reconstruct the game at those points in time into an invisible canvas. We then use the `canvas.toDataURL()` function to extract that data as an image:

```
function saveEvent(event, snake, fruit) {
  var eventObj = sessionStorage.getItem(event);
  // If this is the first time the event is set, create its structure
  if (!eventObj) {
    eventObj = {
      snake: new Array(),
      fruit: new Array()
    };
    eventObj.snake.push(snake);
    eventObj.fruit.push(fruit);
    eventObj = JSON.stringify(eventObj);
```

```
        sessionStorage.setItem(event, eventObj);
    } else {
      eventObj = JSON.parse(eventObj);
      eventObj.snake.push(snake);
      eventObj.fruit.push(fruit);
      eventObj = JSON.stringify(eventObj);
      sessionStorage.setItem(event, eventObj);
    }
    return JSON.parse(eventObj);
  }
```

Each time the player eats a fruit, we call this function, passing it a reference to the `snake` (our hero in this game), and the `fruit` (the goal of this game) objects. What we do is really quite simple: we create an array representing the state of the snake and of the fruit at each event that we capture. Each element in this array is a string representing the serialized array that keeps track of where the fruit was, and where each body part of the snake was located as well.

First, we check if this object currently exists in `sessionStorage`. For the first time we start the game, this object will not yet exist. Thus, we create an object that references those two objects, namely the `snake` and the `fruit` object. Next, we stringify the buffers keeping track of the locations of the elements we want to track. Each time we add a new event, we simply append to those two buffers.

Of course, if the user closes down the browser, that data will be erased by the browser itself, since that's how `sessionStorage` works. However, we probably don't want to hold on to data from a previous game, so we also need a way to clear out our own data after each game.

```
    function clearEvent(event) {
      return sessionStorage.removeItem(event);
    }
```

Easy enough. All we need is to know the name of the key that we use to hold each element. For our purposes, we simply call the snapshots of the snake eating `"eat"`, and the buffer with the snapshot of the snake dying `"die"`. So before each game starts, we can simply call `clearEvent()` with those two global key values, and the cache will be cleared a new each time.

Next, as each event takes place, we simply call the first function we defined, sending it the appropriate data as shown in the following code snippet:

```
    if (fruit.isAt(head.x, head.y)) {
      // Save current game state
```

```
    saveEvent("eat", snake.getBody(), fruit.position);
    fruit.reset();
    snake.grow();
    score.up();
    // Save high score if needed
    setHighScore(document.querySelector("#scores h3:first-child span").
  textContent);
  }
  // …
  if (!snake.isAlive()) {
    saveEvent("die", snake.getBody(), fruit.position);
  }
```

Finally, whenever we wish to display all of these snapshots, we just need to create a separate canvas with the same dimensions as the one used in the game (so that the buffers we saved don't go out of bounds), and draw the buffers to that canvas. The reason we need a separate canvas element is because we don't want to draw on the same canvas that the player can see. This way, the process of producing these snapshots is more seamless and natural. Once each state is drawn, we can extract each image, resize it, and display it back to the user as shown in the following code:

```
// Use each cached buffer to generate each screen shot
function getEventPictures(event, canvas) {
  // Take the buffer from session storage
  var obj = sessionStorage.getItem(event);
  // Create an array to hold the generated images
  var screenShots = new Array();
  if (!obj)
    return screenShots
  obj = JSON.parse(obj);
  var canvas = canvas.cloneNode();
  var renderer = new Renderer(canvas);
  // Go through each game state, and simply draw the data as though it
  // was being drawn for the actual game in action
  for (var i = 0, len = obj.snake.length; i < len; i++) {
    renderer.clear();
    renderer.draw(obj.snake[i], snake.getSkin());
    renderer.draw(obj.fruit[i], fruit.img);
    var screenShot = renderer.toImg();
    screenShots.push(screenShot);
  }
  return screenShots;
}
```

```
// Display a list of images to the user
function drawScreenShots(imgs) {
  var panel = document.querySelector("#screenShots");
  for (var i = 0, len = imgs.length; i < len; i++) {
    var a = document.createElement("a");
    a.target = "_blank";
    a.href = imgs[i].src;
    a.appendChild(imgs[i]);
    panel.appendChild(a);
  }
}
```

Observe that we simply draw the points representing the snake and the fruit into that canvas. All of the other points in the canvas are ignored, meaning that we generate a transparent image. If we want the image to have an actual background color (even if it is just white), we can either call `fillRect()` over the entire canvas surface before drawing the snake and the fruit, or we can traverse each pixel in the `pixelData` array from the rendering context, and set the alpha channel to 100 percent opaque. Even if we set a color to each pixel by hand, but leave off the alpha channel, we'd have colorful pixels, but 100 percent transparent.

Summary

In this chapter we took a few extra steps into the fascinating world of 2D rendering using the long-awaited canvas API. We took advantage of the canvas' ability to export images to make our game more engaging, and potentially more social. We also made the game more engaging and social by adding a persistence layer on top of the game, whereby we were able to save a player's high score.

Two other new powerful features of HTML5, web messaging and IndexedDB, were explored in this chapter, although there were no uses for these features in this version of the game. The web messaging API provides a mechanism for two or more windows to communicate directly through message passing. The exciting bit is that these windows (or HTML contexts) do not need to be in the same domain. Although this could sound like a security issue, there are several systems in place to ensure that cross-document and cross-domain messaging is secure and efficient.

The web storage interface brings with it three distinct solutions for long term data persistence on the client. These are session storage, local storage, and IndexedDB. While IndexedDB is a full-blown, built-in, fully transactional and asynchronous NoSQL object store, local and session storage provide a very simple key-value pair storage for simpler needs. All three of these systems introduce great benefits and gains over the traditional cookie-based data storage, including the fact that the total amount of data that can be persisted in the browser is much greater, and none of the data saved in the user's browser ever travels back and forth between the server and the client through HTTP requests.

In the next chapter we will look at some advanced HTML5 topics, including the next step beyond canvas' 2D rendering context – WebGL. While these topics will be covered in good detail, none of the features that follow will be added to a game. In fact, *Chapter 6, Adding Features to Your Game*, is another rare game in this book that is not built upon a fun HTML5 game, as we have being building together. We will pick up the game building projects in *Chapter 7, HTML5 and Mobile Game Development*, where we conclude the book with a mobile space shooter game.

6
Adding Features to Your Game

This chapter is slightly different than the previous several chapters, in that there is no game associated with this chapter. The reason that we're not building a game with the concepts from this chapter is that the concepts covered are either way too complex for a single chapter (there are entire books dedicated to the topic of WebGL, for example) or they're not a particularly good match for use in a game. Also, some of the features mentioned at the end of the chapter are so new that browser support is still minimal (if any) and the stability of the APIs may not be too reliable. For this reason, we'll simply explain each API, provide meaningful examples, and hope this skin-deep introduction is enough to get you excited about the prospects involved with each API.

The first part of the chapter will cover *four* HTML5 APIs that are very exciting and powerful additions to the browser platform. First and foremost, we'll cover **WebGL**, which brings the power of **OpenGL ES** to the browser, allowing for hardware accelerated 3D graphics rendering without any need for a single plugin. Next, we will discuss how we can use web sockets for a thread-like experience, the video API for native video playback and manipulation right from JavaScript, and geolocation, which allows JavaScript to determine the physical location (geographical location) of a user.

Lastly, we'll wrap up the chapter by looking at the absolute latest features in the HTML5 evolution. These features take CSS to the next level, taking it away from being a mere rectangular-based rendering engine. The first new feature that we'll study is CSS shaders, which allows us to specify how each pixel is to be rendered. This is done using GLSL shaders, which, as we'll see during the WebGL discussion, are independent programs that we write and are run on the GPU, controlling at the lowest level possible how something is to be rendered. With custom shaders, we can do so much more than simple, pre-baked CSS transformations.

Other new CSS features, covered in the second half of the chapter, are CSS columns and CSS regions and exclusions. CSS columns make it beautifully easy to dynamically adjust how many columns of text a container displays. For example, if we want a block of text to be displayed in 3 equal width or height columns, we would normally set up three different containers, then float each container to the left. With columns, we can simply store all of the text inside a single container, then use CSS to generate the columns. Finally, CSS regions and exclusions make it possible to render text inside or around complex patterns, instead of the traditional rectangular shape. Surely you have seen magazines doing this, where a block of text wraps around some shape like the outline of a car or some other object. In the past, doing this effect with plain text (as opposed to using images) has very rarely been attempted in HTML because of the extreme complexity required to pull this off. Now it only takes a few lines of CSS code.

Advanced HTML5 APIs

Although the following APIs and features vary greatly in complexity and learning curve steepness, our goal is to provide at least a thorough introduction to each of these topics. In order to gain a deeper understanding of, and working experience with each topic, it is recommended that you supplement the introduction provided here with other sources.

Since parts of the HTML5 specs and features have not yet reached full maturity, some APIs may not be fully supported in all browsers, even the latest modern browsers. Since this chapter will cover the absolute latest features of HTML5 (as at the time of writing), there is a chance some browsers might not be suitable for the examples covered in the chapter. For this reason, it is recommended that you work on the latest version of whatever the most advanced web browser is. Not only that, but you must also make certain that you check whatever experimental feature and/or security flags your browser has available. The following code snippets were written specifically for, and aimed at Google Chrome, since all of the features described are supported by it. We will make a note of any specific configuration settings required for a feature to work properly but these may or may not be needed as new updates are deployed for new web browsers.

WebGL

Perhaps no other HTML5 feature is as exciting for game developers as WebGL. This new JavaScript API allows us to render high performance, hardware accelerated 2D and 3D graphics. The API is a flavor of OpenGL ES 2.0 and makes use of the HTML5 canvas element in order to bridge the gap between the browser and the graphics processing unit in the user's computer.

While 3D programming is a topic worthy of its own book, the following overview is sufficient to get us started on the most important concepts, and will allow us to get started with 3D game development for the browser platform. For those looking for a good learning resource for OpenGL ES 2, take a look at *OpenGL ES 2.0 Programming Guide by Munshi, Ginsburg, and Shreiner*.

Since WebGL is heavily based on OpenGL ES 2.0, you may be tempted to look for reference and supplemental material about it from OpenGL books and other sources. Keep in mind that OpenGL Version 1.5 and earlier is significantly different than OpenGL 2.0 (as well as OpenGL ES 2.0, from which came WebGL) and may not be a complete source of learning, although it may be a decent starting point.

The major difference between the two versions is the rendering pipeline. In earlier versions, the API used a fixed pipeline, where the heavy lifting was done for us behind the scenes. The newer versions expose a fully programmable pipeline, where we need to provide our own **shader** programs in order to render our models to the screen.

Hello, World!

Before going any further into the theoretical side of WebGL and 3D programming, let's take a quick look at the simplest possible WebGL application, where we'll simply render a yellow triangle against a green background. You will notice that this takes quite a few lines of code. Keep in mind that the problem that WebGL solves is not a trivial one. The purpose of WebGL is to render the most complex of three dimensional, interactive scenes, and not simple, static two dimensional shapes, as illustrated by the following example.

In order to avoid a large code snippet, we'll break down the example into a few separate chunks. Each chunk will be presented in the order in which they are executed.

The first thing we need to do is set up the page where our example will run. The two components here are the two shader programs (more information on what a shader program is will follow) and the initialization of the WebGLRenderingContext object.

```html
<body>

  <script type="glsl-shader/x-fragment" id="glsl-frag-simple">
    precision mediump float;

    void main(void) {
      gl_FragColor = vec4(1.0, 1.0, 0.3, 1.0);
    }
  </script>

  <script type="glsl-shader/x-vertex" id="glsl-vert-simple">
    attribute vec3 aVertPos;

    uniform mat4 uMVMat;
    uniform mat4 uPMat;

    void main(void) {
      gl_Position = uPMat * uMVMat * vec4(aVertPos, 1.0);
    }
  </script>

  <script>
    (function main() {
      var canvas = document.createElement("canvas");
      canvas.width = 700;
      canvas.height = 400;
      document.body.appendChild(canvas);

      var gl = null;
      try {
        gl = canvas.getContext("experimental-webgl") ||
          canvas.getContext("webgl");
        gl.viewportWidth = canvas.width;
        gl.viewportHeight = canvas.height;
      } catch (e) {}
```

```
    if (!gl) {
      document.body.innerHTML =
        "<h1>This browser doesn't support WebGl</h1>";
    }

    var shaderFrag = document.getElementById
      ("glsl-frag-simple").textContent;
    var shaderVert = document.getElementById
    ("glsl-frag-simple").textContent;
  })();
  </script>
</body>
```

The `script` tags of type `glsl-shader/x-vertex` and `glsl-shader/x-fragment` make use of how HTML renders unknown tags. When a browser parses a `script` tag with a `type` attribute that it does not understand (namely a made up type, such as `glsl-shader/x-vertex`), it simply ignores all of the contents of the tag. Since we want to define the contents of our shader programs within our HTML file, but we don't want that text to show up in the HTML file, this slight hack comes in very handy. This way we can define those scripts, have access to them, and not worry about the browser not knowing how to handle that particular language.

As mentioned earlier, in WebGL we need to provide the GPU with a so-called shader program, which is an actual compiled program written in a language called **GLSL** (OpenGL Shading Language), which gives the GPU the instructions required to render our models just the way we want. The variables `shaderFrag` and `shaderVert` hold a reference to the source code of each of these shader programs, which is itself contained inside our custom `script` tags.

Next, we create a regular HTML5 canvas element, inject it into the DOM, and create a `gl` object. Note the similarities between WebGL and the 2D canvas. Of course, beyond this point the two APIs are one from Mars and one from Venus, but until then, the initialization of them is identical. Instead of requesting a 2D Rendering Context object from the canvas object, we simply request a WebGL Rendering Context. Since most browsers (Google Chrome included) are still in experimental stages with WebGL, we must supply the `webgl` string with the experimental prefix when requesting the context. The Boolean `OR` operator separating the two `getContext` calls indicates that we're requesting the context from the experimental prefix, or without the prefix. Whichever call the browser supports, is the call that succeeds.

From this point on, every API call to WebGL is done from this gl object. If the call to the canvas that returns the WebGLRenderingContext object fails, we can make absolutely no calls to WebGL and we might as well halt execution. Otherwise, we can continue on with our program, passing around this object so that we may interact with WebGL.

```javascript
function getShader(gl, code, type) {
  // Step 1: Create a specific type of shader
  var shader = gl.createShader(type);

  // Step 2: Link source code to program
  gl.shaderSource(shader, code);

  // Step 3: Compile source code
  gl.compileShader(shader);

  return shader;
}

function getShaderProgram(gl, shaderFrag, shaderVert) {

  // Step 1: Create a shader program
  var program = gl.createProgram();

  // Step 2: Attach both shaders into the program
  gl.attachShader(program, shaderFrag);
  gl.attachShader(program, shaderVert);

  // Step 3: Link the program
  gl.linkProgram(program);

  return program;
}

(function main() {
  // ...
```

```
var shaderFrag = getShader(gl,
    document.getElementById("glsl-frag-simple").textContent,
    gl.FRAGMENT_SHADER);

var shaderVert = getShader(gl,
    document.getElementById("glsl-vert-simple").textContent,
    gl.VERTEX_SHADER);

var shader = getShaderProgram(gl, shaderFrag, shaderVert);

// Specify which shader program is to be used
gl.useProgram(shader);

// Allocate space in GPU for variables
shader.attribVertPos = gl.getAttribLocation(shader, "aVertPos");
gl.enableVertexAttribArray(shader.attribVertPos);

shader.pMatrixUniform = gl.getUniformLocation
    (shader, "uPMatrix");
shader.mvMatrixUniform = gl.getUniformLocation
    (shader, "uMVMatrix");
})();
```

The next step in this process is to create a vertex and fragment shader, which are then combined into a single shader program. The entire job of the vertex shader is to specify the position of a vertex in the final rendered model and the fragment shader's job is to specify the color of each pixel between two or more vertices. Since these two shaders are needed for any rendering to take place, WebGL combines them into a single shader program.

After the shader program is successfully compiled, it will be sent to the GPU where the processing of fragments and vertices take place. The way we can send input into our shaders is through pointer locations that we specify in the shader program before sending it to the GPU. This step is done by calling the get*Location method on the gl object (the WebGLRenderingContext object). Once we have a reference to those locations, we can later assign a value to them.

Notice that our shader scripts declare variables of type vec4 and mat4. In strongly typed languages such as C or C++, a variable can have a type of int (for integers), float (for floating point numbers), bool (for Boolean values), or char (for characters). In GLSL, there are a few new data types that are native to the language, which are specially useful in graphics programming. These types are vectors and matrices. We can create a vector with two components by using the data type vec2, or vec4 for a vector with four components. Similarly, we can create a 3 x 3 matrix by calling mat3, which essentially creates an array-like structure with three vec3 elements.

```
function initTriangleBuffer(gl) {
  // Step 1: Create a buffer
  var buffer = gl.createBuffer();

  // Step 2: Bind the buffer with WebGL
  gl.bindBuffer(gl.ARRAY_BUFFER, buffer);

  // Step 3: Specify 3D model vertices
  var vertices = [
    0.0,   0.1, 0.0,
    -1.0, -1.0, 0.0,
    1.0,  -1.0, 0.0
  ];

  // Step 4: Fill the buffer with the data from the model
  gl.bufferData(gl.ARRAY_BUFFER, new Float32Array(vertices),
    gl.STATIC_DRAW);

  // Step 5: Create some variables with information about the
    vertex buffer
  // to simplify calculations later on

  // Each vertex has an X, Y, Z component
  buffer.itemSize = 3;

  // There are 3 unique vertices
  buffer.numItems = parseInt(vertices.length / buffer.itemSize);

  return buffer;
}

(function main() {
  // ...

  var triangleVertBuf = initTriangleBuffer(gl);
})();
```

After we have a shader program in place, which will tell the graphics card how to draw whatever points we give it to draw for us, it follows that we now need a few points to draw. Thus, this next step creates a buffer of points that we will draw in a little bit. If you remember *Chapter 4, Using HTML5 to Catch a Snake*, where we introduced the new typed arrays, then this will look familiar to you. The way WebGL stores vertex data is by using those typed arrays, but more specifically, 32 bit floating point arrays.

In this particular case where we're only drawing a triangle, calculating, and keeping track of what all the points are is a trivial task. However, 3D models are not normally drawn by hand. After we draw a complex model using some 3D modeling software of one kind or another, we will be exporting anywhere from a few hundred to several thousand individual vertices that represent the model. In such cases, we will need to calculate how many vertices our model has and it would be a good idea to store that data somewhere. Since JavaScript allows us to add properties to objects dynamically, we take advantage of that and store these two calculations on the buffer object itself.

Finally, let's actually draw our triangle to the screen. Of course, if we haven't written enough boilerplate code already, let's talk about one major component of 3D programming, and write just a little bit of extra code to allow us to finally render our model.

Without getting too deep into the topic of 3D coordinate space and transformation matrices, one key aspect of rendering 3D shapes into a 2D screen (for instance, your computer monitor), we need to perform some linear algebra to convert the points that represent our models from 3D space into a simple 2D space (think x and y coordinates). This is done by creating a couple of matrix structures and performing some matrix multiplication. Then, we just need to multiply each point in our 3D model (our triangle buffer, in this example) by a matrix called the **MVP matrix** (which is a matrix composed of three individual matrices, namely the model, view, and projection matrices). This matrix is constructed by the multiplication of the individual matrices, each representing a step in the transformation process from 3D to 2D.

If you have taken any linear algebra classes before, you will know that multiplying matrices is not as simple as multiplying two numbers. You will also notice that representing a matrix in JavaScript is also not as trivial as defining a variable to type integer. In order to simplify and solve this problem, we can use one of the many matrix utility libraries available in JavaScript. The particular library we'll use in this example is a very powerful one called **GL-Matrix**, which is an open source library created by Brandon Jones and Colin MacKenzie IV.

```
<script src="./glmatrix.js"></script>
...

function drawScene(gl, entityBuf, shader) {
  // Step 1: Create the Model, View and Projection matrices
  var mvMat = mat4.create();
  var pMat = mat4.create();

  // Step 2: Initialize matrices
  mat4.perspective(45, gl.viewportWidth / gl.viewportHeight, 0.1,
    100.0, pMat);
  mat4.identity(mvMat);
  mat4.translate(mvMat, [0.0, 0.5, -3.0]);

  // Step 3: Set up the rendering viewport
  gl.viewport(0, 0, gl.viewportWidth, gl.viewportHeight);
  gl.clear(gl.COLOR_BUFFER_BIT | gl.DEPTH_BUFFER_BIT);

  // Step 4: Send buffers to GPU
  gl.bindBuffer(gl.ARRAY_BUFFER, entityBuf);
  gl.vertexAttribPointer(shader.attribVertPos,
    entityBuf.itemSize, gl.FLOAT, false, 0, 0);
  gl.uniformMatrix4fv(shader.pMatrixUniform, false, pMat);
  gl.uniformMatrix4fv(shader.mvMatrixUniform, false, mvMat);

  // Step 5: Get this over with, and render the triangle already!
  gl.drawArrays(gl.TRIANGLES, 0, entityBuf.numItems);
}


(function main() {
  // ...
```

```
    // Clear the WebGL canvas context to some background color
    gl.clearColor(0.2, 0.8, 0.2, 1.0);
    gl.enable(gl.DEPTH_TEST);

    // WebGL: Please draw this triangle on the gl object,
      using this shader...
    drawScene(gl, triangleVertBuf, shader);
  })();
```

A couple of things about the preceding code are noteworthy. First, you will notice that this is a single frame that's only drawn once. Had we decided to animate our scene (which we most definitely would in a real game), we would need to run the drawScene function inside a request animation frame loop. This loop would involve all of the steps shown, including all of the matrix math that generates our MVP matrix for each and every model that we would render on the scene. Yes, that is a lot of computations to perform multiple times per second, especially on more complex scenes.

Second, observe the usage of our model-view-projection matrices. We first create them as 4 x 4 matrices, then instantiate each of them. The projection matrix's job is to do just that—project the 3D points onto a 2D space (the canvas rendering context), stretching the points as needed in order to maintain the specified aspect ratio of the canvas. In WebGL, the coordinate system of the rendering context goes from zero to one on both axis (the vertical and horizontal axis). The projection matrix makes it possible to map points beyond that limited range.

The model and view matrices allow us to model points relative to the object's center (its own coordinate system) onto the world's coordinate system. For example, say we're modeling a robot. Suppose the robot's head is centered at point (0, 0, 0). From that point, the robot's arms would be, say, at points (-5, 1, 0) and (5, 1, 0) respectively, both relative to the robot's head. But where exactly is the robot placed with respect to the world? And what if we had another robot in this scene, how are they positioned relative to each other? Through the model and view matrices, we can put them both on the same global coordinate system. In our example, we moved the triangle to the point (0, 0, -0.5, -3.0), which is a point somewhere close to the origin of the world coordinate system.

Finally, we bind our matrices to the graphics card, where we later render our scene by calling the draw functions defined in the `WebGLRenderingContext` object. If you look closely at the end of the `drawScene` function, we send some values to the `shader` object. Looking at the two shader programs we wrote earlier (using GLSL), we specified three variables that are used as input into the programs. The observant student will ask where those variables came from (the variables are defined in the vertex shader and are named `aVertPos`, `uMVMat`, and `uPMat`, which are special data types defined in the GLSL language). They come from our JavaScript code and are passed to the shader program in the GPU through calls to `gl.vertexAttribPointer` and `gl.uniformMatrix4fv`.

About 150 lines of code later, we have a yellow triangle rendered against a green background that looks like the following screenshot. Again, I remind you that WebGL is by no means a trivial programming interface and is not the tool of choice for simple drawing that could be done with easier tools, such as the 2DRenderingContext of the canvas element, SVG, and possibly just a simple piece of photo editing software.

Although WebGL takes a lot of boilerplate code to render a very simple shape, as shown in the following screenshot, rendering and animating complex scenes is not much more complicated than that. The same basic steps required to setup a rendering context, create a shader program, and load buffers, are used in creating extremely complicated scenes.

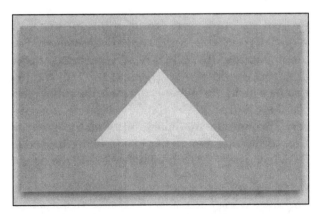

In conclusion, even though WebGL can be a beast of its own for developers just coming in to HTML5 or even game development, the fundamentals are fairly straight forward. For those seeking to deepen their understanding of WebGL (or 3D graphics programming in general), it is recommended that you study up on the subject of three dimensional programming and linear algebra, as well as the principles that are unique to, and a part of, WebGL. As a bonus, go ahead and get acquainted with the GLSL shading language as well, since this is what lies at the heart of WebGL.

Web sockets

If you've ever thought about creating a high performance multiplayer game in HTML5 then the new web sockets API is just the thing you've been looking for. If you haven't done much with socket programming before, this is what you've been missing: instead of establishing a connection to a server each and every time a resource needs to be requested, a socket simply creates a connection once, then the client and server can communicate back and forth over that same connection. To put it another way, imagine making a phone call to someone, saying "Hello", then hanging up the phone after the other person says "Hello" back to you. Then, you call that person again, wait for them to pick up the phone and once you're both ready, you ask the person on the other side of the line how he or she is doing. After receiving an answer, you again hang up the phone. This continues for the duration of the conversation, where you only ask a question at a time (or make a single statement at a time), and most of the time is spent with both of you waiting for the call to come in and connecting the phones.

Now, with socket programming, the above scenario would be like making one phone call, then having the entire conversation without ever hanging up the phone. The only time you would hang up the phone would be when the conversation is finally over, and you and the other person have said good bye, and agreed to put down the phone. In this situation, there is virtually no delay between question and answer—only whatever intrinsic delay is involved in the sound traveling from one phone to another.

In HTML5, the sockets API is divided into two parts, namely a server part and a client part. The server side of the socket is something we will not discuss too much in this book, given the nature of what's involved. The client-side interface is where we will spend most of the discussion, although you will be happy to know that the JavaScript interface for web sockets and web workers is nearly identical.

```
// Step 1: Open connection
var con = new WebSocket
   ("ws://localhost:8888/packt/sockets/multiplayer-game-server");

// Step 2: Register callbacks
con.addEventListener("open", doOnOpen);
con.addEventListener("error", doOnError);
con.addEventListener("message", doOnMessage);
con.addEventListener("close", doOnClose);
```

```
function doOnOpen(event) {
  var msg = document.createElement("p");
  msg.textContent = "Socket connected to " + event.srcElement.URL;
  document.body.appendChild(msg);
}

function doOnError(event) {
  var msg = document.createElement("p");
  msg.textContent = "Error: " + event;
  document.body.appendChild(msg);
}

function doOnMessage(event) {
  var response = JSON.parse(event.data);

  var msg = document.createElement("p");
  msg.textContent = "Message received: " + response.message;
  document.body.appendChild(msg);
}

function doOnClose(event) {
  var msg = document.createElement("p");
  msg.textContent = "Socket connection closed at " +
    event.timeStamp;
  document.body.appendChild(msg);
}

// Step 3: Send a message to the server
con.send("Hello!");
```

As you can see from the preceding code snippet, there aren't too many differences between the web socket interface and the web worker interface. Most notably, perhaps, is the actual interface through which we can post a message to the server. Whereas a web worker uses the postMessage function, a web socket uses the send function. The traditional event handling functions work the exact same way as with workers. There are four events associated with a socket, namely onOpen, onClose, onError, and onMessage. The first two events, onOpen and onClose, are called when the server successfully validates the request and upgrades the connection with the browser and when the server somehow closes a connection with the particular socket, respectively. The onError event is fired when an error occurs on the server application. Finally, when the server pushes a message to the client, the JavaScript handle to the socket is alerted through the onMessage callback function. The event object that is passed to the function, similar to a web worker onMessage event object, has a data attribute with the actual data sent to it, as well as a timestamp attribute indicating when the message was sent.

The connection

Understanding the way a web application connects to a backend server through a web socket is fundamental to learning how the socket API works. The first point to remember is that the protocol that connects the browser to the server is different from the usual HTTP connection. The way a browser keeps the connection open with the server is by using the new WebSocket protocol, which is done by following a few steps. The WebSocket protocol is based on the traditional TCP and uses HTTP to upgrade the connection between a browser and a backend server, as illustrated in the following screenshot:

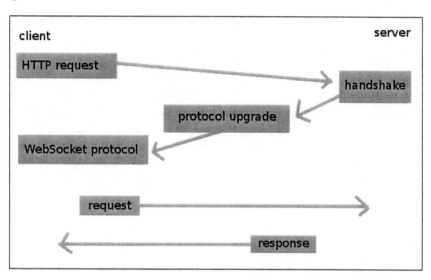

When we create an instance of the WebSocket class in JavaScript, the browser attempts to establish the persistent socket connection with the server. The first thing that happens is that the browser sends an HTTP request to the URI specified in the WebSocket constructor. This request contains an upgrade header, specifying that it wishes to upgrade the connection to using the WebSocket protocol. The server and the browser then perform a typical handshake, which, for the purposes of this book will not be explained in any great detail. If you're interested in implementing your own backend server application to handle this low-level handshake, you can refer to the official web socket documentation online.

To be brief, the client sends this HTTP request to the server, including a header containing a key, which is a simple text string. The server then hashes and encodes that string and sends back an HTTP response, which the browser then validates, and accepts the protocol upgrade if everything is right. If this handshake is successful, the browser proceeds to instantiate the WebSocket object, which we can then use to communicate with the server over the same connection.

The server-side code

A typical use case for web sockets is a multiplayer game where two or more players either play against each other or otherwise share the same game, in real time, but from different locations. One way such a game could be implemented (say, a fighting game such as Street Fighter or Mortal Kombat) is by having two players connecting to the server from separate computers, then the server would receive input from both players and send them the output computed from their actions. Each player's client application would then simply render the data received from the server. For example, player A presses a key on the keyboard that makes the character controlled by player A jump. That data is sent to the server, which is keeping track of where the character is and whether it can jump, and so on. After the server computes what is to be done based on the input it received from player A (in this example, the server determines that player A's character is now performing a jump), it sends the updated state of player A's character to both player A and player B. Their application then simply renders player A's character up in the air. Of course, each player's local instance of the game also renders the state it calculates from a local player's actions in order to provide instant feedback. However, the server-side instance of the game has the ability to invalidate any game state resulting from input from either player, if it is determined to be invalid. This way, both players can experience a very smooth, responsive multiplayer gaming experience, while the integrity of the game remains in check.

Now, depending on the specific language in which the server-side code is implemented, this could either be a trivial task or a real nightmare. Overall, the main thing that this server-side code needs to keep track of is all of the sockets connected to it. Obviously, the complexity of the application will be relative to the goals of the game. However, as far as the web sockets API is concerned, the main point is to pass data back to the client using the `send` interface function and check on input from the `onMessage` function.

The client-side code

As we saw in the previous code snippet, working with the JavaScript `WebSocket` object is very straightforward. Two things to keep in mind, however, are that every call to `WebSocket.send` is asynchronous and whatever data is padded to `WebSocket.send` must be (or will be converted to) a `DOMString`. That means that if we send an object, a function, or anything else to the server, it will be available to the server as a UTF-16 encoded string. If we send a JSON string to the server then all we need to do is parse the data and access the specifics. However, if we simply send an actual object, such as a literal JSON object, the server will receive something such as the following code snippet:

```
// Client code
var con = new WebSocket
   ("ws://localhost:8888/packt/sockets/multiplayer-game-server");
// …

con.send({name: "Rodrigo"});


// Server code
String input = get_input_from_socket();
input.toString() == "[object Object]";
```

Thus, when sending objects through a web socket, JavaScript will not attempt to encode the object, but will instead simply call the object's `toString` function and send the output of that along to the socket.

Video

Being able to play videos directly inside a browser without having to worry about plugins is quite a joyous experience. Not only that, but since the video element is actually a native part of the DOM, that means we can also deal with it the same way as we do with all other DOM elements. In other words, we can apply CSS styles to a video element and the browser is more than happy to make things work for us. For example, suppose we want to create the effect of the video being played on a shiny surface, where the video reflects vertically and the reflection fades out, blending into the background, as in the following screenshot:

Since the browser is in charge of rendering the video, as well as applying CSS styles and effects to all elements being managed by it, we don't have to worry about the logic involved in rendering a video with special effects added to it. Keep in mind, however, that the more CSS we throw on top of the video, the more work the browser will have to do to make the video look the way we want, which may quickly affect performance. However, if all we're adding to the video is a simple detail here and there, then most modern web browsers will have no problem rendering everything at full speed.

```css
<style>
video {
  -webkit-box-reflect: below 1px;
  -webkit-transition: all 1.5s;
}

video {
  -webkit-filter: contrast(250%);
}

div {
  position: relative;
}

div img {
  position: absolute;
  left: 0;
  top: 221px;
  width: 400px;
  height: 220px;
}
</style>

<div>
  <video controls width="400" height="220"
    poster="bunny-poster.png">
    <!-- Video courtesy of http://www.bigbuckbunny.org -->
    <source src="bunny.ogg" type="video/ogg" />
    <source src="bunny.mp4" type="video/mp4" />
    <source src="bunny.webm" type="video/webm" />
  </video>
  <img src="semi-transparent-mask.png" />
</div>
```

Similar to the new HTML5 audio element, there are more or less two ways we can use the tag. One way is to simply create the HTML node, specify the same properties as the `audio` tag, specify one or more `source` nodes, and call it a day. Alternatively, we can use the JavaScript API available to us and programmatically manipulate the playback of the video file.

```javascript
// Step 1: Create the video object
var video = document.createElement("video");
video.width = 400;
video.height = 220;
video.controls = true;
video.poster = "bunny-poster.png";

// Step 2: Add one or more sources
var sources = [
  {src: "bunny.ogg", type: "video/ogg"},
  {src: "bunny.mp4", type: "video/mp4"},
  {src: "bunny.webm", type: "webm"}
];

for (var i in sources) {
  var source = document.createElement("source");
  source.src = sources[i].src;
  source.type = sources[i].type;

  video.appendChild(source);
}

// Step 3: Make video player visible
document.body.appendChild(video);
```

We can also ignore the default controls and manage the playing, pausing, volume adjusting, and so on, on our own by taking advantage of the attributes available to the JavaScript object that references the video element. The following is a list of attributes and functions we can call on a video object.

Attributes

- `autoplay` (Boolean)
- `currentTime` (float—in seconds)
- `paused` (Boolean)
- `controls` (Boolean)
- `muted` (Boolean)
- `width` (integer)
- `height` (integer)
- `videoWidth` (integer—read only)
- `videoHeight` (integer—read only)
- `poster` (string—an image uri)
- `duration` (int—read only)
- `loop` (Boolean)
- `currentSrc` (string)
- `preload` (Boolean)
- `seeking` (Boolean)
- `playbackRange` (integer)
- `ended` (Boolean)
- `volume` (integer—between 0 and 100 exclusive)

Events

`loadstart`	The user agent begins looking for media data, as part of the resource selection algorithm.
`progress`	The user agent is fetching media data.
`suspend`	The user agent is intentionally not currently fetching media data.
`abort`	The user agent stops fetching the media data before it is completely downloaded, but not due to an error.
`error`	An error occurs while fetching the media data.
`emptied`	A media element whose networkState was previously not in the NETWORK_EMPTY state has just switched to that state (either because of a fatal error during load that's about to be reported, or because the load() method was invoked while the resource selection algorithm was already running).

stalled	The user agent is trying to fetch media data, but data is unexpectedly not forthcoming.
loadedmetadata	The user agent has just determined the duration and dimensions of the media resource and the text tracks are ready.
loadeddata	The user agent can render the media data at the current playback position for the first time.
canplay	The user agent can resume playback of the media data, but estimates that if playback were to be started now, the media resource could not be rendered at the current playback rate up to its end without having to stop for further buffering of content.
canplaythrough	The user agent estimates that if playback were to be started now, the media resource could be rendered at the current playback rate all the way to its end without having to stop for further buffering.
playing	Playback is ready to start after having been paused or delayed due to lack of media data.
waiting	Playback has stopped because the next frame is not available, but the user agent expects that frame to become available in due course.
seeking	The seeking IDL attribute changed to true.
seeked	The seeking IDL attribute changed to false.
ended	Playback has stopped because the end of the media resource was reached.
durationchange	The duration attribute has just been updated.
timeupdate	The current playback position changed as part of normal playback or in an especially interesting way, for example, discontinuously.
play	The element is no longer paused. Fired after the play() method has returned, or when the autoplay attribute has caused playback to begin.
pause	The element has been paused. Fired after the pause() method has returned.
ratechange	Either the default Playback Rate or the playback Rate attribute has just been updated.
volumechange	Either the volume attribute or the muted attribute has changed. Fired after the relevant attribute's setter has returned.

For more information on events, visit W3C Candidate Recommendation Media Events at http://www.w3.org/TR/html5/embedded-content-0.html#mediaevents

One final reason that you should be excited about the new HTML5 video element is that each frame of the video can be rendered right into a canvas 2D rendering context, just as if a single frame was a standalone image. This way, we are able to do video processing right on the browser. Unfortunately, there is no `video.toDataURL` equivalent where we could export the video created by our JavaScript application.

```javascript
var ctx = null;
var ctxOff = null;

var poster = new Image();
poster.src = "bunny-poster.jpg";
poster.addEventListener("click", initVideo);
document.body.appendChild(poster);

// Step 1: When the video plays, call our custom drawing function
video.autoplay = false;
video.loop = false;

// Step 2: Add one or more sources
var sources = [
  {src: "bunny.ogg", type: "video/ogg"},
  {src: "bunny.mp4", type: "video/mp4"},
  {src: "bunny.webm", type: "webm"}
];

for (var i in sources) {
  var source = document.createElement("source");
  source.src = sources[i].src;
  source.type = sources[i].type;

  video.appendChild(source);
}

// Step 3: Initialize the video
function initVideo() {
  video.addEventListener("play", initCanvas);
  video.play();
}

// Step 4: Only initialize our canvases once
function initCanvas() {
  // Step 1: Initialize canvas, if needed
  if (ctx == null) {
    var canvas = document.createElement("canvas");
    var canvasOff = document.createElement("canvas");
```

```
      canvas.width = canvasOff.width = video.videoWidth;
      canvas.height = canvasOff.height = video.videoHeight;

      ctx = canvas.getContext("2d");
      ctxOff = canvasOff.getContext("2d");

      // Make the canvas - not video player - visible
      poster.parentNode.removeChild(poster);
      document.body.appendChild(canvas);
   }

   renderOnCanvas();
}

function renderOnCanvas() {
   // Draw frame to canvas if video is still playing
   if (!video.paused && !video.ended) {

      // Draw original frame to offscreen canvas
      ctxOff.drawImage(video, 0, 0, canvas.width, canvas.height);

      // Manipulate frames offscreen
      var frame = getVideoFrame();

      // Draw new frame to visible video player
      ctx.putImageData(frame, 0, 0);
      requestAnimationFrame(renderOnCanvas);
   }
}

function getVideoFrame() {
   var img = ctxOff.getImageData
      (0, 0, canvas.width, canvas.height);

   // Invert the color of every pixel in the canvas context
   for (var i = 0, len = img.data.length; i < len; i += 4) {
      img.data[i] = 255 - img.data[i];
      img.data[i + 1] = 255 - img.data[i + 1];
      img.data[i + 2] = 255 - img.data[i + 2];
   }

   return img;
}
```

The idea is to play the video offscreen, meaning that the actual video player is never attached to the DOM. The video still plays, but the browser never needs to blitz each frame to the screen (it only plays in memory). As each frame is played, we draw that frame to a canvas context (just like we do with images), take the pixels from the canvas context, manipulate the pixel data, then finally draw it back on to the canvas.

Since a video is nothing more than a sequence of frames played one after the other, giving the illusion of animation, we can extract each frame from an HTML5 video and use it with the canvas API just like any other image. Since there isn't a way to draw to the video element, we simply keep on drawing each frame from the video player into a plain canvas object, achieving the same result—but with carefully crafted pixels. The following screenshot illustrates the result of this technique:

One way to achieve this result is to create two canvas elements. If we only draw to the same canvas (draw the frame from the video, then manipulate that frame, then draw the next frame, and so on), the customized frame would only be visible for a fraction of a second. It would only be visible until we quickly drew the next incoming frame. In turn, this next frame would only be visible for as long as we looped through that frame's pixel data and redrew that frame again. You get the idea, the result would be messy, and not at all what we want.

So instead we use two canvas contexts. One context will be in charge of only displaying the pixels we work on (also known as, the manipulated pixels) and the other context will never be visible to the user and will serve the purpose of holding each frame as it comes straight from the video. This way, we're only drawing to our main, visible canvas once per iteration and all that's ever displayed in this canvas context is the manipulated pixels. The original pixels (also known as, the pixels from the original video that's playing in memory) will continue to be streamed to the offscreen canvas context as fast as they can.

Geolocation

Although 3D graphics are awesome, as is a socket-based, multiplayer game, neither technology is necessarily new. Geolocation, on the other hand, is somewhat of a more recent phenomenon. With it, we are able to use JavaScript to determine the physical location (geographical location) of a user. Having such a tool at our disposal opens up new possibilities of awesome, highly innovative game concepts.

Now, whenever a new feature comes out that promises to be able to track down exactly where a user is physically located, most people (except for developers, of course) get at least a little scared about it. After all, how creepy would it be to play a very dark, survival horror game, knowing that other people playing the game can see exactly where you live. Luckily for us, the entire geolocation API is opt-in-based, meaning that the user is prompted about the application attempting to capture the user's location and the browser only allows the application to continue to capture the GPS location of the user if and when the user accepts the request from the application.

As shown in the following screenshot, when attempting to use the geolocation API, the browser will somehow alert the user about it and ask for permission to continue. If the user decides not to share his or her location with the application, the browser will not share the location with the application.

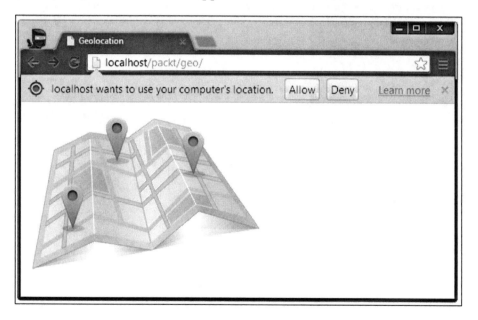

Although each browser implements this request step slightly differently, especially with regards to how this notification and request is graphically conveyed to the user, there is no way for the application to use the geolocation API to forcefully or secretly collect this piece of information.

```javascript
function getGeo(position) {
  var geo = document.createElement("ul");
  var lat = document.createElement("li");
  var lon = document.createElement("li");

  lat.textContent = "Latitude: " + position.coords.latitude;
  lon.textContent = "Longitude: " + position.coords.longitude;

  geo.appendChild(lat);
  geo.appendChild(lon);
  document.body.appendChild(geo);
}

function doOnPermissionDenied(message) {
  var p = document.createElement("p");

  p.textContent = "Permission Denied Error: " + message;
  document.body.appendChild(p);
}

function doOnPositionUnavailable(message) {
  var p = document.createElement("p");

  p.textContent = "Position Unavailable Error: " + message;
  document.body.appendChild(p);
}

function doOnTimeout(message) {
  var p = document.createElement("p");

  p.textContent = "Operation Timeout Error: " + message;
  document.body.appendChild(p);
}
```

```
function doNoGeo(positionError) {
  switch (positionError.code) {
    case positionError.PERMISSION_DENIED:
      doOnPermissionDenied(positionError.message);
      break;

    case positionError.POSITION_UNAVAILABLE:
      doOnPositionUnavailable(positionError.message);
      break;

    case positionError.TIMEOUT:
      doOnTimeout(positionError.message);
      break;
  }
}

// Ask the user if you may use Geolocation
navigator.geolocation.getCurrentPosition(getGeo, doNoGeo);
```

The first part of the API involves asking the user for permission to get his or her location. This is done by calling the getCurrentPosition function on the geolocation attribute of the global navigator object. The function takes two arguments, namely a callback function to be called if the user allows the browser to share the user's location and a callback function to be called if the user denies the application's request.

If the user accepts the request from the application to share the geolocation, the callback is invoked with a Geoposition object passed in to it. This object has *nine* properties that we can use:

- timestamp: When the callback function was invoked
- coords: An instance of class Coordinates
- accuracy: How accurate the GPS coordinate is (in meters)
- altitude: In meters
- altitudeAccuracy: How accurate the altitude is (in meters)
- heading: In degrees clockwise from north
- latitude: As a double
- longitude: As a double
- speed: In meters per second

There are only three attributes in the position object that are required to be present. These are the latitude and longitude values, along with the accuracy attribute. All other values are optional and will be available if the hardware in use supports them. Keep in mind, also, that this feature is equally available on mobile devices, so it is possible and likely that the user's position changes somewhat during the course of the application's usage. Thankfully, once the user has agreed to have his or her position shared with the application, any subsequent calls to get the current position will be successful right away. Of course, the user can just as well clear the permissions for a given domain right from the browser, so any subsequent calls to get the position may fail (if the user has disabled the feature altogether) or result in a new request for permission (in case the user simply cleared the permissions cache on the browser).

As you can see from the following screenshot, Google Chrome displays a different icon on the address bar when a page is using geolocation to let the user know about it. By clicking this special icon, the user can reset the permissions, or block or allow the application on a more long term basis.

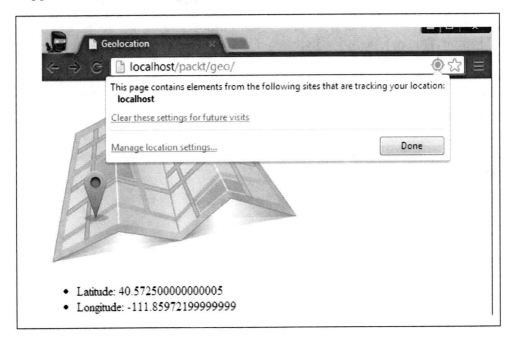

A Google Maps example

Possibly the most common use case for geolocation these days involves rendering a position to a map. Thankfully, Google offers a terrific, free API that we can tap into for the purposes of doing just that. With this mapping service, we can capture a user's geolocation, then render a marker on the map right where the user is located (or somewhere within the accuracy distance of where the user is). While the Google Maps API is rather robust, we will simply cover a fairly trivial example of how we can go about obtaining the user's location then render that coordinate point on a map.

The general idea where the maps API is based is simple: create a map object to be rendered inside some HTML container object, specify where this map is to be centered (so that we can know the general area within the map that is immediately visible to the user), and add markers to it. Marker objects take at least two attributes, namely a reference to a map object and a GPS coordinate point. In our example, we'll center the map on the user's GPS coordinate and also place a marker on that same location.

```
// Step 1: Request permission to get the user's location
function initGeo() {
   navigator.geolocation.getCurrentPosition(renderToMap, doNoGeo);
}

// Step 2: Render the user's location on a map
function renderToMap(position) {
  var container = document.createElement("div");
  container.id = "myContaier";
  container.style.width = window.innerWidth + "px";
  container.style.height = window.innerHeight + "px";

  document.body.appendChild(container);

  // Define some point based on a GPS coordinate
  var coords = new google.maps.LatLng(
    position.coords.latitude,
    position.coords.longitude);

  // Specify how we want the map to look
  var options = {
    zoom: 16,
    center: coords,
    mapTypeControl: false,
    mapTypeId: google.maps.MapTypeId.ROADMAP
  };
```

```
  // Create a map, and inject it into the DOM element referenced
  var map = new google.maps.Map(container, options);

  // Create a marker and associate it with our map
  var marker = new google.maps.Marker({
    position: coords,
    map: map,
    title: "Where's me?"
  });
}
```

While the preceding example might not be the most exciting piece of software you've seen, it does a great job illustrating two powerful points. First, the geolocation API is powerful, yet, it is also possibly the easiest of all other HTML5 APIs in terms of all the functionality it offers and everything you need to know in order to use it. Second, the preceding snippet shows how open the web platform is and how much we can potentially accomplish simply by taking advantage of other people's work.

Running the preceding code will result in a very nice looking map covering the entirety of the screen, with the central point of the map being the user's current location, as shown in the following screenshot. Keep in mind that Google Maps is just one example of the many free APIs that we can use in conjunction with such powerful HTML5 features as geolocation.

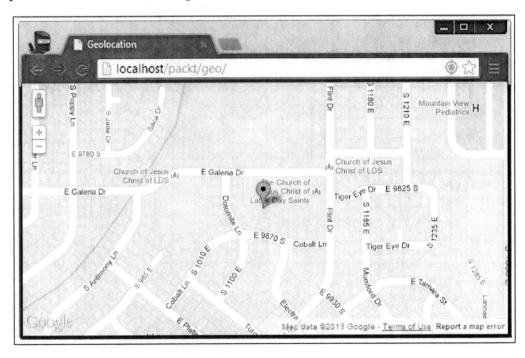

Upcoming CSS features

One of my favorite things about the Open Web is that it is also a living web. As new ideas arise and as new needs manifest themselves, it becomes a matter of time until new features are introduced into a spec. A perfect example of this is CSS, where recently there have been a few new features added to the spec. Best of all, most browser vendors are quite proactive at bringing these new features to their browsers.

In this next section we will look at three new features of CSS, namely CSS shaders, CSS columns, and CSS regions and exclusions. To give you an idea of how active the development of these features is, we will discuss the first feature **CSS shaders**, which was recently renamed as CSS custom filters. Talk about a fast moving development life cycle.

Programming in the bleeding edge

Although most of the content in this book is somewhat new and state of the art, the majority of the HTML5 features and APIs discussed so far are fairly stable. By that, I mean that just about any major browser should be able to handle these features without any problems. However, the following CSS features are literally fresh out of the oven. To be more specific, all three of these features are still being baked, with the recipe being worked on until it reaches a more stable level of refinement.

With that said, this section may require that you use the absolute most recent browsers, using the latest possible version, and you may even be required to delve into the settings section of your browser of choice so that any advanced flags are set in order for these new and experimental features to work. All of the code examples for the rest of this chapter were written for and tested in Google Chrome Canary (nightly builds). As of this writing, after a fresh install of Google Chrome Canary, the following flags had to be manually enabled:

- Enable `experimental WebKit features`
- Enable `CSS shaders`

You likely won't need to enable the `WebGL` flag, as this particular flag has been enabled by default for a while, but in case the flag is disabled, you can make it available in the same manner. To view all the available flags that can be set on Google Chrome, simply type the following command in the browser's address bar (where you normally enter a website's URL): `chrome://flags`.

Once in the flags page, you will see a list of flags, along with a description of what each flag does. Look for the two flags related to `experimental WebKit features` and `CSS shaders`, and be sure that they are enabled. As you can tell from the following screenshot, beware that carelessly setting and unsetting flags may affect the way that Google Chrome behaves and performs. Be sure to change the least amount of flags to avoid doing anything to cause the browser to work less than optimally and make sure you keep track of any flags you change, so that you can revert your changes, should anything bad happen as a result.

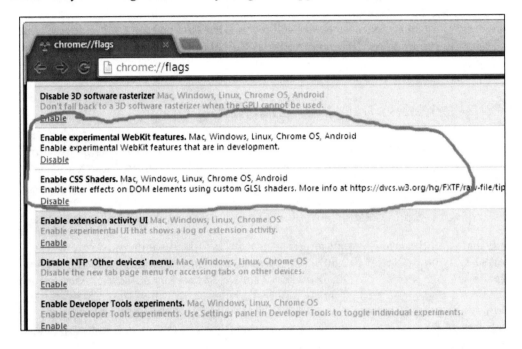

One final note about developing with these absolute bleeding edge APIs is that, given the nature of an experimental API, there may be browser specific syntax and features as well as significant performance differences between different browsers. Since not all browsers start adopting new APIs at the same time, a great percentage of users are not able to view your latest and greatest code until APIs become stable enough—which sometimes takes longer than we'd like them to.

CSS shaders

Currently, this is the absolute latest feature added to CSS. The original idea behind CSS shaders was to allow a designer to use GLSL shaders to render arbitrary HTML elements. Instead of simply specifying an element's background color, border style, box shadow, and so on, we can now take care of how each pixel of an element is rendered.

More recently, this feature was merged into the existing CSS filters spec, which specifing a handful of pre-baked filters that we can apply to an element. For example, we can apply a blur filter to an image element, letting the browser process the image dynamically, as it gets served from the server to the web application. However, instead of relying only on whatever filters a browser decides to make, we can now cook our own filters and have the CSS rendering engine use those. Thus, the current name of this new CSS API is (for now, anyway) **custom CSS filters**.

Using CSS filters is pretty easy. After all, they are nothing more than a regular CSS property. As of this writing, there are *nine* different filters that we can apply, not only to images, but also to anything that can receive CSS styling. If a filter is added to an element with one or more children nodes in it, as is the nature of CSS, the filter effect will cascade down to any and all child elements, unless one or more of them specify their own filters, or deliberately specify that no filtering should be applied to it and its children.

The current list of CSS filters that can be used are as follows:

- `blur`: Applies a Gaussian blur
- `brightness`: Increases the brightness of the element by applying more or less white color
- `contrast`: Adjusts the contrast of the element
- `drop-shadow`: Applies a drop shadow effect to the element
- `grayscale`: Converts the colors of the element into grayscale
- `hue-rotate`: Applies a hue rotation in degrees based on a color circle
- `invert`: Inverts the colors of the element
- `opacity`: Applies transparency to the element
- `saturate`: Increases the saturation of the element
- `sepia`: Converts the colors of the element into sepia

Keep in mind that, although these filters are in fact mere CSS attributes, in reality they are each a separate function that the browser performs on the elements matched by the CSS query. Thus, each filter function takes one or more arguments, which, behind the scenes, are variables being passed to pre-defined shader programs.

```
<style>
div {
  margin: 10px;
  padding: 0;
  border: 1px solid #ddd;
  background: #fafafa;
  width: 400px;

  transition: all 3.3s;
  filter: invert(1);
}

div:hover {
  -webkit-filter: invert(0) blur(3px) contrast(150%);
}

h2 {
  margin: 0;
  padding: 10px;
  font-size: 4.75em;
  color: #aaa;
  text-shadow: 0 -1px 0 #555, 0 1px 0 #fff;
}
</style>

<div>
  <h2>CSS Filters</h2>
  <img src="strawberry.jpg" width="400" height="350" />
</div>
```

In the following screenshot, the image on the left is a regular piece of HTML, with a heading and an image. On the right, we applied a CSS filter that inverted the colors. That entire effect was achieved with a single line of code.

Note that we can apply multiple filters to the same element by just simply listing additional filters as the value of the CSS property. Also, keep in mind that even though it only takes a single line of code to add one of these exciting filters to our applications, each filter used means work that the browser will need to do on top of all that it's already doing. Thus, the more we use these filters, the more we can expect performance to drop accordingly.

Using custom filters

In order to input our own filtering functions for the browser to use when rendering our application, we need to create the shader program that does what we want. Thankfully, these shader programs are written in the same shading language that we use in WebGL. If you thought learning JavaScript, CSS, and HTML was a lot of work already, I'm sorry to say, but go ahead and add GLSL to the list of languages you must master (or find someone who's already mastered it) in order to take full advantage of the HTML5 revolution.

To specify custom shaders to be used for our CSS filters, we simply call the custom function as the value of the filter attribute, pass in our vertex and fragment shaders, followed by any possible variables to be used by the vertex shader. External variables used by the fragment shader are passed in from the vertex shader, so we can't pass anything into it directly from CSS.

```
div {
  margin: 10px;
  padding: 0;
  border: 1px solid #ddd;
  background: #fafafa;
  width: 400px;

  filter: custom(url(simple-vert-shader.glsl)
    mix(url(simple-frag-shader.glsl) normal source-atop,
    16 32,
    lightPosition 0.0 0.0 1.0;
}
```

There are three parts to the preceding filter definition. First, we call `custom` to indicate that we'll be using our own shaders. The first argument we pass to this function is the vertex shader. The extension of this file is not important, as the contents of the file will be compiled and sent to the GPU. A lot of the time, you will see other developers using file extensions for their shaders such as `.glsl` or `.vs` and `.fs` (for vertex shader and fragment shader, respectively). Note that the fragment shader is sent through the `mix()` function, as opposed to just being sent directly through the `url()` function, as is the case with the vertex shader. Lastly, we specify the number of rows and columns that will make up the element's content mesh. The vertices that make up this mesh are created by the browser automatically. Finally, the last set of arguments passed with our custom filter are uniform values (accompanied by their names) for the vertex shader to use.

Since GLSL itself is beyond the scope of this book, we will stay away from a thorough example of these custom shaders. Instead, we will look at a symbolic example, which will use dummy shaders. Without the proper background knowledge and experience with graphics programming, shader programming, and other 3D graphics topics, it would be rather challenging to explain our way through a custom shader program.

The following shader programs take three inputs from CSS, namely a value between 0.0 and 1.0 representing the amount of red, green, and blue to be applied to each pixel in the image. As a quick and brief crash course in OpenGL Shading Language (GLSL), I'll just say this: a uniform is like a global variable that we can pass in to the vertex shader. The vertex shader is called once per vertex and determines where each vertex is positioned. In order to send values to the fragment shader, the vertex shader can use a varying variable. If we define a variable of whatever type in the vertex shader that has the `varying` keyword before it, that means that whatever value is assigned to it will be available to the fragment shader, provided that the fragment shader also defines a varying variable of the same name and type. Thus, if we want a value to be passed to the fragment shader directly from CSS, we can simply send the value to the vertex shader, then use `varying` to pass the value through to the fragment shader. The fragment shader is called once per pixel and determines what color to apply to that pixel.

```
// ----------------------------------------------------
// Vertex shader: simple-vert-shader.glsl
// ----------------------------------------------------
precision mediump float;

// Built-in attribute
attribute vec4 a_position;

// Built-in uniform
uniform mat4 u_projectionMatrix;

// Values sent in from CSS
uniform float red;
uniform float green;
uniform float blue;

// Send values to fragment shader
varying float v_r;
varying float v_g;
varying float v_b;

void main() {

  v_r = red;
  v_g = green;
  v_b = blue;

  // Set the position of each vertex
  gl_Position = u_projectionMatrix * a_position;
}
```

The only two things the preceding vertex shader does are pass our values from CSS to the fragment shader and set the vertex position of each vertex on our content mesh.

```
// --------------------------------------------------
// Vertex shader: simple-vert-shader.glsl
// --------------------------------------------------
precision mediump float;

// Input from vertex shader
varying float v_r;
varying float v_g;
varying float v_b;

void main() {

  // Set the color of each fragment
  css_ColorMatrix = mat4(v_r, 0.0, 0.0, 0.0,
    0.0, v_g, 0.0, 0.0,
    0.0, 0.0, v_b, 0.0,
    0.0, 0.0, 0.0, 1.0);
}
```

With that shader program in place, all we need to do is call it from within our HTML file. The three parameters we need to pay attention to are the red, green, and blue uniforms. Whatever values we send in for those three color channels, it will reflect on the rendering of whatever elements we apply this filter to.

```
<style>
div {
  margin: 10px;
  padding: 0;
  border: 1px solid #ddd;
  background: #fafafa;
  width: 400px;
```

```
  /**
   * We can leverage CSS transitions to make our simple
   * shaders seem even more impressive
   */
  transition: filter 1.0s;

  filter: custom(url(simple-vert-shader.glsl)
    mix(url(simple-frag-shader.glsl)
    normal source-atop),
    16 32,
    red 1.0, green 0.0, blue 0.0);
}

div:hover {
  filter: custom(url(simple-vert-shader.glsl)
    mix(url(simple-frag-shader.glsl)
    normal source-atop),
    16 32,
    red 1.0, green 1.0, blue 0.0);
}

h2 {
  margin: 0;
  padding: 10px;
  font-size: 4.75em;
  color: #aaa;
  text-shadow: 0 -1px 0 #555, 0 1px 0 #fff;
}
</style>

<div>
  <h2>CSS Filters</h2>
  <img src="strawberry.jpg" width="400" height="350" />
</div>
```

With this setup in place, our `div` element will render one particular way by default. In this case, we only turn on the red channel on every pixel within the DOM node. When we hover over the element, however, we apply the same shader, but with a completely different color. This time we make every pixel look extra yellow. With the help of CSS transitions, we can smoothly gradate those two states, giving a simple, yet quite cozy effect. Of course, the more you know about GLSL, the more fancy and powerful you can make these custom shaders. And as an added bonus, we don't have to worry about all of the setup work involved in using shaders in WebGL. The default abstraction provided by the browser is quite useful, making custom shaders very reusable, since people using our shaders only need to keep track of a couple of CSS attributes. Best of all, since shader programs are, at least at this CSS level, pure text files, we can learn how other people's shaders work by inspecting their source code. By using our custom shader, we can easily control which color channels are turned on or off at an individual pixel level, as shown in the following screenshot. This pixel by pixel manipulation is not only limited to images, but is rather performed on each pixel of whatever DOM element we apply the filter to—text, images, containers, and so on.

Beware, however, that since this technology is so hot off the oven, there are very few tools, if any, to help us develop, debug, and maintain GLSL shaders. You will quickly notice that when an error is found within your shaders, you will simply see an unfiltered HTML document. If your shader programs fail to compile, for example, the browser will not bother letting you know what happened, or where, or maybe even why. Thus, writing custom CSS filters can be the most challenging aspect of web development at the moment, since browsers are not yet very useful in offering a hand in the process.

CSS columns

If you have been using the internet for at least a few weeks, or if you have seen at least a couple of dozen different websites, you will certainly have noticed the rectangular nature of HTML documents. Although it is possible to use a combination of HTML, JavaScript, and CSS to create very robust designs, web designers have been waiting for many moons for a simple solution to create multicolumn designs.

With the new CSS columns feature, we can create a regular block of text, then tell the CSS engine to display that block in two or more columns. Everything else is handled by the browser very efficiently. For example, say we want a block of text to be displayed into four equal width columns, with 20 pixels between each column. This can be achieved with two intuitive lines of code (vendor prefix may be required, but is deliberately ignored in this example).

```
<style>
div {
  column-count: 4;
  column-gap: 20px;
</style>

<div>
  <p>Lorem ipsum dolor sit amet, consectetuer adipiscing elit, sed
diam nonummy nibh euismod tincidunt ut laoreet dolore magna aliquam
erat volutpat. Ut wisi enim ad minim veniam, quis nostrud exerci
tation ullamcorper suscipit lobortis nisl ut aliquip ex ea commodo
consequat. Duis autem vel eum iriure dolor in hendrerit in vulputate
velit esse molestie consequat, vel illum dolore eu feugiat nulla
facilisis at vero eros et accumsan et iusto odio dignissim qui blandit
praesent luptatum zzril delenit augue duis dolore te feugait nulla
facilisi.</p>

  <p>Nam liber tempor cum soluta nobis eleifend option congue nihil
imperdiet doming id quod mazim placerat facer possim assum. Typi non
habent claritatem insitam; est usus legentis in iis qui facit eorum
claritatem. Investigationes demonstraverunt lectores legere me lius
quod ii legunt saepius.</p>

  <p>Claritas est etiam processus dynamicus, qui sequitur mutationem
consuetudium lectorum. Mirum est notare quam littera gothica, quam
nunc putamus parum claram, anteposuerit litterarum formas humanitatis
per seacula quarta decima et quinta decima. Eodem modo typi, qui nunc
nobis videntur parum clari, fiant sollemnes in futurum.</p>
</div>
```

With the preceding setup, the browser knows that we wish to render our text into four columns, with 20 pixels separating each column on the sides. Observe that no mention is ever made about how wide to make each column. In this case, the browser calculates the space available inside the `div` container, subtracts the total width needed for the column gap (the space between two columns, not including the space between a column and the container), then divides the remaining width into the total number of columns. This way, as we resize the browser window, the columns will automatically resize and everything else will retain its dimensions.

After we specify a column gap width, the browser can determine how wide to make each column (if we specify a fixed number of columns) or a number of columns to display (if we specify a width for each column) based on the available space for the columns, as shown in the following screenshot. It doesn't normally make sense to specify both a column width and a number of columns.

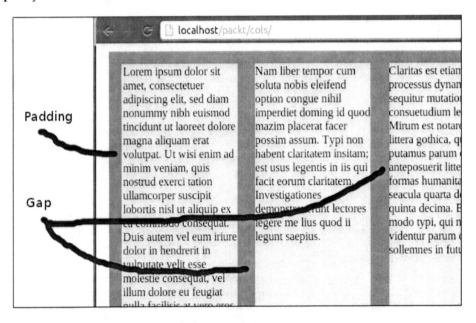

Alternatively, we can simply tell the browser how wide we want each column, and optionally how much gap to have between two columns. What the browser would do in this situation is the opposite. It would calculate the remaining space available for rendering the columns, then render as many columns as it can in that space, given the width constraint we have specified.

```
<style>
div {
  column-width: 200px;
  column-gap: 20px;
}
</style>
```

The column rule

Similar to the concept of a border around a box, as in border: 1px solid #333, CSS columns come with the concept of a rule. Simply put, a column rule is a single border that is drawn vertically between two columns. A rule can be styled much like a border and is rendered right between the two columns, making use of the space provided by a column-gap. If the space available for a column rule is greater than the space provided by a column gap, the gap is rendered properly and the rule is ignored.

```
<style>
div {
  column-count: 3;
  column-gap: 20px;
  column-rule-width: 1px;
  column-rule-style: dashed;
  column-rule-color: rgb(255, 10, 10);
}
</style>
```

Again, similar to a border property, we can specify each attribute related to a column rule, or short hand the definition in the same order as a border (width, style, and color, respectively). Valid values for a border style include the following:

- none: No border
- dotted: The border is a series of dots
- dashed: The border is a series of short line segments
- solid: The border is a single line segment
- double: The border is two solid lines. The sum of the two lines and the space between them equals the value of 'border-width'
- groove: The border looks as though it were carved into the canvas
- ridge: The opposite of 'groove': the border looks as though it were coming out of the canvas

 For more information on the table border styles, you can visit http://www.w3.org/TR/CSS2/tables.html#table-border-styles

Column breaks

Sometimes, we may want a bit of control over where exactly the content breaks into a new column. For example, if we have several blocks of text, each preceded by heading of some sort. It may not look too good if the last line in a column is a lonely heading meant to introduce the next section. The column break property gives us this ability where we can specify column breaks before or after an element.

By specifying where a column should or should not break into the next column, we can have more control over how each column is rendered and populated, as demonstrated in the following screenshot:

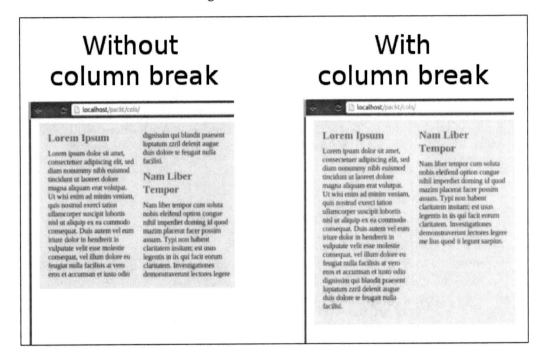

The same properties used to control page breaks in CSS are also used to control the breaking of columns. There are three properties we can use to control column break, namely `break-before`, `break-after`, and `break-inside`. The first two are fairly self-explanatory—we can use break before or after to indicate the behavior before or after a particular element, such as always break the column, never break, or insert the column break where it should normally be inserted. Break inside, on the other hand, specifies what should be the behavior inside a multiline block of text, instead of simply at its beginning or end.

```
<style>
div {
  -webkit-column-count: 3;
  -webkit-column-gap: 20px;
  -webkit-column-rule: 1px solid #fff;
  padding: 20px;
  margin: 10px;
  background: #eee;
}

div p {
  margin: 0 0 10px;
  -webkit-column-break-inside: auto;
}

div h2 {
  margin: 0 0 10px;
  color: #55c;
  text-shadow: 0 1px 0 #fff;
  -webkit-column-break-before: always;
}
</style>

<div>
  <h2>Lorem Ipsum</h2>
  <p>Lorem ipsum dolor sit amet, consectetuer adipiscing elit, sed
diam nonummy nibh euismod tincidunt ut laoreet dolore magna aliquam
erat volutpat. Ut wisi enim ad minim veniam, quis nostrud exerci
tation ullamcorper suscipit lobortis nisl ut aliquip ex ea commodo
consequat. Duis autem vel eum iriure dolor in hendrerit in vulputate
velit esse molestie consequat, vel illum dolore eu feugiat nulla
facilisis at vero eros et accumsan et iusto odio dignissim qui blandit
praesent luptatum zzril delenit augue duis dolore te feugait nulla
facilisi.</p>

  <h2>Nam Liber Tempor</h2>
  <p>Nam liber tempor cum soluta nobis eleifend option congue nihil
imperdiet doming id quod mazim placerat facer possim assum. Typi non
habent claritatem insitam; est usus legentis in iis qui facit eorum
claritatem. Investigationes demonstraverunt lectores legere me lius
quod ii legunt saepius.</p>
```

```
<h2>Claritas est etiam</h2>
<p>Claritas est etiam processus dynamicus, qui sequitur mutationem
consuetudium lectorum. Mirum est notare quam littera gothica, quam
nunc putamus parum claram, anteposuerit litterarum formas humanitatis
per seacula quarta decima et quinta decima. Eodem modo typi, qui nunc
nobis videntur parum clari, fiant sollemnes in futurum.</p>
</div>
```

Note how the column break property is applied to the h2 tag, which now becomes the element that controls the breaking of each column. Of course, if we had specified a greater number of columns in this block of text than there were headings tags, then obviously the text inside the paragraph tags would end up breaking into new columns. This behavior can also be controlled, although in this particular case we simply set the column-break-inside property to auto, making it clear that we would like the content of each paragraph tag to spill over into other columns if needed.

CSS regions and exclusions

Two new text-related features of CSS are regions and exclusions. Regions behave somewhat similar to columns, in that we specify how a particular block of text is to render and flow. The main difference between regions and columns is that columns are restricted to equal width implied rectangles, whereas regions specify a separate content source and define where that content is to flow. For example, we can tell CSS to render text from a given source into three separate div elements, along with an arbitrary SVG polygon. Each of these elements need not be related in any particular way—one can be absolutely positioned, one can be transformed, and so on. The text would then flow from one element into the next, following the order in which each element is defined within the HTML file. Exclusions, on the other hand, do the exact opposite. Instead of defining areas where text flows into, they describe areas or shapes where text is to go around.

The whole reason for these two separate, yet closely related APIs, is to push the envelope of where we can take the visual design of web applications. Until now, the only way to achieve this sort of effect was through external software, and hopefully a very specific plugin that allowed such software or technology to be executed inside a browser. Now that the browser has grown a bit more mature, we can pull off these magazine-like effects right from the stylesheet.

Regions

The way regions work is somewhat similar to columns, yet it is fundamentally different. In general, all that regions do is specify a content source, then assign a CSS expression as the destination of that content. The content is moved from the element specified as the source and flowed into all elements assigned as destinations. If one or more elements don't receive any content because there wasn't enough content, these elements will behave just like a regular *empty* element. Other than the CSS property that identifies an element as a destination, there is nothing else about that element that is different from any other regular HTML elements.

```
<style>
h2, p {
   margin: 0 0 10px;
}

#src {
   flow-into: mydiv;
}

.container {
   flow-from: mydiv;

   border: 1px solid #c00;
   padding: 0.5em;
   margin: 0.5em;
}

.col1, .col2, .col3 {
   float: left;
   width: 50%;
}

#one {
   height: 250px;
}

#two, #three {
   height: 111px;
}
```

```
.col3 {
  clear: both;
  width: 100%;
}
</style>

<div id="src">
  <h2>Lorem Ipsum</h2>
  <p>Lorem ipsum dolor sit amet, consectetuer adipiscing elit, sed
diam nonummy nibh euismod tincidunt ut laoreet dolore magna aliquam
erat volutpat. Ut wisi enim ad minim veniam, quis nostrud exerci
tation ullamcorper suscipit lobortis nisl ut aliquip ex ea commodo
consequat. Duis autem vel eum iriure dolor in hendrerit in vulputate
velit esse molestie consequat, vel illum dolore eu feugiat nulla
facilisis at vero eros et accumsan et iusto odio dignissim qui blandit
praesent luptatum zzril delenit augue duis dolore te feugait nulla
facilisi.</p>

  <h2>Nam Liber Tempor</h2>
  <p>Nam liber tempor cum soluta nobis eleifend option congue nihil
imperdiet doming id quod mazim placerat facer possim assum. Typi non
habent claritatem insitam; est usus legentis in iis qui facit eorum
claritatem. Investigationes demonstraverunt lectores legere me lius
quod ii legunt saepius.</p>

  <h2>Claritas est etiam</h2>
  <p>Claritas est etiam processus dynamicus, qui sequitur mutationem
consuetudium lectorum. Mirum est notare quam littera gothica, quam
nunc putamus parum claram, anteposuerit litterarum formas humanitatis
per seacula quarta decima et quinta decima. Eodem modo typi, qui nunc
nobis videntur parum clari, fiant sollemnes in futurum.</p>
</div>

<div class="col1">
  <div class="container" id="one"></div>
</div>
<div class="col2">
  <div class="container" id="two"></div>
  <div class="container" id="three"></div>
</div>
<div class="col3">
  <div class="container" id="four"></div>
</div>
```

Here, we assign the contents of the element with an `id` property of `src` as the content provider, so to speak. This is done by assigning the new CSS property `flow-into`, which is assigned a string that we can use to identify this particular region content source. That means that the contents of that element will not be rendered where they are within the DOM, but will instead be distributed among all elements with a CSS property of `flow-from`, with a value matching the keyword used by the element with the `flow-into` property.

```
#src {
   flow-into: description-text;
}

div.description {
   flow-from: description-text;
}
```

Once a region source is defined, and a region chain is created, the browser takes care of distributing the contents throughout all the regions. Each region can be uniquely styled and can be a unique element altogether. For example, a region source can be defined and two targets can be created. One target can be a standard `div` element and the other can be an SVG shape. CSS regions can also be combined with exclusions, which we'll discuss in the next section.

As illustrated in the following screenshot, four elements are styled and floated about, while a region source is put in charge of filling up those regions. In case of region resizing, because of the browser window itself being resized, the user agent takes care of refreshing the content, flowing into the newly resized regions.

Lorem Ipsum

Lorem ipsum dolor sit amet, consectetuer adipiscing elit, sed diam nonummy nibh euismod tincidunt ut laoreet dolore magna aliquam erat volutpat. Ut wisi enim ad minim veniam, quis nostrud exerci tation ullamcorper suscipit lobortis nisl ut aliquip ex ea commodo consequat. Duis autem vel eum iriure dolor in hendrerit in vulputate velit esse molestie consequat, vel illum dolore eu feugiat nulla facilisis at vero eros et accumsan et iusto odio dignissim qui blandit

praesent luptatum zzril delenit augue duis dolore te feugait nulla facilisi.

Nam Liber Tempor

Nam liber tempor cum soluta nobis eleifend option

congue nihil imperdiet doming id quod mazim placerat facer possim assum. Typi non habent claritatem insitam; est usus legentis in iis qui facit eorum claritatem. Investigationes demonstraverunt lectores legere me lius quod ii legunt saepius.

Claritas est etiam

Claritas est etiam processus dynamicus, qui sequitur mutationem consuetudium lectorum. Mirum est notare quam littera gothica, quam nunc putamus parum claram, anteposuerit litterarum formas humanitatis per seacula quarta decima et quinta decima. Eodem modo typi, qui nunc nobis videntur parum clari, fiant sollemnes in futurum.

Exclusions

The way exclusions work is very similar to how we normally make text flow around images or any other inline elements. The main difference is that we can take it a step further and specify a few details in CSS that tells the text exactly how to flow.

```
<style>
img {
  width: 300px;
  height: 60px;
  display: inline-block;
  float: left;
}
</style>

<div>
  <img src="lipsum-logo.png" />
  <h2>Lorem Ipsum</h2>
  <p>Lorem ipsum dolor sit amet, consectetuer adipiscing elit, sed
diam nonummy nibh euismod tincidunt ut laoreet dolore magna aliquam
erat volutpat. Ut wisi enim ad minim veniam, quis nostrud exerci
tation ullamcorper suscipit lobortis nisl ut aliquip ex ea commodo
consequat. Duis autem vel eum iriure dolor in hendrerit in vulputate
velit esse molestie consequat, vel illum dolore eu feugiat nulla
facilisis at vero eros et accumsan et iusto odio dignissim qui blandit
praesent luptatum zzril delenit augue duis dolore te feugait nulla
facilisi.</p>
</div>
```

This trivial snippet simply tells the rest of the content inside that div element to flow around the image from its right side. Even if we had an SVG object in the place of that image, and this object was a polygon shaped like a triangle pointing to the right, the text would wrap around the object treating it like a rectangle.

However, with the magic of CSS exclusions, we can add properties to the image tag or the SVG object that would alter the way its outer shape is interpreted. By default, since any HTML element has an x and y position, along with a width and height attribute, every element is treated like a rectangle. Using the shape property changes that.

```
<style>
h2, p {
  margin: 0 0 10px;
}

svg {
  float: left;
  width: 300px;
  height: 400px;
  shape-outside: polygon(0 0, 100% 50%, 0 100%);
}

svg polygon {
  fill: #c33;
}
</style>

<div>
  <svg xmlns="http://www.w3.org/2000/svg">
    <polygon points="0, 0, 300, 200, 0, 400"></polygon>
  </svg>

  <h2>Lorem Ipsum</h2>
  <p>Lorem ipsum dolor sit amet, consectetuer adipiscing elit, sed
diam nonummy nibh euismod tincidunt ut laoreet dolore magna aliquam
erat volutpat. Ut wisi enim ad minim veniam, quis nostrud exerci
tation ullamcorper suscipit lobortis nisl ut aliquip ex ea commodo
consequat. Duis autem vel eum iriure dolor in hendrerit in vulputate
velit esse molestie consequat, vel illum dolore eu feugiat nulla
facilisis at vero eros et accumsan et iusto odio dignissim qui blandit
praesent luptatum zzril delenit augue duis dolore te feugait nulla
facilisi.</p>
</div>
```

One thing that might be a bit tricky about CSS exclusions is that it simply defines a shape or path for the text to flow around and not necessarily a shape or path to be rendered. In other words, the two highlighted lines of code in the previous code example are completely independent. The only reason that the two polygon definitions resemble each other closely is for visual effects. If we had used an image, a div, or any other HTML element inside that block of text, the CSS shape-outside property would still cause the text to flow around that element the same way, no matter what physical shape that element has. Simply adding a CSS shape attribute to an element will not alter its own visual properties.

Running the previous code example produces an output similar to the following screenshot. Again, remember that the relationship between the path that the text follows and the shape of the element displayed, where no text is allowed to enter, is purely coincidental and intentional. If instead of an SVG polygon we had an image element, the text would still follow that arrow shape, but the rectangular image would float on top of any text that followed a path intersecting the image's boundaries. Strictly speaking, exclusions only deal with how text flows within a given block of text. Whether anything is rendered along the path that the text follows is up to the designer, and is a separate issue from exclusions, as shown in the following screenshot:

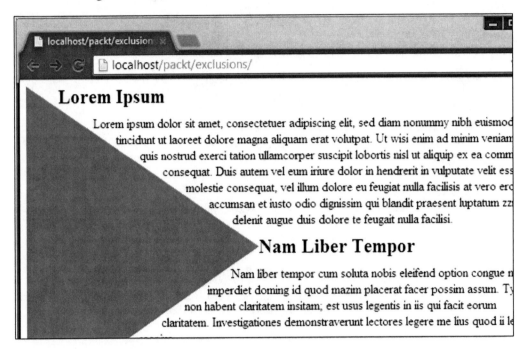

If the ultimate goal is to simply define a path for text to follow, such as in the previous example, we don't need to use SVG, or any specific HTML element. Simply having an element present and assigning basic floating attributes to that element is enough for exclusions to work with. Remember, the only significant part of exclusions is the shape attribute.

```
<style>
.shape {
  display: inline-block;
  float: left;
  width: 300px;
```

```
  height: 400px;
  shape-outside: polygon(0 0, 100% 50%, 0 100%);
}
</style>

<div>
  <span class="shape"> </span>

  <h2>Lorem Ipsum</h2>
  <p>Lorem ipsum dolor sit amet, consectetuer adipiscing elit, sed
  diam nonummy nibh euismod tincidunt ut laoreet dolore magna aliquam
  erat volutpat. Ut wisi enim ad minim veniam, quis nostrud exerci
  tation ullamcorper suscipit lobortis nisl ut aliquip ex ea commodo
  consequat. Duis autem vel eum iriure dolor in hendrerit in vulputate
  velit esse molestie consequat, vel illum dolore eu feugiat nulla
  facilisis at vero eros et accumsan et iusto odio dignissim qui blandit
  praesent luptatum zzril delenit augue duis dolore te feugait nulla
  facilisi.</p>
</div>
```

Alternatively, we can use the companion property to shape-outside, namely shape-inside. Intuitively, this property defines the opposite as its counterpart. Whereas a shape-outside property tells the browser where text needs to flow around (outside), a shape-inside property tells the browser the area where the text must stay within. All property values are the same for both attributes. The only difference between the two attributes is that in shape-outside, text is placed well outside of the placeholder element. With shape-inside, any text to be guided within the shape defined is placed as a descendant node of the shape element.

```
<style>
.shape {
  display: block;
  width: 300px;
  height: 400px;
  shape-inside: polygon(0 0, 100% 50%, 0 100%);
}
</style>

<div>
  <h2>Lorem Ipsum</h2>
  <span class="shape">
```

```
    <p>Lorem ipsum dolor sit amet, consectetuer adipiscing elit, sed
diam nonummy nibh euismod tincidunt ut laoreet dolore magna aliquam
erat volutpat. Ut wisi enim ad minim veniam, quis nostrud exerci
tation ullamcorper suscipit lobortis nisl ut aliquip ex ea commodo
consequat. Duis autem vel eum iriure dolor in hendrerit in vulputate
velit esse molestie consequat, vel illum dolore eu feugiat nulla
facilisis at vero eros et accumsan et iusto odio dignissim qui blandit
praesent luptatum zzril delenit augue duis dolore te feugait nulla
facilisi.</p>
  </span>
</div>
```

In comparison with shape-outside, the shape-inside property contains its own
contents within itself, as opposed to shape-outside, which is nothing but a block
around which its sibling elements must flow, as shown in the following screenshot:

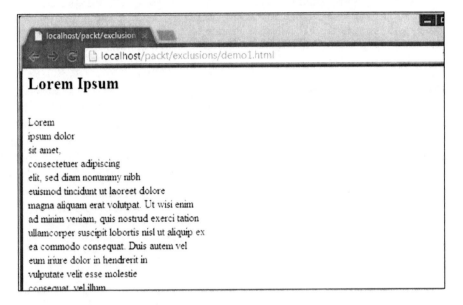

Finally, in anticipation of the question that these two properties beg to be asked, yes,
we could very well combine an exclusion that defines a shape-outside property, and
one that defines a shape-inside property. Observe that a shape-inside exclusion is
nothing more than a block level element, just like any other. Viewing the source code
of an HTML file without any CSS instructions will make a shape-inside exclusion
impossible to be told apart from an ordinary block of text. Thus, we could very well
use a shape-inside excluded element as a shape-outside exclusion. The same
element can have both CSS attributes, since their effect is mutually exclusive. Any
text inside the element would be bound to the shape-inside exclusion declaration,
whereas any content around the element would be associated with the effects of the
shape-outside attribute.

```
<style>
h2, p {
  margin: 0 0 10px;
}

#wrap {
  width: 50%;
  height: 100%;
  float: left;

  shape-inside: polygon(0 0, 100% 50%, 0 100%);
  shape-outside: polygon(0 0, 100% 50%, 0 100%);
}
</style>

<div>
  <h2>Lorem Ipsum</h2>

  <div id="wrap">
    <p>Lorem ipsum dolor sit amet, consectetuer adipiscing elit, sed
diam nonummy nibh euismod tincidunt ut laoreet dolore magna aliquam
erat volutpat. Ut wisi enim ad minim veniam, quis nostrud exerci
tation ullamcorper suscipit lobortis nisl ut aliquip ex ea commodo
consequat. Duis autem vel eum iriure dolor in hendrerit in vulputate
velit esse molestie consequat, vel illum dolore eu feugiat nulla
facilisis at vero eros et accumsan et iusto odio dignissim qui blandit
praesent luptatum zzril delenit augue duis dolore te feugait nulla
facilisi.</p>
  </div>

  <h2>Nam Liber Tempor</h2>
  <p>Nam liber tempor cum soluta nobis eleifend option congue nihil
imperdiet doming id quod mazim placerat facer possim assum. Typi non
habent claritatem insitam; est usus legentis in iis qui facit eorum
claritatem. Investigationes demonstraverunt lectores legere me lius
quod ii legunt saepius.</p>

  <h2>Claritas est etiam</h2>
  <p>Claritas est etiam processus dynamicus, qui sequitur mutationem
consuetudium lectorum. Mirum est notare quam littera gothica, quam
nunc putamus parum claram, anteposuerit litterarum formas humanitatis
per seacula quarta decima et quinta decima. Eodem modo typi, qui nunc
nobis videntur parum clari, fiant sollemnes in futurum.</p>
</div>
```

Defining shapes

Conveniently, possible values for shape properties are the same as basic SVG shapes. The four available shapes are rectangle, ellipse, circle, and polygon. Point values can be represented as length values or percentage values. The syntax for each of these shapes is very consistent and is of the form `<shape>([value]{?})`. For example:

- `rectangle(x, y, width, height)`: Defines a sharp rectangle with the top left corner of the shape being positioned at point x, y

- `rectangle(x, y, width, height, round-x, round-y)`: Defines a rectangle with the option of rounding its corners

- `ellipse(x, y, radius-x, radius-y)`: Defines an ellipse centered at point x, y

- `circle(x, y, radius)`: Defines a circle of a given radius, center at point x, y

- `polygon(p1-x p1-y, p2-x p2-y, (...))`: Defines a polygon given three or more pairs of x, y positions

Summary

This chapter presented some of the more complex and cutting edge HTML5 APIs. The major highlight was the new 3D rendering and graphics programming API—WebGL. We also took a look at HTML5's new video playback capabilities as well as the ability to manipulate each frame of a video played natively on the browser. Finally, we got our feet wet with the latest and greatest CSS improvements and additions. This involved such APIs as CSS shaders, columns, and regions and exclusions.

In the next chapter, we conclude our journey into the fascinating world of HTML5 game development by delving into mobile web development with HTML5. We will learn what makes mobile game development different from the traditional desktop application development. We will also learn two HTML5 APIs to help us along the way. The game that we will build to illustrate these concepts is a 2D space shooter that is completely mobile-friendly.

7

HTML5 and Mobile Game Development

In this last chapter we will take a look at the ever so important concept of not only developing for multiple browsers and platforms, but also of developing an application with multiple devices in mind. It used to be that web development was all about supporting multiple browsers. Then it became all about taking advantage of the latest technologies available and creating applications that resembled a native desktop application. Today, we must not only remember those same concepts that allow us to make our applications available to as many people as possible, but we must also remember that the standard desktop computer is not the only machine accessing our web applications.

While creating an HTML5-based game or application, we must be able to envision our users connecting through the desktop computer, net-books, HTML5-ready video game systems, smart phones, tables, television sets, and soon their smart watches, smart glasses, and possibly their smart toasters, fish tanks, and so on. Needless to say, there are quite a few differences between these devices, other than their size, shape, and suggested retail price.

As we develop the last game in this book, lets take a look at some of the most important concepts related to mobile game development with HTML5. We'll first look at fundamental differences between a desktop machine and a mobile device (specifically, a smart phone and a tablet). The two HTML5-related APIs discussed in the chapter are media queries (which allows us to adjust CSS properties based on the current state of the device viewing the application) and JavaScript touch events, with their corresponding event handlers. Finally, we'll conclude the chapter with a discussion on how to go about developing and optimizing a game for a desktop browser as well as a mobile device, with a single code base.

Desktop versus mobile

At first sight, the careless web developer might be led to believe that, because many of today's smart phones are in fact quite a lot smarter than most fifth graders, that their fancy web applications and games will run just fine on a mobile device. Do not be deceived! Although it is true that your smart phone is indeed smarter than you were when in fifth grade (in fact, most not-so-smart phones today have more computer power than the hardware that NASA used to take Neil A. Armstrong, Michael Collins, and Edwin E. Aldrin to the moon in 1969), it is in many instances no match to the average desktop computer from which most people surf the internet and play games online.

There are several significant differences between a desktop browser and a mobile browser. For this reason, we need to develop our applications with these differences in mind. After all, no matter how large the group of people only using the internet strictly from a mobile device or from a desktop browser, we have no reason to limit our reach to only one of those groups.

One key aspect of mobile-friendly development that we must keep in mind, which doesn't always apply to games, is that one's mobile strategy is often inherently different from a desktop strategy for reasons beyond hardware limitations and differences. For example, use case on a mobile device is substantially different than the use case on a desktop version of a journal application. Since it is much harder and slower to type on a small device, users are less likely to spend hours typing a journal entry on a phone application as opposed to its desktop counterpart, where a full-sized keyboard is available. Thus, the entire mobile experience must be considered with a different persona in mind.

Finally, because the human-computer interaction is different in a mobile device, the presentation of the application must be considered with these features in mind. For example, while navigating a website, most people would generously move the mouse cursor about the screen in an attempt to discover what can be clicked and what can be interacted with. Every time an action element is hovered, the mouse pointer changes (normally from an arrow icon to a pointing index finger) hinting to the user that an action can be initiated by clicking on such item. On a mobile device, however, no such thing exists. Thus, the design must take this into account, so that users aren't confused, intimidated, or worse yet, hesitant to use your game or application.

The rest of this section will present a few major implementation considerations for your mobile strategy as well as a couple of current best practices. Both sections apply equally well to mobile games and mobile applications (non-gaming applications, that is). Albeit not extensive, this list of considerations and best practices should be sufficient to get you thinking in the right direction, and pointed towards a successful mobile campaign.

Major implementation considerations

Perhaps the most distinguishing feature that sets a mobile device apart from a desktop computer is the fact that the mobile device is always accessible. Once the user has left his or her house, the desktop machine is parked until possibly many hours later. The mobile device, on the other hand, can be as far away from the user as his or her pocket. So at any moment, the user can pull out the mobile device and start playing your game or using your application.

Very importantly, a continuation of this always accessible use case is that a user will play your game for a very small amount of time—while waiting for the elevator, while standing in line at the store, or while trying to drown out an awkward moment during a first date. Thus, your game must accommodate these brief, very brief, playing sessions and it must do so in a way that the player can still make progress in the game while playing it in sessions of 30 to 120 seconds at a time.

Some important considerations for your mobile game that are more related to the physical nature of mobile devices include its limited screen size, the possibility to change screen orientation effortlessly, limited computing power (relative to a desktop computer, of course), limited battery power, and browser differences (no, those haven't gone away yet on mobile devices, either).

Screen size and orientation

The most obvious difference between a desktop computer and a mobile device is its size. Even though most modern devices can simulate large screen resolutions, the physical screen size is still rather limited. Not only that, but also at any moment the user can rotate the device sideways, expecting a responsive feedback of some sort from the application.

In web design in general, the standard solution to the problem of smaller and varying screen sizes is a technique called responsive design. The main tool used today to implement responsive design is the new CSS media query API (which we discuss later in the chapter). Simply put, this API allows us to load different stylesheets or sets of CSS rules based on, among other things, screen size, proportions, and orientation.

For example, we can define a CSS stylesheet for the case when the screen is wider than it is taller (which, by definition, would make it a landscape viewport) and have a second style sheet designed for the case when the screen is taller than it is wider (making it a portrait view). Media queries would allow us to automatically and dynamically load one of these two stylesheets based on the current screen state. That is, if the user was to manually resize the browser window, the style sheet would trigger in real time.

As for screen orientation changes, DOM-based web applications have it easier, because the browser itself if able to rotate everything, so it faces the right direction. On a canvas-based application (either 2D canvas or WebGL), a screen rotation also rotates the browser's coordinate system, but not the canvas'. Thus, if you want a particular game to play horizontally on a landscape view, and vertically on a portrait view, you'll need to manage the rotation of the canvas' coordinate system by hand.

Most importantly, however, is the fact that when designing a mobile-friendly, or a mobile version of a game, the screen size will be significantly smaller. That means that fewer elements can be crammed into a particular view. Less information needs to be presented, since less information can be conveyed at once.

The two common solutions to this problem are to develop one application with two separate presentation layers (or two separate views or templates), only serving the view that's appropriate to the device requesting it (serving the mobile template when a template accesses the application and the full template when a desktop browser requests the application) and developing a single application with a single template, but making this template responsive, as described previously. The less popular alternative is to develop two separate applications altogether, where each application focuses on a given paradigm (mobile and desktop).

Normally, the mobile template is a shrunk down version of the full template where not all elements are necessarily displayed, as represented by the following illustration:

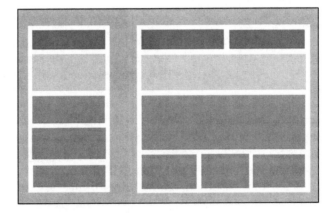

Computing power

As mentioned before, today's mobile devices have gotten quite powerful. Even more amazing is the fact that the tendency is for them to continue to improve, jamming more computing power into less physical space. However, the best smart phone today is no match against even an average power gaming PC. For most web applications, this difference can often be neglected but certainly not for more complex games.

One specific disadvantage that mobile devices have against desktop computers in this area is that the gap between the computing power of a lower-end mobile device and an average mobile device is quite large, as compared to a low-end desktop computer and a mere average one. Thus, when considering the capabilities of your game's users, remember that a large amount of those players will have very limited devices.

Battery life

Believe it or not, the most used feature of a smart phone is, well, to make and receive phone calls. With such an important function being the mobile device's primary use, it would be quite tragic to keep the device from performing such a task because a game uses up all of the device's battery power. For this reason, one very important characteristic of a mobile application (including games and mobile web applications) is how well it conserves power.

The more data the application needs to process, the more electricity it will require to do so. If the game spends much of its time performing complex calculations, it is likely to quickly drain the device's battery sooner than one would like it to. It is imperative that your mobile games use the least possible amount of power so that the player can enjoy the game as much as possible, while still saving enough battery power so that the device can serve its most fundamental purpose – to make phone calls.

Browser differences

If you thought all your browser compatibility issues would go away once you started focusing your web development efforts on mobile devices, think again. Not only are there differences between the various mobile browsers themselves (just as there are differences on their desktop counterparts), but also not every HTML5 API and feature available on a given desktop browser is available on the same browser's mobile version.

Some features are in fact available on a mobile browser, but the performance is still a very long way from being acceptable. One simple example that we will see in the game developed in this chapter is CSS animations. Depending on how creative you get with the animation, the mobile browser might have a very hard time handling the animation, while on a desktop browser the computations and rendering power needed to display the animation smoothly and consistently are quite trivial.

In summary, when defining the concrete way in which your mobile application is to be implemented, keep in mind that some APIs and features will simply have to be thrown out, lest the application performs at unacceptable levels.

Best practices

Now that you're ready to take the theory just discussed, where the rubber meets the road, let's discuss a few best practices on how to do just that. While a complete book could be dedicated to this topic, the following selection covers what I believe to be the top five most important best practices for mobile web development. Again, these concepts apply to generic web applications as well as games.

Degrade gracefully and enhance progressively

Up to a couple of years ago, any discussion about adding new and cutting edge functionality to a web application was built around the topic of graceful degradation. More recently, that ideology has shifted more towards the other end of the spectrum, where the suggested way of building multiplatform and multidevice applications is with progressive enhancement.

In this context, graceful degradation refers to building the full-blown application first (the latest and greatest desktop browser), then scaling it down so that it works on a less capable browser as well as on mobile devices. Similarly, progressive enhancement refers to building the mobile version of the application first, then making it work on the desktop browser. Whichever approach is taken, the end result is the same—one application that functions equally well on both platforms.

While much can be said about both of these approaches, in practice none is particularly better than the other. The only difference is simply where you start. Hopefully, the application is well planned for, so that each version is already envisioned before construction begins, so that starting at either end will take the application to the same place. Normally, however, the ideal approach to take depends largely on the type of project in question.

In the case of most games, as was indeed the case with the 2D space shooter game built for this chapter, it is much easier to develop the desktop version first then remove whatever functionality is not supported by, or appropriate for, mobile devices.

For example, the main rendering loop of our game is based on the new `requestAnimationFrame` function. Now, not all browsers expose this function yet, while others expose it through a different interface. Gracefully degrading this functionality would mean to use the function where available and use a fallback where it isn't available.

```
window.requestAnimationFrame = (function() {

  // Check if the unprefixed version is present
  if (window.requestAnimationFrame) {
    return window.requestAnimationFrame;
  }
```

```
// Check for WebKit based implementation
if (window.webkitRequestAnimationFrame) {
  return window.webkitRequestAnimationFrame;
}

// Check for Mozilla based implementation
if (window.mozRequestAnimationFrame) {
  return window.mozRequestAnimationFrame;
}

// Check for Microsoft based implementation
if (window.msRequestAnimationFrame) {
  return window.msRequestAnimationFrame;
}

// Check for Opera based implementation
if (window.oRequestAnimationFrame) {
  return window.oRequestAnimationFrame;
}

// If nothing else, simulate the functionality with
// something similar - a custom timer
return function(callback) {
  var fps = 1000 / 60;
  var timestamp = Date.now();

  setTimeout(function(){
    callback(timestamp);
  }, fps);
};
})();
```

On the other hand, a progressive enhancement approach would start out with the lowest common denominator first, not promising any special bells and whistles to anyone, but adding those in as permitted by the client technology.

For example, suppose we want to make extensive use of CSS animations. Specifically, we wish to use a very large image for the background, then animate its position and size continually using keyframe animation. On a mobile device, this could consume a lot of processing power, causing severe performance problems. Thus, we decide not to use these animations in such cases.

Enhancing the application progressively in this case would mean that we start out with a static image for the background. The CSS file defining the animation and applying it to the application is not loaded by default.

```
// --------------------------------
// Default Stylesheet: style.css
// --------------------------------
.background-img {
  background: url("/img/bg.png");
}


// --------------------------------
// HTML Template: template.html
// --------------------------------
<div id="container" class="background-img"></div>
```

Once that minimum functionality is in place, we can test the environment in order to determine if we should load the CSS file, injecting the more robust functionality.

```
// --------------------------------
// Enhanced Stylesheet: enhanced.css
// --------------------------------

@-webkit-keyframes animagedBg {
  from {
    background-position: 0 0;
  }
  to {
    background-position: 1300% 600%;
  }
}

.anim-background {
  -webkit-animation: animagedBg;
  -webkit-animation-duration: 500s;
  -webkit-animation-timing-function: linear;
  -webkit-animation-iteration-count: infinite;
}

// --------------------------------
// JavaScript Detection: main.js
// --------------------------------

// Returns true if the browser is mobile
```

```
function isMobile(userAgent) {
  var mobileAgents = [
    "ANDROID",
    "BLACKBERRY",
    "IPHONE",
    "IPAD",
    "IPHONE",
    "OPERA MINI",
    "IEMOBILE"
  ];

  return mobileAgents.indexOf(userAgent.toUpperCase()) >= 0;
}

var mobile = isMobile(navigator.userAgent);

// If the browser is not mobile, add enhanced CSS functionality
if (!mobile) {
  var container = document.querySelector("#container");
  container.classList.add("anim-background");
}
```

Now, it wouldn't be particularly difficult to build the game with the animated background first, then remove it when a particular device was detected. There wouldn't necessarily be any added value taking this approach either.

In summary, whatever approach makes more sense to your specific application and design goals and objectives, the key principle is to keep user experience in mind. Never present the user of your game or application with an unusable product or feature. Either downgrade the feature to something useful or upgrade it when you are sure that the user's environment can make proper use of the feature.

Finger-friendly design

Another very important design consideration that is so easy to overlook is the size of the various elements. Although making text large enough is important, this is somewhat easier to get right. Plus, text size is fairly easy to adjust dynamically, so users can tweak things until they're comfortable with the exact size of the text in your application. However, coming from the point-and-click world, where action targets are big enough if the mouse pointer can fit on top of it, we may not realize that different people have vastly different finger sizes. Nothing can possibly be more frustrating to a big-fingered user, than to miss a click target because the target is too small. When the first touch-sensitive mobile applications came out several years ago, users probably considered carrying a finger sharpener along with their device, so that those tiny touch targets could be reached.

In the following illustration, the screenshot on the left is an example of items that are too small for a user to touch, as well as items that are too close together. The better solution, as shown on the screenshot on the right, makes the interface more forgiving and harder for the user to mess up.

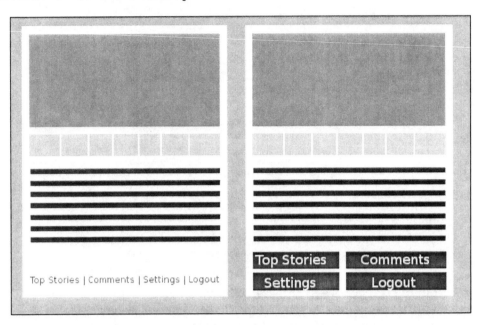

If you look at the developer guides published by the various mobile platform makers, you will find specific pixel dimensions that are suggested as the minimum size for widgets that can be touched as well as minimum distances between two or more touchable elements. While there is no perfect size of any particular widget, we must always design with this issue in mind.

Save battery life

No matter how amazing your mobile game might be, the minute that users realize that the game is rudely demanding on their device's battery, the game will immediately be frowned upon. If the user is running low on power, but they know that your game is very friendly with power consumption, your application will definitely get extra love.

Now, the main source of energy inefficiencies in mobile apps is extensive, unnecessary hardware use. For example, if an application pulls the GPS multiple times per second, it will probably run down the battery fairly quickly. However, in an HTML5 application, direct hardware access is not as readily available.

In the case of a web application, the main way to save energy is to do as much caching as possible. The main point of caching here would be to avoid extra network activity. Not only would the extra processing require more energy, but it would also force the user to spend what is often limited bandwidth. As an added bonus, caching would also make your application behave much faster.

Plan for offline

A very large amount of mobile gamers today have a limited amount of internet access from their mobile device. Any extra use of that precious data plan might be a costly deal for the user. As a result, many users actively disable internet access on their device. As a result of that, you should never make the assumption that your games will have continuous access to the internet.

Again, the best solution to this use case is to use caching to your benefit. First, by making fewer server round trips, even if each batch is larger, you will be saving expensive bandwidth that the user is trying to save. Second, the application can seem much faster and more responsive if HTTP requests are saved up for a moment when the application is not doing anything meaningful (such as displaying a game-related message or waiting for the user to input information).

Offering a desktop version

There are many reasons why a user might want to checkout a mobile application's non-mobile version. Perhaps it is because of missing functionality, maybe the user has a good enough mobile device that can actually handle the full version just fine or maybe the user wants to access the full version from a mobile device just out of curiosity. Whatever the reason, adding a link to the full-sized version of your application is perhaps the easiest thing you can do, so why not do it for the minority of users who might actually use it!

Understanding media queries

Media queries have been around since HTML4 and CSS2. Originally, the CSS media attribute was used to specify a different stylesheet to be loaded based on the media type loading the page, such as screen, TV, projection, or handheld. In HTML5, media queries also allow for expressions that check for other properties of the user agent viewing the document such as viewport width, height, resolution, and so on.

A **media query** is made up of two parts, namely a media type declaration and one or more expressions that evaluate to either true or false. Any CSS rules contained nested within the media query declaration are applied whenever any of the media query expressions evaluate to true. Alternatively, every CSS rule inside a stylesheet referenced by a link tag whose media attribute contains a **truthy** media query expression is applied to the specified media type.

```
// -------------------------------
// Media queries on the HTML file
// -------------------------------
<link rel="stylesheet"
  media="screen and (min-device-width: 960px)"
  href="default-style.css" />


// -------------------------------
// Media queries within a CSS file
// -------------------------------
@media screen and (min-device-width: 960px) {
  html, body {
    margin: 0;
    padding: 0;
  }

  /* ... */
}
```

According to the specification, a browser is expected to, but not required to, continue to evaluate the expressions in media queries and update the CSS rules as changes take place in the browser environment. In other words, if two media queries are specified in a page—one for a window with a width below a certain size and one with a width above that value—the browser is not required to load the corresponding style sheet if the user manually resizes the browser width without refreshing the page. However, since this isn't a very common use case, it should not be of much concern to web designers. Besides, most modern browsers do in fact re-evaluate media query expressions in real time.

There are nine media types that can be specified and targeted from a media query. Alternatively, the keyword all can be used to indicate all media types. The allowed media types in CSS media types are as follows:

- braille: Used for braille tactile feedback devices
- handheld: Used for handheld devices
- print: Used for printers

- projection: Used for projectors
- screen: Used for computer screens
- tty: Used for media using a fixed-pitch character grid
- tv: Used for televisions
- embossed: Used for paged braille printers
- speech: Used for speech synthesizers

The two operators that can be used to connect two or more expressions are the logical AND and OR operators, indicated by the and keyword and a comma character respectively. Additionally, the logical NOT operator can be used to negate an expression. This operator is indicated by the not keyword.

```
// Applies media queries to:
// viewport width between [200px, 450px] OR wider than or
    equals to 1200px
@media
  all and (min-width: 200px) and (max-width: 450px),
  (min-width: 1200px) {
  /* ... */
}

// Applies media queries to:
// non-printer viewport width between [200px, 450px]
// OR any media type wider than or equal to 1200px
@media
  not print and (min-width: 200px) and (max-width: 450px),
  all (min-width: 1200px) {
  /* ... */
}
```

The 13 values that can be checked inside media query expressions are width, height, device-width, device-height, orientation, aspect-ratio, device-aspect-ratio, color, color-index, monochrome, resolution, scan, and grid. So long as the expression makes sense, any combination of these values can be used in an expression. This is when some basic Boolean logic comes in handy as well as a bit of common sense.

Finally, the units that can be used along with each expression are the same as CSS units. We can use fixed units (such as pixels, centimeters, or inches) or relative units (such as percentages or ems). As a refresher, the following list describes the possible units used in CSS, and thus, in media query expressions:

- %: percentage
- in: inch

- cm: centimeter
- mm: millimeter
- em: em (1 em = height of current font size)
- ex: ex (1 ex = height of a font)
- pt: point (1 point = 1/72 inch)
- pc: pica (1 pica = 12 points)
- px: CSS pixels

The rest of this section will contain a more detailed explanation of each of the valid values used in media queries, along with examples for each.

width

When queried against a continuous media type, the value refers to the total viewport (visible window area) width of the device, including any rendered scroll bars. When queried against a paged media type, the total width measured against is the width of the output page.

Optionally, the prefixes `min` and `max` can be used with the `width` keyword, allowing us to specify ranges, rather than discrete values.

```
@media all and (min-width: 250px) {
  body {
    background: red;
  }
}

@media all and (max-width: 249px) {
  body {
    background: blue;
  }
}
```

The preceding snipped specifies two media queries that apply to all media types. When the output width is less than 250 (exclusive), the background color is set to blue. Otherwise, the background color becomes red. As is the case with most modern browsers, we can resize the browser window manually and the new CSS rules will apply automatically. Otherwise, the properties are tested and set at the time the browser renders the page the first time.

In the following illustration, the window on the left is not quite wide enough to trigger the first media query on the previous snippet, which causes the second snippet to evaluate to true. By simply resizing the browser window (which can be done by maximizing the browser or possibly by simply turning the mobile device into landscape mode), the second media query will be invalidated and the first one will become enabled.

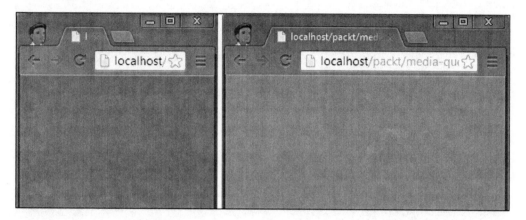

Note that the units used in the previous media query evaluation are CSS pixels. When setting special rules for media types where pixels don't apply very easily, we can use other units such as `in` (inches) or `cm` (centimeters), as seen in the following example:

```
@media print and (min-width: 7.0in) {
  h1 {
    color: red;
  }
}

@media print and (max-width: 6.5in) {
  h1 {
    color: blue;
  }
}
```

The output of the previous code snippet can be seen in the following screenshot. Note that the minimum and maximum width in question is not necessarily the width of the page in which the printing takes place, but rather the width of the box formed by the paper width minus any margins set by the printer. In this case, a sheet of paper of 8.5 inches in width, minus a single inch from the left and right margins, makes an effective width of 6.5 inches in portrait mode. The landscape version of that same page, which is 11 inches wide, produces a box width of 9 inches, which is wide enough to trigger the first media query.

The top print preview on the following screenshot represents a page being printed in portrait mode. That is, its width (in this case) is no more than 6.5 inches. The preview on the bottom is wider than 7.0 inches which causes a different media query to enable, thus changing the stylesheet settings for the page to be printed.

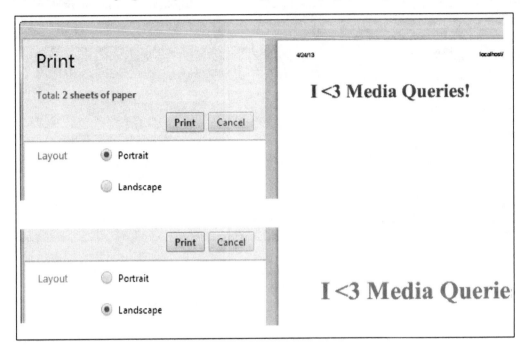

height

Similar to the `width` property, the `height` property refers to the viewport height of a continuous media type, including rendered scroll bars. For paged media types, this refers to the effective page box available to the output media. Needless to say, the value of a height property cannot be a negative unit. Again, just like the `width` property described previously, we can also add the modifier prefixes `min` and `max` to this property in order to specify ranges of values, rather than unit-perfect single values.

```
@media all and (min-height: 500px) {
  article {
    width: 100%;
    float: none;
  }
}
```

```
@media all and (max-height: 499px) {
  article {
    width: 33%;
    float: left;
  }
}
```

device-width

Similar to the `width` property, the device-width refers to the entire physical window or page, regardless of the current browser window's width or available output width of a paged media.

```
@media all and (min-device-width: 1601px) {
  h1 {
    color: red;
  }
}

@media all and (max-device-width: 1599px) {
  h1 {
    color: green;
  }
}

@media all and (device-width: 1600px) {
  h1 {
    color: blue;
  }
}
```

In the previous code example, if the screen width (not browser width) is exactly 1600px, the last media query will be active, regardless of any browser resizing. The same goes for a page—if the entire width of the page calculates to exactly 1600px wide, the corresponding media query will match. Anything more or less than that and one of the other two media queries will be used instead. Again, the keywords `min` and `max` are valid modifiers that we can use in conjunction with this property.

The answer to the question about when to choose device-width or width and vice-versa is simple: whenever the design of your application calls for it. In most cases, the end result is the same. The only time when width is more appropriate than device-width is when the user might use their browser windowing in a customized size (not maximized) and the design is intended to reflow and auto adjust to the current width of the browser. On the other hand, if a design is meant to remain the same on a certain monitor width (or range of widths) regardless of the current browser state, then device width might be a more elegant and efficient way to go about it.

device-height

Finally, the last possibility with querying the rectangular sides of a display, device-height works exactly the same as device-width (other than the size measured). Although the same result can be achieved with the other viewport queries described so far, out of the four queries described so far, device-height might be the ideal candidate (along with device-width) to identify mobile orientation (portrait or landscape).

orientation

Since media queries don't allow for comparison between two attributes (for example, if width is greater than or equal to height), orientation allows us to determine which way a media type is rotated. Had there been comparison operators included in the CSS media query engine, we could easily determine if a page was in landscape mode. To do that, we simply need to determine if the width is greater than the height. If the two sides are of the same length (a square viewport), the specification determines the media to be in portrait mode. However, since such an approach is not possible directly with media queries, we can instead use the much more intuitive orientation attribute.

The two possible values for the attribute are, with little surprise, `portrait` and `landscape`. The prefixes `min` and `max` are not allowed with this query, since it doesn't make sense to classify something as being at least landscape or no more than portrait.

```
@media all and (orientation: portrait) {
  body {
    backgroundcolor: red;
  }
}

@media all and (orientation: landscape) {
  body {
    backgroundcolor: green;
  }
}

@media all and
  not (orientation: portrait) and
  not (orientation: portrait) {
  body {
    backgroundcolor: blue;
  }
}
```

In the previous example, we check if the media is either landscape or portrait. Whatever the orientation evaluates, the media query becomes activated. Note that the third query attempts to set a third orientation based on erroneous conclusions. One might imagine that the way to determine if something is landscape or portrait is to take the ratio between the two—if the width is greater than the height then the media is in landscape mode, otherwise it is in portrait mode. You can imagine how someone might conclude that if both sides (width and height) are the same, that the orientation is neither landscape nor portrait. However, it is important to remember that a square figure is not landscape, but is indeed portrait. The key is to remember that there are only two possible values for this property, precisely because there are only two possible states that a media can be in at a time.

aspect-ratio

The aspect ratio property allows us to check for the proportion of the media's width relative to its height (in this order). This property takes into account the actual ratio between the width and height media query values, meaning that dynamic changes to the viewport width and height affect this property directly. The min and max keywords can be used in the evaluation of this property.

```
// Aspect ratio is exactly twice as high as wide
@media all and (aspect-ratio: 1/2) {
  h1 {
    color: blue;
    font-size: 1.0em;
  }
}

// Aspect ratio is at least three times as high as wide
@media all and (min-aspect-ratio: 1/3) {
  h1 {
    color: red;
    font-size: 0.5em;
  }
}

// Aspect ratio is no more than four times as wide as high
@media all and (max-aspect-ratio: 4/1) {
  h1 {
    color: green;
    font-size: 3.0em;
  }
}
```

```
// Aspect ratio is an exact square
@media all and (aspect-ratio: 1/1) {
  h1 {
    color: yellow;
    font-size: 2.0em;
  }
}

// Aspect ratio is no more than half as high as wide - ERROR!
@media all and (max-aspect-ratio: 1/0.5) {
  h1 {
    color: green;
    font-size: 3.0em;
  }
}
```

The previous code snippet demonstrates various ways to calculate aspect ratio. Keep in mind that the value of this attribute must always read as a single fraction, with no floating point numbers involved. Simply said, the value must be in the form of an integer, followed by a slash, followed by a second integer. The first integer refers to the width value and the second to the height. Together, they form a ratio.

The first media query in the previous example tests for a viewport that is exactly two width units for every one width unit. Put it another way, that expression checks for a viewport that is twice as high as it is tall or half as wide as it is wide. In contrast, the last media query attempts to generate the same result, but in reverse. The attempt there was to query a media type that was at most twice as wide as it is tall. This expression would raise a silent expression (the expression would be ignored), because the format is not appropriate. Instead of checking for 1/0.5, the proper way would be to make it 2/1, making the width length twice as large as the height.

When specifying a desired value for a media query aspect-ratio expression, the number on the left refers to the width relative to the height, which is represented by the value on the right. Both numbers must be positive integers and the larger of the two values can be on either side. Alternatively, both values can be the same, which would test for a square aspect ratio (1/1).

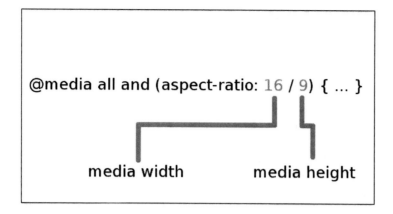

device-aspect-ratio

Checking for device-aspect-ratio works the exact same way as the aspect-ratio, as explained previously, with the only difference being that the `width` and `height` references are based on the device-width and device-height, as explained in their respective sections.

Again, as with device-width and device-height, this is a great way to check for the underlying fingerprinting of the device accessing the application, which is independent of the current state of the browser window at the time the media query is tested. As far as responding to user actions, testing for aspect-ratio might be a better solution than device-aspect-ratio as the user might change the dimensions of the browser window independently of the device-screen-ratio. However, in order to determine the device's true aspect ratio, the alternative would be to use device-aspect-ratio.

Also, keep in mind that it is quite possible to define redundant media queries when querying the aspect ratio. In a case such as this, as is the case with CSS, the last matching expression overrules previous duplicated expressions and values.

```
// Aspect ratio evaluates to 1/1
@media all and (device-aspect-ratio: 1/1) {
  h1 {
    color: blue;
    font-size: 3.0em;
  }
}

// Aspect ratio evaluates to 1/1
@media all and (device-aspect-ratio: 1/1) {
```

```
  h1 {
    color: red;
    font-size: 3.0em;
  }
}

// Aspect ratio evaluates to 1/1
@media all and (device-aspect-ratio: 2/2) {
  h1 {
    color: green;
    font-size: 0.5em;
  }
}

// Aspect ratio evaluates to 1/1
@media all and (device-aspect-ratio: 10/10) {
  h1 {
    color: purple;
    font-size: 0.5em;
  }
}

// Aspect ratio evaluates to 1/1
@media all and (device-aspect-ratio: 2000/2000) {
  h1 {
    color: orange;
    font-size: 10.5em;
  }
}

// Aspect ratio evaluates to 1/1
@media all and (device-aspect-ratio: 17/17) {
  h1 {
    color: transparent;
    font-size: 0.0em;
    display: none;
  }
}
```

The previous code example shows six media query expressions, all of which evaluate to the same aspect ratio. Whether the original expressed ratio is a duplicate of a previous value or a different value that reduces to the same ratio, the end result is the same. When equal ratios are found and no other expression breaks the tie by further qualifying the whole expression, then the last occurrence of the duplicate expression becomes the only active query for values not unique to the previous expressions. For example, if two or more expressions evaluate to the same aspect ratio, whatever CSS attributes that both expressions had in common are given priority to the last occurrence of the query. Unique values between each expression get cascaded to the final evaluation.

```
// Aspect ratio evaluates to 1/1
//   Properties set: color, font-size
//   Properties overridden: none
@media all and (device-aspect-ratio: 1/1) {
  h1 {
    color: blue;
    font-size: 1.5em;
  }
}

// Aspect ratio evaluates to 1/1
//   Properties set: color, border, padding
//   Properties overridden: color
@media all and (device-aspect-ratio: 1/1) {
  h1 {
    color: red;
    border: 1px solid green;
    padding: 20px;
  }
}

// Aspect ratio evaluates to 1/1 and anything landscape
//   Properties set: color
//   Properties overridden: color
@media all and (min-device-aspect-ratio: 1/1) {
  h1 {
    color: green;
  }
}
```

In the previous code snippet, three separate media queries evaluate to the same aspect ratio. The last query also uses a `min` modifier, meaning that it matches any aspect ratio that is not 1/1 (as well as any aspect ratio that is exactly 1/1), but the device width is still larger than the height (in other words, any media types of aspect ratio 1/1 and any media types of orientation landscape).

In this case, when a media type is `landscape` (remember a square or 1/1 aspect ratio is never considered landscape), only the third query matches the current state. Thus, only the color attribute is assigned to the `h1` tag specified in that media query. However, when the aspect ratio is in fact 1/1, then all three of media queries evaluate to true, thus all three queries are applied to the elements they specify.

The first query only sets a color of the tag to green. The second query resets that tag color and additionally applies a few more attributes to the tag. Finally, the third query again resets the tag color, but doesn't touch any other property. The final result for these composite queries for a media type with a 1/1 aspect ratio can be seen in the following code snippet.

```
@media all and (device-aspect-ratio: 1/1) {
  h1 {
    color: green;
    border: 1px solid green;
    padding: 20;
  }
}
```

color

This media query attribute checks for the number of bits per color component used by the output device. For example, if the output device uses an 8-bit color system, where it uses 2 bits to represent the red, green, blue, and alpha components, then the color attribute in the media query expression is 2. The `min` and `max` modifiers can also be used to test for this as well.

```
@media all and (color: 2) {
  h1 {
    color: green;
    border: 1px solid green;
    padding: 20;
  }
}
```

If the output device is not a color device then the value of the color attribute will be zero.

```
@media all and (color: 0) {
  h1 {
    color: green;
    border: 1px solid green;
    padding: 20;
  }
}
```

```
// This query produces the exact same result as the previous one
@media all and (min-color: 1) {
  h1 {
    color: green;
    border: 1px solid green;
    padding: 20;
  }
}
```

In some instances, where the output device uses different bit counts per color component, the color attribute refers to the smallest value of bits per component. For example, if the output device uses an 8-bit color system and it uses 3 bits for the red component, 3 for the green component, and 2 for the blue component then the value used as the color attribute for the media query will be 2.

color-index

The `color-index` attribute returns the number of colors used by the output device. For example, a device with 256 colors would match the following media query exactly:

```
@media all and (color-index: 256) {
  h1 {
    color: green;
    border: 1px solid green;
    padding: 20;
  }
}
```

As with the color attribute, values specified for the color-index attribute cannot be negative. Also, if the output device does not use a color lookup table, the value for color-index is zero.

monochrome

If an output device is monochrome, this media query attribute refers to the number of bits per pixel used by device. This is similar to color, but only applies to monochrome devices and, for obvious reasons, only for a single pixel, as opposed to the lowest color component.

```
@media all and (monochrome: 1) {
  h1 {
    color: black;
    border: 1px solid black;
    padding: 20;
  }
}
```

If the device is not monochrome, this attribute will match a value of zero. Also, we can use the `min` and `max` modifier keyword to target ranges. Alternatively, a single Boolean expression can be used to determine whether the device is monochrome or not.

```
@media not all and (monochrome) {
  h1 {
    color: red;
    border: 1px solid purple;
    padding: 20;
  }
}

// This query produces the exact same result as the previous one
@media all and (color) {
  h1 {
    color: red;
    border: 1px solid purple;
    padding: 20;
  }
}
```

resolution

Contrary to what one might be led to believe, the resolution attribute does not query the screen resolution as in the resolution we can set to our monitor through the operating system. Instead, the resolution attribute queries the pixel density (or dot density in the case of a printer) measured in dpi (dots per inch or pixels per inch) as well as dpcm (dots or pixels per centimeter).

```
@media all and (resolution: 300dpi) {
  h1 {
    color: black;
    border: 1px solid black;
    padding: 20;
  }
}
```

The `min` and `max` modifiers are valid in this query expression. If the output device does not use square pixels, using `min-resolution` queries against the least dense dimension of the output device. When a `max-resolution` query is issued, the most dense dimension of the output device is used to evaluate the expression.

scan

When rendering on a television, the scan attribute queries the scanning of the device. The only possible values are `progressive` and `interlace`. Using the `min` and `max` modifiers does not make sense in the context of a television's scan process and thus makes an invalid expressions.

```
@media all and (scan: interlace) {
  h1 {
    color: black;
    border: 1px solid black;
    padding: 20;
  }
}

@media all and (scan: progressive) {
  h1 {
    color: red;
    border: 1px solid red;
    padding: 20;
  }
}
```

grid

A grid output device is one that is not a bitmap-based device. Querying the `grid` attribute returns true when the output device is not bitmap-based. The only possible values to query against are 1 and 0. The `min` and `max` modifiers are not valid in this query.

Examples of grid-based devices include any device that uses a character grid, such as those older calculators or even older model cell phones with fixed fonts.

```
// Evaluates to true on grid-based devices
@media all and (grid) {
  h1 {
    color: black;
    border: 1px solid black;
    padding: 20;
  }
}

// Evaluates to true on grid-based devices
@media all and (grid: 1) {
  h1 {
    color: black;
```

```
      border: 1px solid black;
      padding: 20;
  }
}

// Evaluates to true on bitmap-based devices
@media all and (grid: 0) {
  h1 {
    color: black;
    border: 1px solid black;
    padding: 20;
  }
}

// Evaluates to true on bitmap-based devices
@media not all and (grid) {
  h1 {
    color: black;
    border: 1px solid black;
    padding: 20;
  }
}
```

Understanding touch events

Although similar in nature to an ordinary mouse click, a touch event allows us
to interact with the computer primarily through a point and respond manner.
However, touches are far more flexible than clicks and thus open up the stage for a
whole new type of game.

Fundamentally, a touch is different than a click in that more than one touch is possible
on the same surface, at the same time. Also, a touch is generally different than a click
in that it allows for a larger target area as well as varying pressure. I say generally
because not all devices detect the touch area with high precision (or with any precision
at all) or touch pressure. Similarly, some mouse or other equivalent input devices
actually do offer pressure sensitivity, although most browsers don't have use of such a
feature, neither do they expose that data through a click event object.

For compatibility purposes, most mobile browsers respond to touch events
when JavaScript code expects a touch. In other words, a click handler can
be triggered by the user touching the screen. In this case, a regular click
event object is passed to the registered `callback` function and not a touch
event object. Furthermore, the experience might differ between a drag
event (the `dragMove` event) and a touch move event. Finally, multiple
touches may or may not trigger simultaneous click event listeners.

There are three events related to touch, namely touch start, touch move, and touch end. Touch start and touch end can be related to the mouse down and mouse up events respectively, while a touch move event is similar to a drag move event.

touchstart

This event is triggered when the touch area detects a new touch, whether or not one or more touch events have already started and have not yet ended.

```
document.body.addEventListener("touchstart", doOnTouchStart);

function doOnTouchStart(event) {
  event.preventDefault();

  // ...
}
```

The object passed into the registered `callback` function is an instance of the `TouchEvent` class, which contains the following attributes:

touches

An instance of the `TouchList` class which looks like an ordinary array and contains a list of all touches that have been touched down on the touch device and have not yet been removed, even if other active touches have moved about the screen or input device. Each element in this list is an instance of type `Touch`.

changedTouches

An instance of the `TouchList` class containing a list of touch objects representing all new touch points that have been introduced since the last touch event. For example, if two touch objects have already been detected (in other words, two fingers have been pressed against the touch device) and a third touch is detected, only this third touch is present in this touch list. Again, every touch-related element contained by this touch list is of type `Touch`.

targetTouches

An instance of the `TouchList` class containing a list of touch objects representing all touch points that have been captured by a given DOM node. For example, if multiple touches have been detected throughout the screen but a particular element registered for a touch start event and captured this event (either from the capture or bubble stage), only touch events captured by this node will be present in this touch list. Again, every touch-related element contained by this touch list is of type `Touch`.

touchend

Similar to a mouse up event, a `touchend` event is fired when any of the registered touch events leave the input touch device.

```
document.body.addEventListener("touchend", doOnTouchEnd);

function doOnTouchEnd(event) {
  event.preventDefault();

  // ...
}
```

Just like a `touchstart` event, the object passed into the registered `callback` function is an instance of the `TouchEvent` class, which contains the same three `TouchList` attributes. The context of the `touches` and `targetTouches` attributes are the exact same as their version found in `touchstart`. However, the `changedTouches` touch list has a slightly different meaning in this event.

Although the `TouchList` object inside a `touchend` event is the exact same as the one in `touchstart`, the list of touch objects contained here represents touches that have left the touch input device.

touchmove

The `touchmove` event, analogous to a `drag` event, is fired whenever at least one of the registered touch objects changes position without triggering a `touchend` event. As we'll soon see each touch object is uniquely tracked so that it is possible to determine if any of the registered touch objects have moved and which ones have actually displaced.

```
document.body.addEventListener("touchmove", doOnTouchMove);

function doOnTouchMove(event) {
  event.preventDefault();

  // ...
}
```

Again, just like a `touchend` event, the object passed into the registered `callback` function is an instance of the `TouchEvent` class, which contains the same three `TouchList` attributes. The context of the `touches` and `targetTouches` attributes are the exact same as their version found in `touchstart`. The touch objects in the `changedTouches` list in the `touchmove` event represent previously registered touches that have moved about the input device.

One important thing about the touchmove event is that it can be associated with a drag event. If you notice, the default behavior for a drag event is to scroll the page in the direction of the scroll. In some applications involving dragging across the screen with a finger, this behavior may not be desired. For this reason, the event. preventDefault() method is called, which produces the effect of alerting the browser that no scrolling is desired. If, however, the intention is to scroll the screen with a touchmove event, provided that the element being touched supports such behavior, this can be accomplished by omitting the call to the prevent default function.

The touch object

Now, you may have noticed that each TouchList object holds instances of a very specific object which is an instance of the Touch class. This is important because the input device needs to keep track of individual touches. Otherwise, the list of changedTouches would not be accurate thus limiting what we can accomplish with the API.

The way that each touch can be uniquely identified is by having the input device assign a unique ID to each event it captures. This ID remains the same for the same touch object until that object is released (in other words, when that particular touch leaves the input device).

Lets take a look at all the other properties of the Touch class and see what other important information is contained therein.

identifier

A unique integer identifier for a particular touch event contained in the current touches TouchList. This number remains the same until a touch event leaves the input device, which allows us to track each touch individually even if many other touch objects are starting, moving, and ending while the one particular touch object can be singled out and kept appropriately.

Note that sometimes the value of this attribute may match the array index value of the touch object within a TouchList object. Sometimes the identifier property might even match the order in which each touch was detected by the input device. As an attentive programmer, you must never assume that these two values will always be the same.

For example, suppose that the first time a touch is detected by the device it has an identifier ID of zero (and since this is the first touch in the **TouchList**, it will obviously be indexed into the list with an index value of zero). Now a second touch is detected, making it the second object in the **TouchList** array, which would give it an index key of one. Suppose this touch also receives an identifier of one so that all three values match (touch order, array order, and identifier value). Now, after moving these two touches around the input device, suppose the first touch object is released and a new touch event is detected. Now there are again two touch objects in the **TouchList**, but their values are completely different than the first two touch elements. While the second touch event still has the same identifier (in this example, the identifier was one), it's now (possibly) the first element in the **TouchList**.

Although at times the order in which a touch is detected, the touch's position in the **TouchList** array, and the touch's unique identifier number may all match (assuming that the input device even assigns specific identifier values), you should never use any of these assumptions to track individual touches. A touch should always be tracked by its unique identifier attribute when more than one touch is being tracked. If only a single touch is tracked, that touch will always be the first element in the TouchList object.

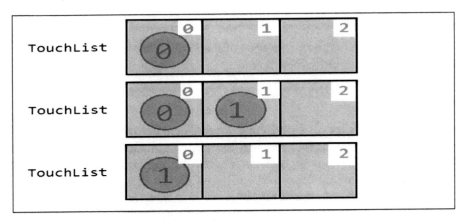

In summary, the order in which touches are detected and assigned to the TouchList object is unpredictable and should never be assumed. The proper way to track individual touch objects is through the identifier property assigned to each object. Once a touch event is released, the value of its former identifier property can be reassigned to a consequent touch, so be sure to keep that in mind as well.

screenX

The `screenX` coordinate refers to the point in the browser viewport that was touched relative to the origin of the system display. The origin of the browser's viewport is not taken into account in this calculation at all. Point (0, 0) is the upper left corner of the monitor, and however many pixels to the right of it is touched, that's where this attribute will refer.

screenY

The `screenY` coordinate refers to the point down from the system's screen (monitor), independent of where the browser is relative to that. If the screen is, say, 800 pixels in height and the browser is set up with a height of, say, 100 pixels located exactly 100 pixels below the top of the screen, then at touch a the half-way point between the browser's viewport's top and bottom left corners would result in the touch's `screenY` coordinate being 150.

Think about it, the browser's viewport has 100 pixels in height so that it's midpoint is exactly 50 pixels below its origin. If the browser is exactly 100 pixels below the screen's origin, that midpoint is 150 pixels below the screen's vertical origin.

The `screenX` and `screenY` attributes almost look like they don't take the browser's coordinate system into account whatsoever. With that, since the origin the browser bases its calculations off of its screen's origin, then it follows that a point returned by `screenX` and `screenY` will never be less than zero, since there is no way we can touch a point outside the screen's surface area and still have the screen detect that point.

clientX

Similar to `screenX`, `clientX` coordinate refers to the offset from a touch location from the browser's viewport's origin, independent of any scrolling within the page. In other words, since the origin of the browser's viewport is its upper left corner, a touch 100 pixels to the right of that point corresponds to a `clientX` value of 100. Now, if the user scrolls that page, say, 500 pixels to the right, then a touch to the right of the browser's left border by 100 pixels would still result in a `clientX` value of 100, even though the touch occurred at point 600 within the page.

clientY

The `clientY` coordinate refers to the point down from the browser's viewport origin, independent of where within the page the touch occurred. If the page scrolls an arbitrary amount of pixels to the right and to the bottom and a touch is detected at the very first pixel to the right of the upper left corner of the browser's viewport and exactly one pixel down, the `clientY` value would be calculated as 1.

The `clientX` and `clientY` attributes don't take the web page's coordinate system into account whatsoever. With that, because this point is calculated relative to the browser's frame, it follows that a point returned by `clientX` and `clientY` will never be less than zero since there is no way we can touch a point outside the browser's viewport surface area and still have the browser detect that point.

pageX

Finally, the coordinate represented by `pageX` refers to the point within the actual page where the touch was detected. In other words, if a browser is only, say, 500 pixels wide but the application is 3000 pixels wide (meaning that we can scroll the application's content to the right by 2500 pixels), a touch detected exactly 2000 pixels from the browser's viewport's origin would result in a `pageX` value of 2000.

In the world of gaming, a better name for `pageX` would probably be `worldCoordinateX` since the touch takes into account where within the world the touch event took place. Of course, this only works when the web page physically scrolls, not when a representation of a scroll has taken place. For example, say we render a world onto a 2D canvas and the world is actually much larger than the width and height of the canvas element. If we scroll the virtual map by an arbitrary amount of pixels but the canvas element itself never actually moved, then the `pageX` value will be meaningless with respect to the game's map's offset.

pageY

And to conclude, the `pageY` coordinate refers to the point where the touch was detected below the browser's viewport's origin, plus any scrolled offsets. As with the other touch point locations, it is impossible to obtain a negative value for the `pageX` and `pageY` attributes since there is no way to touch a point in the page that has not been scrolled to yet, especially a point behind the origin of the page where we cannot ever scroll to.

The following illustration shows the difference between screen, client, and page location. The screen location refers to the location within the screen (not browser window), with the origin being the upper left corner of the display. Client location is similar to screen location, but places the origin at the top left corner of the browser viewport. Even if the browser is resized and moved half way across the screen, the first pixel to the right of the browser viewport will be point (0, 0). Page location is similar to client location but takes into account any scrolling within the browser viewport. If the page is scrolled down 100 pixels vertically and none horizontally, the first pixel to the right of the left margin of the browser viewport will be (100, 1).

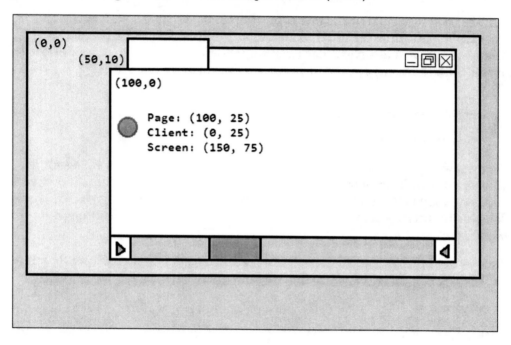

radiusX

When a touch is detected by the input device, an ellipse is drawn around the touch area by the input device. The radius of that ellipse can be accessed through the radiusX and radiusY attributes, hinting at how much area is covered by the touch. Keep in mind that the accuracy of the ellipse that describes the area touched is determined by the device used, so mileage may vary greatly here.

radiusY

In order to get the radius across the horizontal axis of the ellipse formed by the touch detected by the input device, we can use the `radiusY` attribute. With that information, we can add an extra depth to the types of applications we can create using touch as input.

As an example application, the following code snippet detects as many touches as the input device can handle simultaneously, keeping track of the radius of each touch, then displaying each touch at its approximate size.

First, we need to set up the document viewport to be the same width and height as the device as well as set initial zoom levels. We also want to disable pinching gestures, because in this particular sample application, we want that gesture to act as any other touch movement and not have any special meaning.

```
<meta name="viewport"
  content="width=device-width, initial-scale=1.0,

    user-scalable=no" />
```

The meta viewport tag allows us to define specific width and height values for the viewport, or use the optional device-width and device-height attributes. If only a width or height value is specified, the other is inferred by the user agent. The tag also allows us to specify a default zoom level as well as disable zooming through gestures or other means.

Next, we need to make sure the root DOM node in the application stretches the entire width and height of the display so that we can capture all touch events within it.

```
<style>
body, html {
  width: 200%;
  height: 100%;
  margin: 0;
  padding: 0;
  position: relative;
  top: 0;
  left: 0;
}

div {
  position: absolute;
  background: #c00;
  border-radius: 100px;
}
</style>
```

We set the body tag to be as wide as the viewport and remove any margin and padding from it so that touches near the edge of the screen would not be missed by the element's event handling. We also style the div elements to look round, have a red background color, and be absolutely positioned so that we can place one anywhere a touch is detected. We could have used a canvas element instead of rendering multiple div tags to represent each touch but that is an insignificant detail for this demo.

Finally, we get down to the JavaScript logic of the application. To summarize the structure of this demonstration, we simply use a global array where each touch is stored. Whenever any touch event is detected on the document, we flush that global array that keeps track of each touch, create a div element for each active touch, and push that new node to the global array. At the same time as this is happening, we use a request animation frame look to continuously render all the DOM nodes contained in the global touches array.

```javascript
// Global array that keeps track of all active touches.
// Each element of this array is a DOM element representing
   the location
// and area of each touch.
var touches = new Array();

// Draw each DOM element in the touches array
function drawTouches() {
  for (var i = 0, len = touches.length; i < len; i++) {
    document.body.appendChild(touches[i]);
  }
}


// Deletes every DOM element drawn on screen
function clearMarks() {
  var marks = document.querySelectorAll("div");

  for (var i = 0, len = marks.length; i < len; i++) {
    document.body.removeChild(marks[i]);
  }
}


// Create a DOM element for each active touch detected by the
// input device. Each node is positioned where the touch was
// detected, and has a width and height close to what the device
// determined each touch was
```

```
function addTouch(event) {
  // Get a reference to the touches TouchList
  var _touches = event.touches;

  // Flush the current touches array
  touches = new Array();

  for (var i = 0, len = _touches.length; i < len; i++) {
    var width = _touches[i].webkitRadiusX * 20;
    var height = _touches[i].webkitRadiusY * 20;

    var touch = document.createElement("div");
    touch.style.width = width + "px";
    touch.style.height = height + "px";
    touch.style.left = (_touches[i].pageX - width / 2) + "px";
    touch.style.top = (_touches[i].pageY - height / 2) + "px";

    touches.push(touch);
  }
}

// Cancel the default behavior for a drag gesture,
// so that the application doesn't scroll.
document.body.addEventListener("touchmove", function(event) {
  event.preventDefault();
});

// Register our function for all the touch events we want to track.
document.body.addEventListener("touchstart", addTouch);
document.body.addEventListener("touchend", addTouch);
document.body.addEventListener("touchmove", addTouch);

// The render loop
(function render() {
  clearMarks();
  drawTouches();

  requestAnimationFrame(render);
})();
```

An example of multi touch taking into account the radius of each touch is illustrated as follows. By touching the side of a closed fist to a mobile device, we can see how each part of the hand that touches the screen is detected with their relative size and area of contact.

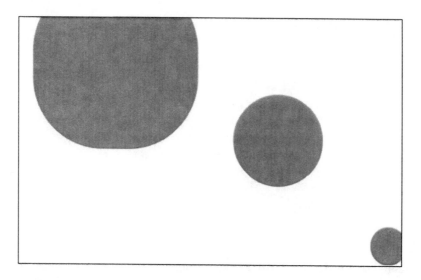

rotationAngle

Depending on the way a touch is detected, the ellipse that represents the touch might be rotated. The `rotationAngle` attribute associated with each touch object is the clockwise angle in degrees that rotates the ellipse to most closely match the touch.

force

Some touch devices are capable of detecting the amount of pressure applied to the surface of the input surface by the user. When this is the case, the force attribute represents that pressure with a variable between 0.0 and 1.0, where 1.0 represents the maximum pressure that the device can handle. When a device doesn't support force sensitivity, this attribute will always return 1.0.

Since the value of the force attribute is always between zero and one, we can conveniently use this to render elements with a varying degree of opacity (with zero being a completely transparent—invisible—element and one being completely rendered).

```
var width = _touches[i].webkitRadiusX * 20;
var height = _touches[i].webkitRadiusY * 20;
var force = _touches[i].webkitForce;

var touch = document.createElement("div");
touch.style.width = width + "px";
touch.style.height = height + "px";
touch.style.left = (_touches[i].pageX - width / 2) + "px";
touch.style.top = (_touches[i].pageY - height / 2) + "px";
touch.style.opacity = force;

touches.push(touch);
```

target

When a touch event is detected, the DOM element, where the touch was first detected, is referenced through the `target` attribute. Since a touch object is tracked until the touch ends, the target attribute will reference the original DOM element where the touch was first started for the duration of the touch life cycle.

The game

As we discussed at the beginning of this chapter, there are several considerations that must be kept in mind when designing and building a game to be played on a mobile device as well as on a desktop browser. As we write this final game in this book, we will apply those principles and best practices making a game to be playable on both a mobile device and an HTML5-ready browser.

The approach taken in this particular project is to design for desktop first then add mobile-specific APIs and functionality later. The number one reason for this decision was because it is much easier to test and debug an application on a desktop browser using existing tools and common practices, then add the things needed to make the code run smoothly on mobile as well.

The final game is a traditional two-dimensional space shooter, where the player controls a single ship that can move around the screen and always shoots up in the same direction. Random enemy space ships come from all sides of the screen, attempting to hit the player's ship, thus giving damage to the player's ship until it explodes.

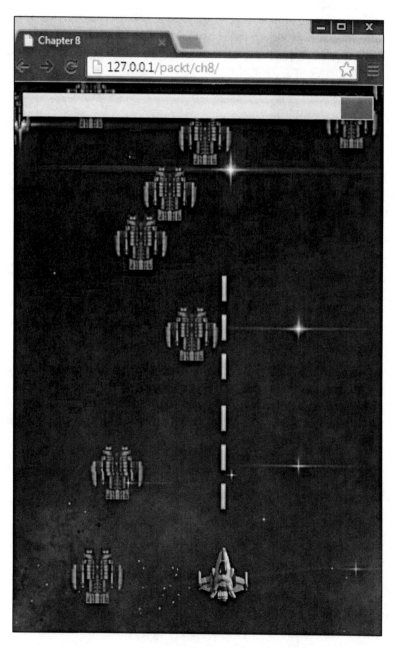

Code structure

Given the complexity of this game, the structure of the code has to be carefully considered. For simplicity, we will use a component-based approach so that adding feature upon feature is much easier, especially when it comes down dynamically adding the input handling mechanism. Since the game needs to be played equally well on a mobile device as well as on a desktop (in other words, the game needs to take and handle mouse and keyboard input as well as touch input, depending on the environment in which it is played), being able to add a specific component to the game on the fly is a very important feature.

If you're not familiar with component-based game development, don't worry too much about it. The general idea of component-based development is to separate each piece of functionality from a class and make that functionality its own class. What this allows us to do is to create individual objects that represent individual pieces of functionality, such as moving, rendering, and so on.

The final project structure for this game is as follows, where the list of files and directories shows the root of the project folder:

/css

This is where the single stylesheet file is stored. This stylesheet defines all the styling for both the desktop and mobile versions, although there are very few differences between the two. The way to add CSS features to a version of the game is to declare these features inside CSS classes then assign those classes to DOM elements when appropriate.

The first thing we want to declare in this stylesheet is the viewport, making sure that every pixel within the screen is part of the document, so that we can capture input events everywhere on our document. We also want to keep the document from somehow growing larger than the viewport which would introduce scrollbars to the game, which in this case is not desired.

```
body, html {
  width: 100%;
  height: 100%;
  margin: 0;
  padding: 0;
  overflow: hidden;
}

body {
  background: url("../img/space-bg-01.jpg") repeat;
}
```

Two features that we want in our game, if the device running it supports it, are transitioned effects of DOM elements as well as animating the background image. In order to add that functionality only where appropriate (for example, adding this feature to some mobile devices might slow down the game play to unplayable levels, given the amount of processing the mobile browser would need to do in order to produce the CSS animation and transitions), we create the CSS animation and add it to a custom class. When we determine that the device can handle the animation, we simply add the class to the document.

```
/**
 * Make the background image continually move up and to the left,
 * giving the illusion that the game world is scrolling at an
   angle.
 */
@-webkit-keyframes NebulaBg {
  from {
    background-position: 0 0;
  }
  to {
    background-position: 1300% 600%;
  }
}


/**
 * Add the animation to this class, and add a transition
 * to any box-shadow applied to whatever element this class is
   attached to.
 */
.animBody {
  -webkit-transition: box-shadow 8s;

  -webkit-animation: NebulaBg;
  -webkit-animation-duration: 500s;
  -webkit-animation-timing-function: linear;
  -webkit-animation-iteration-count: infinite;
}
```

Finally, in order to simplify some of the game user interface, we create some of the game elements as ordinary DOM elements, as opposed to rendering equivalent elements directly in the canvas where the rest of the game is rendered.

The only game element we're building as a DOM element is the energy bar for the player's ship, which indicates how much energy the ship has left. This energy bar is composed of a container element containing a `div` element inside of it. The width of this nested `div` represents the amount of energy the player has left, which can be a value between 0-100%.

```
.energyBar {
  position: absolute;
  top: 2%;
  left: 4%;
  z-index: 99999;
  width: 92%;
  height: 25px;
  border: 1px solid #ff5;
  background: #c00;
  overflow: hidden;
}

.energyBar div {
  background: #ff5;
  height: 100%;
  width: 100%;
  -webkit-transition: width 0.2s;
}
```

/img

Inside this folder we store all the image assets used in the game. Since all of these images are rendered inside a canvas, we could have very well combined all of the images into a single image atlas. This would be a very nice optimization, especially as the game grows and the number of image assets grows. Since most browsers limit the number of parallel HTTP requests that an application makes to the same server, we can only fetch a limited amount of images at the same time. This means that if there are too many individual image files being fetched from the same server, the first 4-8 requests are processed (the default number of parallel connections to the same server varies from browser to browser but is usually around 6 or so) while the rest of them wait in a queue.

Thus, it is easy to see how creating a single image atlas asset is a much better choice over downloading multiple individual image files. Even if the total image file size of the atlas is greater than the total size of all the other images combined, the big gain is in the transfer latency. Even if the game doubles in individual image assets at some point in time, we would still only have to download a single image atlas (or a few separate atlases which can all be downloaded simultaneously).

Since not everybody is highly talented when it comes to creating awesome looking graphics for your games and even fewer people have the time to create each image to be used in the game. Many game developers find it worthwhile to buy graphics from digital artists.

In this game, all of the graphics were downloaded from websites where artists share their creations for free or very low costs. The website address to this wonderful community is http://opengameart.org.

/js

As mentioned earlier, this game is built on a component-based model. The file structure is divided into four main categories; namely components, entities, widgets, and general purpose code. Each of these pieces of code are meant to be somewhat generic and reusable. The gluing together of all these pieces is done in a file called main.js.

/components

The components directory is where we store all of the components used in the game. In the context of game development, a component is a very specific class that may contain its own data and performs a very specific function. For example, when designing a class to represent the player, instead of having this class handle the rendering of the player's ship, moving, performing collision detection, and so on, we can break down each piece of functionality from this class into many individual smaller classes—or components.

Commonly, each component in your game implements a common interface so we can take advantage of object-oriented techniques. Although classical inheritance and other object-oriented techniques can be simulated in JavaScript, we simply copy the same base interface for each component and make the assumption in our client code that every component follows the same interface.

```
// Namespace the component in order to keep the global namespace
  clean
var Packt = Packt || {};
Packt.Components = Packt.Components || {};

Packt.Components.Component = function(entity) {
  var entity = entity;

  this.doSomething = function() {
};
```

Every component in this game has two things in common. They all live within the `Pack.Components` object simulating a package-based structure and they all hold a reference to the parent entity that uses the service provided by the component.

The first component that we'll create will be the `sprite` component, which is responsible for rendering an entity. As we'll see in our discussion about entities, an entity only keeps track of its own position in the game world and has no notion of its width and height. For this reason, the `sprite` component also keeps track of the entity's physical size as well as the image that represents the entity visually.

```
var Packt = Packt || {};
Packt.Components = Packt.Components || {};
Packt.Components.Sprite = function
  (pEntity, pImgSrc, pWidth, pHeight) {
  var entity = pEntity;
  var img = new Image();
  img.src = pImgSrc;

  var width = pWidth;
  var height = pHeight;
  var sWidth = pWidth;
  var sHeight = pHeight;
  var sX = 0;
  var sY = 0;
  var ctx = null;

  // Inject the canvas context where the rendering of the entity
  // managed by this component is done
  function setCtx(context) {
    ctx = context;
  }

  // Public access to the private function setCtx
  this.setCtx = setCtx;

  // If the image used to render the entity managed by this
    component
  // is part of an atlas, we can specify the specific region
  // within the atlas that we want rendered
  this.setSpriteCoords = function(x, y, width, height) {
    sX = x;
    sY = y;
    sWidth = width;
    sHeight = height;
  };
```

```
// Render the entity
this.update = function() {
  if (ctx && entity.isActive()) {
    var pos = entity.getPosition();
    ctx.drawImage(img, sX, sY, sWidth, sHeight, pos.x, pos.y,
      width, height);
  }
};

// Return both values at once, instead of using two getter
   functions
this.getSize = function() {
  return {
    width: width,
    height: height
  };
};
};
```

Once the functionality to render an entity is in place, we can now move on to adding a component to allow the player to move the entity about the screen. Now, the whole point of using components is to allow for maximum code reuse. In our case, we want to reuse the component that makes a player move so that we can have each enemy ship move about the game world using the same functionality.

To make the entity move, we use a very standard Move component which moves the entity based on its direction vector and a constant speed at which the entity is to move in this given direction. The Vec2 data type is a custom general purpose class discussed later in the chapter. Basically, this class represents a vector where it holds two variables representing the two components of a vector and defines a very handy function to normalize the vector when needed.

```
var Packt = Packt || {};
Packt.Components = Packt.Components || {};

Packt.Components.Move = function(entity, speed) {
  var entity = entity;
  var speed = speed;
  var direction = new Packt.Vec2(0, 0);

  // Move the entity in the direction it is facing by a constant
     speed
```

```
    this.update = function() {
      var pos = entity.getPosition();
      direction.normalize();

      var newPos = {
        x: pos.x + direction.get("x") * speed,
        y: pos.y + direction.get("y") * speed
      };

      entity.setPosition(newPos);
    };

    // Allow the input mechanism to tell the entity where to move
    this.setDirection = function(x, y) {
      direction.set(x, y);
    };
  };
```

Now, the way that both a player and an enemy can use this same Move component to move their entities is slightly different. In the case of an enemy, we can simply create some raw artificial intelligence to set the direction of the enemy's entity every so often and the Move component takes care of updating the entity's position as needed.

In order to make the player's ship move, however, we want the player himself or herself to tell the entity where to go. To accomplish this, we simply create an input component that listens for human input. However, since the player might be playing this game from a device that may support either mouse events or direct touch events, we need to create two separate components to handle each case.

These components are identical in every way, except for the fact that one registers for mouse events and the other for touch events. While this could have been done inside a single component, and conditional statements dictated which events to listen for instead, we opted for separate components in order to make the code less coupled to any particular device.

```
    var Packt = Packt || {};
    Packt.Components = Packt.Components || {};

    Packt.Components.TouchDrag = function(entity, canvas) {
      var entity = entity;
      var canvas = canvas;
      var isDown = false;
      var pos = entity.getPosition();
```

```
canvas.getCanvas().addEventListener
  ("touchstart", doOnTouchDown);
canvas.getCanvas().addEventListener("touchend", doOnTouchUp);
canvas.getCanvas().addEventListener("touchmove", doOnTouchMove);

// Set a isDown flag on the entity, indicating that the player
  is currently
// touching the entity that is to be controlled
function doOnTouchDown(event) {
  event.preventDefault();
  var phy = entity.getComponent("physics");
  var touch = event.changedTouches;

  if (phy) {
    isDown = phy.collide(touch.pageX, touch.pageY, 0, 0);
  }
}


// Whenever the player releases the touch on the screen,
// we must unset the isDown flag
function doOnTouchUp(event) {
  event.preventDefault();
  isDown = false;
}


// When the player drags his/her finger across the screen,
// store the new touch position if and only if the player
// is actually dragging the entity
function doOnTouchMove(event) {
  event.preventDefault();
  var touch = event.changedTouches;

  if (isDown) {
    pos.x = touch.pageX;
    pos.y = touch.pageY;
  }
}


// Reposition the player's entity so that its center is placed
// right below the player's finger
this.centerEntity = function() {
  if (isDown) {
    var sprite = entity.getComponent("sprite");
```

```
        if (sprite) {
          var size = sprite.getSize();
          var x = pos.x - size.width / 2;
          var y = pos.y - size.height / 2;

          entity.setPosition({x: x, y: y});
        }
      }
    };

    this.getPosition = function() {
      return pos;
    };
  };
```

Next, let's look at a very crucial component of any game with moving entities, namely the `physics` components whose sole responsibility in life is to tell if two entities collide. This is done in a very simple and efficient fashion. In order for an entity to be able to use the `physics` component, it must also have a `sprite` component since the `physics` component needs to know where each entity is located as well as how tall and wide each entity is. With a `sprite` component, we're able to extract both pieces of information about each entity.

The way to check whether two entities collide is very simple. The component itself stores a reference to an entity so the function that performs the check needs to know the position and size of the entity we're checking against for collision. Once we have the location and dimensions of both entities, we simply check if one entity's right side is to the left of the other's left side, if one's left side is to the right of the other's right side, or if one's bottom is above the other's top, and if one's top is below the other entity's bottom. If any of these tests passes (in other words, the conditional check returns positive) then we know that there is no collision, since it is impossible for two rectangles to be intersecting each other, and yet any of those four statements are true about them. Similarly, if all of those tests fail, we know that the entities are intersecting each other and a collision has occurred.

```
var Packt = Packt || {};
Packt.Components = Packt.Components || {};

Packt.Components.Physics = function(entity) {
  var entity = entity;

  // Check if these two rectangles are intersecting
  this.collide = function(x, y, w, h) {
    var sprite = entity.getComponent("sprite");
```

```
      if (sprite) {
        var pos = entity.getPosition();
        var size = sprite.getSize();

        if (pos.x > x + w) {
          return false;
        }

        if (pos.x + size.width < x) {
          return false;
        }

        if (pos.y > y + h) {
          return false;
        }

        if (pos.y + size.height < y) {
          return false;
        }

        return true;
      }

      return false;
    };

    // Return the entity's location and dimensions
    this.getBodyDef = function() {
      var pos = entity.getPosition();
      var sprite = entity.getComponent("sprite");
      var size = sprite.getSize() || {width: 0, height: 0};

      return {
        x: pos.x,
        y: pos.y,
        width: size.width,
        height: size.height
      };
    };
  };
};
```

The last two components used in the game are very simple and are slightly more unique to this particular type of game than the other components. These components are the Strength component and the LaserGun component, which gives entities the ability to shoot laser beams at other entities.

The `Strength` component isolates the management of the player's own energy as well as all enemy ships and everybody's lasers. This component is used to determine if an entity is still alive and how much damage it can cause on other entities upon contact. If an entity is no longer alive (if its strength has gotten below zero) then it is removed from the game altogether, as is the case with lasers every time they collide with another entity.

```
var Packt = Packt || {};
Packt.Components = Packt.Components || {};
Packt.Components.Strength = function(pEntity, pHP, pEnergy) {
  var entity = pEntity;
  var hp = pHP;
  var energy = pEnergy;

  // This is how much damage the entity causes to other entities
  // upon collision between the two
  this.getHP = function() {
    return hp;
  };

  // This represents how much energy the entity has left. When
  // the energy gets to or below zero, the entity dies
  this.getEnergy = function() {
    return energy;
  };

  // Update the entity's energy levels
  this.takeDamage = function(damage) {
    energy -= damage;
    return energy;
  };
};
```

The `LaserGun` component is slightly more involved because it contains a collection of entities that it manages. Each time a laser beam is fired by the entity containing the laser gun, a new entity is created to represent that laser beam. This entity is similar to all the other entities in the game since it also contains a `sprite` component to draw itself a `Move` component and a `physics` component as well.

Each time the laser gun updates itself, it needs to move all of its lasers forward and remove any of its laser beams from its control if the laser has gone outside the screen area.

```
var Packt = Packt || {};
Packt.Components = Packt.Components || {};
```

```
Packt.Components.LaserGun = function(entity, canvas, maxShots) {
  var entity = entity;
  var MAX_SHOTS = maxShots;
  var canvas = canvas;
  var shots = new Array();
  var shotsPerSec = 1000 / 15;
  var timeLastShot = 0;

  // Move all lasers forward, and remove any lasers outside
  //   the screen
  this.update = function() {
    for (var i = 0, len = shots.length; i < len; i++) {
      try {
        shots[i].update();
        var shotPos = shots[i].getPosition();

        if (shotPos.y < -100) {
          shots.splice(i, 1);
        }
      } catch (e) {}
    }
  };

  // Create a new laser entity, and assign all of the components
  // it will need in order to actually destroy other ships
  this.add = function(x, y) {
    var time = Date.now();

    // Don't add a new laser until at least some time has passed,
    // so that we don't fire too many lasers at once
    if (time - timeLastShot >= shotsPerSec) {

      // Restrict the amount of lasers that can be on the screen
      //   at once
      if (shots.length < MAX_SHOTS) {
        var shot = new Packt.Entity
          (Packt.ENTITY_TYPES.BULLET, x, y);
        var spriteComp = new Packt.Components.Sprite(
          shot, "./img/laser-blue.png", 8, 32);
        spriteComp.setCtx(canvas.getContext());
        var strengthComp = new Packt.Components.Strength
          (shot, 10, 0);
        var physComp = new Packt.Components.Physics(shot);
        var mockMove = new Packt.Components.Move(shot, 15);
```

```
          shot.addComponent("sprite", spriteComp);
          shot.addComponent("move", mockMove);
          shot.addComponent("physics", physComp);
          shot.addComponent("strength", strengthComp);

          shot.setOnUpdate(function() {
            mockMove.setDirection(0, -1);
            mockMove.update();
          });

          shots.push(shot);
        }

        timeLastShot = time;
      }
    };

    // Return a list of active shots
    this.getShots = function() {
      return shots;
    };
  };
```

With all of our major components in place, we're ready to take a look at the other classes in the game. Remember, though, that the whole purpose of using components is to simplify development and to loosen the coupling between individual pieces of functionality. Thus, if we wanted to add more components to the game, say, an explosion effect component, for example, all we'd need to do is follow the same basic structure of a component and we'd be ready to simply plug it into the main game logic script.

/entities

Entities are the main building blocks of the game. They are the generalized representation of anything that we can interact with — the player's ship, enemy ships, or laser beams. Some people call their entities objects, characters, or actors, but the idea behind them is the same.

In our game, we don't extend the base entity class in order to create a distinction between ships and lasers. The only thing that sets them apart are the components they use and how those components are used.

The structure of our game entities is basic and to the point. Each entity keeps track of its own position within the game world, a flag that indicates its state (whether the entity is active or not—dead or alive), a list of components, and an update function. Also, for simplicity, each entity declares a `draw` function which delegates the actual drawing to the `sprite` component, if the entity happens to have one. We also define a few general purpose functions inside each entity so as to make adding, removing, and using components a bit easier. Finally, each entity allows for a custom update function, so that each instantiated entity can update itself differently.

```javascript
var Packt = Packt || {};
Packt.ENTITY_TYPES = {
  SHIP: 0,
  BULLET: 1
};

Packt.Entity = function(type, x, y) {
  var type = type;
  var pos = {
    x: x,
    y: y
  };

  var isActive = true;
  var components = new Object();

  // Make this function empty by default, and allow the user to
    override it
  var update = function(){};

  // Add a component to this entity if one by this name has not
    yet been added
  function addComponent(key, component) {
    if (!components[key]) {
      components[key] = component;
    }

    return component;
  }

  // Attempt to remove an entity by its name
  function removeComponent(key) {
    if (components[key]) {
      return delete components[key];
    }
```

```
      return false;
    }

    // Return a reference to a component
    function getComponent(key) {
      return components[key] || null;
    }

    // Draw this component
    function draw() {
      if (components.sprite) {
        components.sprite.update();
      }
    }

    // Expose these functions through a public interface
    this.addComponent = addComponent;
    this.removeComponent = removeComponent;
    this.getComponent = getComponent;
    this.getPosition = function() {
      return pos;
    };

    this.setPosition = function(newPos) {
      pos = newPos;
    };

    this.isActive = function() {
      return isActive;
    };

    this.setActive = function(active) {
      isActive = active;
    };

    this.draw = draw;
    this.update = update;
    this.update = function() {
      update();
    };
    // Save a reference to a new update callback function
    this.setOnUpdate = function(cb){
      update = cb;
    };
  };
```

As you can see, this entity class is really quite bare bones. It takes into account what our game needs to do, what is used in the game, and it encapsulates the most common functionality based on that. From here we can instantiate an entity and add components to it, making it a very unique entity, based on all that it potentially can and cannot do.

/widgets

The only widget used in this game is the `EnergyBar` widget. The whole point of widgets is to simplify the management of different user interface elements. The way in which each widget decides how to display the elements they represent is their own business and any client code using them should only be concerned about the interface through which it can communicate with the widget.

What the `EnergyBar` widget does is display a horizontal bar across the top of the page representing how much energy the player has left. Each time the player is hit by an enemy ship, its energy levels drop by some amount. When that energy meter goes to zero, the player dies, and the game is over.

One way this energy bar could have been rendered was through the canvas API, where the widget was rendered directly on the game canvas. While this is a very acceptable solution as well as a very common one, I decided to just use a plain old DOM element instead. This way the styling can be changed much more easily through CSS and nothing else would need to be changed within the code. In other words, while someone worked on the actual code, a second person could work on styling the widget and all they'd need to access would be the stylesheet associated with it.

```
var Packt = Packt || {};
Packt.Widgets = Packt.Widgets || {};

Packt.Widgets.EnergyBar = function(cssClass) {
  var energy = 100;

  // Create the DOM element to represent this widget on screen
  var container = document.createElement("div");
  container.classList.add(cssClass);

  var bar = document.createElement("div");
  bar.style.width = energy + "%";
  container.appendChild(bar);

  // Return the DOM element so it can be appended to the document
  this.getElement = function() {
    return container;
  };
```

```
    // Increase the player's energy level and update the DOM element
    // that represents it on screen. To decrease the energy level,
simply
    // pass a negative number to this function
    this.addEnergy = function(amount) {
      energy += amount;
      bar.style.width = energy + "%";
    };

    // Set the energy level directly, instead of just adding to
    // or removing from it
    this.setEnergy = function(amount) {
      energy = amount;
      bar.style.width = energy + "%";
    };
  };
```

When an `EnergyBar` widget is instantiated, it creates its own DOM element that represents the widget, adding any CSS classes and IDs associated with it. The member attribute energy represents the amount of energy that an entity has and the width of one of the DOM elements created by the widget matches to the percentage of energy it contains. After a widget's element has been added to the document, we can simply communicate with the widget class through its public interface and the DOM elements displayed on the document get updated accordingly.

Canvas.js

With the exception of the `EnergyBar` widget, everything else rendered to the screen in this game is rendered through a canvas, using the 2D rendering context. In order to keep things together and make the code more organized, we create a very simple abstraction over the canvas API. Instead of keeping track of a canvas variable referencing some DOM element, along with its accompanying context reference, we encapsulate the canvas element, the JavaScript reference to it, and the reference to the rendering context all inside a single object.

```
// Namespace the canvas abstraction
var Packt = Packt || {};

// Construct a canvas of an arbitrary size
Packt.Canvas = function(w, h) {
  var width = w;
  var height = h;
  var canvas = document.createElement("canvas");

  canvas.width = width;
```

```
    canvas.height = height;

    var ctx = canvas.getContext("2d");

    this.getCanvas = function() {
      return canvas;
    };

    this.getContext = function() {
      return ctx;
    };

    this.getWidth = function() {
      return width;
    };

    this.getHeight = function() {
      return height;
    };

    // Allow the client to clear the entire rendering buffer without
    // needing to know how things are done under the hood, and
      without
    // anyone needing to worry about the width and height of the
      canvas
    this.clear = function() {
      ctx.clearRect(0, 0, width, height);
    };
  };
```

We also hide some of the detailed functionality of the canvas API by adding a few helper functions, such as getWidth, getHeight, and clear, so that other areas in the code can interact with the canvas through this simplified interface.

One other reason that an abstraction such as this can be very handy is that it would greatly simplify things if we decided to use two or more canvases. Suppose we wanted to render a widget into its own canvas. Without an abstraction like this, we would now have four separate variables to keep track of in our code.

A common optimization pattern in HTML5 game rendering with the 2D canvas is to separate the rendering into layers. For example, things that don't change very frequently from frame to frame (such as the background graphics of a level) can be re-rendered much less frequently than dynamic objects that may need to be rendered at a different location each frame (the player and the enemies that are trying to kill the hero). Instead of redrawing each and every pixel of the background graphics each frame, since most of those pixels are the exactly same as the previous frame, we can draw the entire background scene onto its own canvas and absolutely position it behind another canvas that only draws on smaller parts of it, making it much easier to redraw every frame.

Since the background layer doesn't change too often, if at all, we can render more complex graphics onto it and not have to worry about redrawing anything there very often. Although the foreground layer normally needs to be cleared and redrawn every single frame, we can still maintain a good frame rate because we're normally only rendering on a small portion of the foreground canvas, which doesn't take as much processing as it would to redraw the background layer every frame.

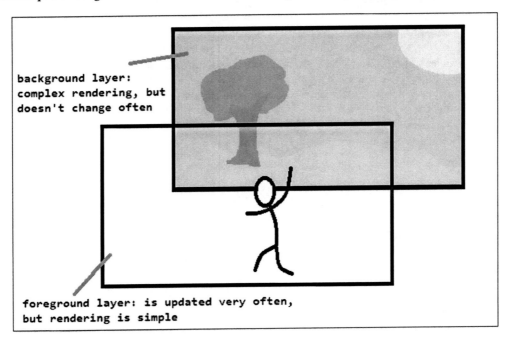

Now it becomes easy to see how valuable a simple canvas abstraction can be when using more advanced rendering techniques. In most cases, even if we're just rendering on a single canvas, being able to encapsulate all the loose variables associated with a canvas often makes things more efficient, especially when you need to pass the canvas and the canvas context around to other functions and classes.

EnemyManager.js

Since the player of our game will only control a single entity throughout the entire game, creating an instance of the entity class and letting the player control that entity is trivial. The challenge is finding a way to create enemy entities, move them around, and manage them as the game progresses. To solve this problem, we create an EnemyManager class, whose job is to create enemy entities when needed and manage their existence.

While this may seem like a complex task, it becomes more manageable if we break down the task into smaller pieces. The responsibilities that the EnemyManager class has include creating a new enemy entity and adding it to a list of active entities that it stores, updating each entity individually, and removing any dead entities from the entity list it manages.

```
// Namespace the enemy manager object
var Packt = Packt || {};

Packt.EnemyManager = function(canvas) {
  var entities = new Array();
  var canvas = canvas;
  var worldWidth = canvas.getWidth();
  var worldHeight = canvas.getHeight();

  // By returning the list of active enemies to the client code,
  // we can pass on the responsibility of rendering each entity,
  // as well as allow other components to interact with the
    entities
  this.getEntities = function() {
    return entities;
  };

  // Create a new entity at a certain screen location, along
  // with a list of components
  function addEnemies(x, y, components) {
    var entity = new Packt.Entity(Packt.ENTITY_TYPES.SHIP, x || 0,
      y || -100);
    for (var c in components) {
      entity.addComponent(c, components[c]);
    };

    var strengthComp = new Packt.Components.Strength
      (entity, 0.5, 25);
    var physComp = new Packt.Components.Physics(entity);
    var mockMove = new Packt.Components.Move
      (entity, (Math.random() * 5 >> 0) + 2);
```

```
    var enemySprite = "./img/enemy-red.png";

    // Randomly assign a different skin to the sprite component
    if (parseInt(Math.random() * 100) % 2 == 0) {
      enemySprite = "./img/spaceship.png";
    }

    var spriteComp = new Packt.Components.Sprite
      (entity, enemySprite, 64, 64);

    spriteComp.setCtx(canvas.getContext());
    spriteComp.setSpriteCoords(0, 0, 64, 64);
    entity.addComponent("sprite", spriteComp);
    entity.addComponent("move", mockMove);
    entity.addComponent("physics", physComp);
    entity.addComponent("strength", strengthComp);

    // Randomly assign a starting direction to each entity
    var randPathX = (Math.random() * 100 % 10) - 5;
    var randPathY = (Math.random() * 100 % 50) + 10;
    entity.setOnUpdate(function() {
      mockMove.setDirection(randPathX, 1);
      mockMove.update();
    });

    entities.push(entity);
  }

this.add = addEnemies;

// Remove dead entities from our management
this.remove = function(entity) {
  for (var i = 0, len = entities.length; i < len; i++) {
    if (entities[i] === entity) {
      entities.splice(i, 1);
      return entity;
    }
  }

  return null;
};
```

```
// Update each entity's position, and remove dead entities
this.update = function() {
  var enemiesDeleted = 0;
  for (var i = 0, len = entities.length; i < len; i++) {
    try {
      entities[i].update();

      var pos = entities[i].getPosition();

      if (pos.y > worldHeight + 100 || !entities[i].isActive())
      {
        entities.splice(i, 1);
        enemiesDeleted++;
      }

      if (pos.x < -100) {
        pos.x = worldWidth + 50;
        entities[i].setPosition(pos);
      } else if (pos.x > worldWidth + 100) {
        pos.x = -50;
        entities[i].setPosition(pos);
      }
    } catch (e) {}
  }

  if (enemiesDeleted > 0) {
    for (var i = 0; i < enemiesDeleted; i++) {
      var offset = (Math.random() * 100 >> 0) %
        (worldWidth / 75 >> 0);
      var x = 50 * offset + 25 + (25 * offset);
      var y = 0 - Math.random() * 100 - 100;
      addEnemies(x, y, {});
    }
  }
};
};
```

Because we are using a component-based architecture, these three tasks aren't complex at all. In order to create a new entity, we simply instantiate the class and add the necessary components it needs to function. To add variety to the game, we can randomly assign a different sprite to each entity created as well as randomly tweak the properties of each entity, such as making it move faster, cause more damage, look bigger, and so on.

Removing dead entities is even easier. All we need to do is iterate over the list of active entities and remove them from the list if the active flag for an entity is unset. One thing we could also do is remove any entities that wander too far off the screen area, so that we don't need to manage entities that can't possibly be hit by the player's lasers.

Finally, the update function takes the job of updating each active entity's position (or rather, it tells each entity to update its own position based on the direction they're headed), simulate some basic artificial intelligence by moving each entity forward, then removing any dead entities.

GameLoop.js

The game loop class takes care of running the game's logic for each frame. The main added value that we get from using a class such as this is that we can encapsulate this boilerplate functionality and reuse it with different settings with minimal effort.

```
// Namespace the game loop class
var Packt = Packt || {};

Packt.GameLoop = function(fps) {
  var fps = fps;
  var frameDelay = 1000 / fps;
  var lastFrameTime = 0;
  var isRunning = true;

  // By default, the game tick is empty, indicating that we expect
    the client
  // to provide their own update function
  var update = function(){};

  // Once the game loop object is set to running, this function
    will be called
  // as close to the specified frame rate as it can, until the
    client code
  // sets the object's running state to false
  function run(time) {
    if (isRunning) {
      var delta = time - lastFrameTime;

      if (delta >= frameDelay) {
        update();
        lastFrameTime = time;
      }
```

```
      requestAnimationFrame(run);
    }
  }

  // Allows client code to start/stop the game loop
  this.setRunning = function(running) {
    isRunning = running;
    return isRunning;
  };

  this.isRunning = function() {
    return isRunning;
  };

  this.run = run;

  // Allows client code to override default update function
  this.setOnUpdate = function(cb){
    update = cb;
  };
};
```

When we create an instance of this class, we tell it how fast we want the game loop to run in terms of frames per second and the class takes care of the rest. Once this is set up, the class will class its own update class at whatever frequency we tell it to. As an added bonus, we can also specify our own update function to be executed every time the game loop ticks.

PhysicsManager.js

Similar to the `EnemyManager` class, the `PhysicsManager` class is responsible for isolating complex functionality so that the client code is cleaner and the functionality can be reused elsewhere. Since this class is a bit more involved, we won't be showing the complete source code for it in the book. As with the other chapters, check out Packt's website for this book.

In summary, the `PhysicsManager` class takes a reference to all of the enemy entities (which it can get from the `EnemyManager` object), all of the player's laser beams, and the player's entity itself. Then, inside its update method, it checks for collision between all of those entities.

Vec2.js

Since the `physics` engine of this game makes extensive use of vector structures and since JavaScript doesn't provide native vector data types, we decided to create our own. This simple class represents a vector with two components and provides a function to normalize the vector. This is especially useful when we want to move an entity in whichever direction it faces.

main.js

Finally, we bring it all together in a file that we might as well call `main.js`. This file looks an awful lot like me when I go to a fast food restaurant: take one of everything and see how it all goes together. First we instantiate a canvas object, then the player entity, an `EnemyManager` object, a `PhysicsManager` object, and finally, a game loop object. After everything is wired up, we start the game loop and the game is set in motion.

```
(function main(){
  var WIDTH = document.body.offsetWidth;
  var HEIGHT = document.body.offsetHeight;
  var MAX_ENEMIES = 100;

  // The main canvas where the game is rendered
  var canvas = new Packt.Canvas(WIDTH, HEIGHT);
  document.body.appendChild(canvas.getCanvas());

  // The energy widget
  var playerEnergy = new Packt.Widgets.EnergyBar("energyBar");
  document.body.appendChild(playerEnergy.getElement());

  // The player entity, along with its required components
  var player = new Packt.Entity(Packt.ENTITY_TYPES.SHIP,
    canvas.getWidth() / 2, canvas.getHeight() - 100);

  var playerLaserGunComp = new Packt.Components.LaserGun
    (player, canvas, 10);
  var playerStrengthComp = new Packt.Components.Strength
    (player, 0, 100);
  var playerMoveComp = new Packt.Components.Drag(player, canvas);
  var playerPhysComp = new Packt.Components.Physics(player);
  var playerSpriteComp = new Packt.Components.Sprite
    (player, "./img/fighter.png", 64, 64);
  playerSpriteComp.setCtx(canvas.getContext());
  playerSpriteComp.setSpriteCoords(64 * 3, 0, 64, 64);
  player.addComponent("sprite", playerSpriteComp);
```

```
player.addComponent("drag", playerMoveComp);
player.addComponent("physics", playerPhysComp);
player.addComponent("strength", playerStrengthComp);
player.addComponent("laserGun", playerLaserGunComp);

// Override the player's update function
player.setOnUpdate(function() {
  var drag = player.getComponent("drag");
  drag.centerEntity();

  var pos = player.getPosition();
  var laserGun = player.getComponent("laserGun");
  laserGun.add(pos.x + 28, pos.y);
  laserGun.update();
});


// The enemy manager
var enMan = new Packt.EnemyManager(canvas);
for (var i = 0; i < MAX_ENEMIES; i++) {
  var offset = i % (WIDTH / 75 >> 0);
  var x = 50 * offset + 25 + (25 * offset);
  var y = -50 * i + 25 + (-50 * i);
  enMan.add(x, y, {});
}

// The physics manager
var phy = new Packt.PhysicsManager();
phy.setPlayer(player);

// The game loop, along with its overriden update function
var gameLoop = new Packt.GameLoop(60);
gameLoop.setOnUpdate(function() {
  // Check if game is over
  if (playerStrengthComp.getEnergy() < 0) {
    document.body.classList.add("zoomOut");

    var ctx = canvas.getContext();
    ctx.globalAlpha = 0.01;

    gameLoop.setRunning(false);
  }
```

```
    // Add everyone to the physics manager to check for collision
    var enemies = enMan.getEntities();
    for (var i = 0, len = enemies.length; i < len; i++) {
      phy.addEnemy(enemies[i]);
    }

    var playerLasers = playerLaserGunComp.getShots();
    for (var i = 0, len = playerLasers.length; i < len; i++) {
      phy.addPlayerShots(playerLasers[i]);
    }

    // Update positions
    enMan.update();
    player.update();

    // Check for collisions
    phy.checkCollisions();

    // Draw
    canvas.clear();
    for (var i = 0, len = enemies.length; i < len; i++) {
      enemies[i].draw();
    }

    for (var i = 0, len = playerLasers.length; i < len; i++) {
      playerLasers[i].draw();
    }

    player.draw();
    playerEnergy.setEnergy(playerStrengthComp.getEnergy());
  });

  // Get the game going
  gameLoop.run();
})();
```

The main reason for the self-invoked main function is to privately scope all of the variables contained within the function is to prevent users from manipulating the game from a browser's JavaScript console. Had the game variables all been stored in the global scope, anyone with access to that would be able to manipulate the game state. Also, since this function is merely a setup function, this would be the perfect place to put any conditional logic to load alternate resources based on the user agent executing the script.

index.html

The host page for this game could not be any briefer. All that we do in this file is load all of our resources. Since different components sometimes depend on other components or other modules defined in our game (and since JavaScript provides no mechanism to load individual components into a script), the order in which our JavaScript resources are loaded is important.

```html
<!doctype html>
<html>
  <head>
    <meta charset="utf-8" />
    <title>2D Space Shooter</title>
    <link rel="stylesheet" href="./css/style.css" />
  </head>

  <body class="animBody">
    <script src="./js/Vec2.js"></script>
    <script src="./js/components/Sprite.js"></script>
    <script src="./js/components/Move.js"></script>
    <script src="./js/entities/Entity.js"></script>
    <script src="./js/Canvas.js"></script>
    <script src="./js/GameLoop.js"></script>
    <script src="./js/components/TouchDrag.js"></script>
    <script src="./js/components/Physics.js"></script>
    <script src="./js/components/Strength.js"></script>
    <script src="./js/components/LaserGun.js"></script>
    <script src="./js/PhysicsManager.js"></script>
    <script src="./js/EnemyManager.js"></script>
    <script src="./js/widgets/EnergyBar.js"></script>
    <script src="./js/main.js"></script>
  </body>
</html>
```

Mobile optimizations

In this final section, let's take a look at a few aspects of the game that we could (and should) optimize particularly for deployment on mobile devices. Although some of the following optimizations discussed also overlap in terms of desktop optimizations, they are especially impactful in mobile web development.

Combine resources

Although it is a good practice to write loose, modular code, we must not stop there. Before deploying the application to a production server, we would be wise to at least combine all of those files into a single file. The easiest way to do this would be by simply concatenating each file and serving up that larger file instead of multiple ones.

The reason this is preferred over sending multiple individual files to the client is because after a certain amount of concurrent connection to the same server, the browser will queue consequent connections and the total time it will take to load all of the files will increase.

Also, after all of the resources have been combined into a single resource, we should also use one of the many available tools that lets us compress, minify, obfuscate, and uglify our code. Anything we can do to reduce the code to the smallest possible amount of bytes is a big win for a mobile player. One particularly powerful tool for the job is the popular open source Closure Compiler developed by Google. Among its many features, the Closure Compiler also offers a function that analyzes the final code and removes any unreachable, dead code. Doing this will further reduce the final size of the application code making it especially handy for download over limited network connections, such as those found in most mobile devices today.

Track touches by IDs

The way we wrote our component to handle user input through touch makes the assumption that only one touch will be used at all times. While this assumption may hold true for most of the time in our game, it may not be the case in other games. The TouchDrag component always looks for the touch information on the very first touch object found within the changed touches list. The only issue with that is that the original touch may not always be the first array element within its parent array.

To change this, all we need to do is keep track of the touch ID of the finger that first touches the screen, then reference that touch based on its identification value.

```
Packt.Components.TouchDrag = function(entity, canvas) {
  var touchId = 0;

  // When a successful touch is first captured, cache the touch's
    identification
  function doOnTouchDown(event) {
    event.preventDefault();
    var phy = entity.getComponent("physics");
    var touch = event.changedTouches;
```

```
    if (phy) {
      touchId = touch.identifier;
      isDown = phy.collide
        (touch[touchId].pageX, touch[touchId].pageY, 0, 0);
    }
  }


  // Clear the touch flag on the entity, as well as the touch id
  function doOnTouchUp(event) {
    event.preventDefault();
    isDown = false;
    touchId = 0;
  }


  // Always move the entity based on the cached touch id
  function doOnTouchMove(event) {
    event.preventDefault();
    var touch = event.changedTouches;

    if (isDown) {
      pos.x = touch[touchId].pageX;
      pos.y = touch[touchId].pageY;
    }
  }
};
```

By tracking the original touch and only responding to it, we can guarantee fidelity in the touch input, even if multiple touches are initiated on the screen. This would also be the proper way of tracking separate touches for the purposes of implementing gestures or other input triggers based on an arbitrary combination of touches.

Use CSS animations with caution

There is a strange phenomenon that sometimes happens in mobile browsers when we are too generous with some of the newer CSS properties. For example, if we add a box shadow to an element, we can still get pretty strong performance. Optionally, if we add a CSS transition to some other element, performance could still be maintained. However, if both of these properties are assigned together then performance all of a sudden drops down to barely playable conditions.

Since there is no formula that describes which properties should and should not be used, and which combinations should be avoided, the advice here is to use the least amount of CSS properties possible and add them slowly. In the case of our game, where the desktop version makes heavy use of CSS animations to render the background, we need to consider the implications that this may have on a mobile device. After trying the effect on the two most popular mobile platforms today and seeing performance drop severely, we concluded that the particular animation we wanted, along with a constantly rendering canvas, was too much for a mobile processor to handle.

One way to determine if a particular CSS animation is too demanding on a mobile device is to use profiling tools such as Google Developer Tools and take note of the sort of work that the browser needs to do in order to achieve the desired animation. In cases such as this game, where a background detail was so computationally intensive to generate that it conflicted with the calculations required to simply play the game, we might well opt for a less demanding alternative. In this game, instead of loading the CSS animation onto the document body, we simply display a still background graphic.

Use separate canvases for each game layer

As briefly discussed earlier, one powerful optimization technique in HTML5 rendering is to use more than one canvas. The point is to render less frequently those things that only need to be rendered every once in a while. Those things that need to be rendered much more often, we render by themselves in a dedicated canvas context so that no CPU (or CPU) power is used to render details around these elements.

For example, the background scene of a game generally stays the same for several frames. Instead of clearing the entire canvas context, only to redraw those exact same pixels, on their exact same prior location, we can just render a background scene on a dedicated canvas and only render that scene again when the screen scrolls, or the scene otherwise changes. Until then, that canvas need not be bothered. Any movable objects and entities that need to be rendered multiple times per second can just be rendered on a second canvas, with a transparent background, so that the background layer can be seen through.

In this game, we could very well have rendered the image used as the background graphic onto a dedicated background layer, then provide the background animation to the canvas this way. However, since HTML5 provides a similar function that produces the same effect, we opted for that instead.

Use image atlases

The idea behind image atlases is really quite brilliant. Since the canvas API specifies a function that allows us to draw onto the canvas context from a source image specifying the area within the image that the pixel copying is to take place, we can simply use one master image from which all of our graphics assets can be drawn.

Instead of sending multiple loose images from the server down to the client, we can simply bundle all of our images into a single atlas file then draw each asset from a certain section of this larger collage.

Following is an image atlas with many smaller images inside it placed side by side, allowing us to retrieve each individual image from a single image asset. One of the main benefits of this technique is that we only need one HTTP request to the server in order to gain access to all of the images used within the atlas.

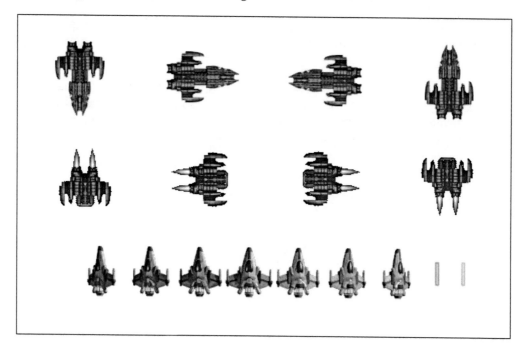

Of course, the challenge in using this technique is that we would need a way to know where each particular image is located within the atlas file. While doing this by hand might not seem too cumbersome on a small project such as this one, the complexity of this task gets unruly very fast.

There exist many open source tools available to solve this very problem. These tools take individual loose image files, bundle them up in the smallest possible atlas that can be generated from the list of images provided, and also generate a JSON file that we can use to map each loose image to their new representation within the atlas.

Summary

This chapter was dedicated to mobile development with the new HTML5 APIs available. We talked about the huge opportunity for game developers in the open web platform with regards to mobile devices as well as some of the main challenges associated with it. We talked about some best practices with mobile web development, which include degrading gracefully and enhancing progressively, designing for all finger sizes, saving battery life wherever possible, planning for offline game play, and offering a desktop version of your application.

The final two APIs presented in this chapter were CSS media queries and JavaScript touch events. Media queries allow us to check for other properties of the user agent viewing the document, such as viewport width, height, resolution, orientation, and so on. Depending on the properties set on the user agent executing our application, we can use media queries to load different CSS rules and documents, effectively modifying the document style at run time. The new JavaScript touch events are different from mouse events, in that multiple touches are allowed at the same time as well as pressure detection, touch size, and rotation angle.

Now that you have been introduced to the new features of HTML5, including the latest CSS and JavaScript APIs, the next step is for you to get some keyboard time and start developing your own games for the largest and most exciting computing platform of all time—the open web. Happy gaming!

Index

G

Geolocation
about 219, 243-246
Google Maps example 247, 248
Geolocation API 31
Geoposition object
about 245
properties 245
getItem(key) 193
GL-Matrix 228
GLSL (OpenGL Shading Language) 223
Google Chrome 220
Google Chrome Canary 249
Google Maps 247, 248
Google Web Toolkit. *See* GWT
grid attribute 301
GWT
about 105
URL 105

H

height attributes 290
HTML
about 7
history 8
HTML5
about 9, 10, 34
browser features 16-18
game development 35, 36
no plug-ins 34
powerful capabilities 34
semantic document structure 10-13
wide adoption 34
HTML5 web forms API
about 60
form validation 75
new input types 60
using, in game 77
HTML elements, Typography game
about 48
data attributes 51
email input, web form 49, 50
range input, web form 48
web form 48
Hyper Text Markup Language. *See* HTML

I

IDBFactory 199
IDBOpenDBRequest 200-202
IDBTransaction
about 202, 203
readonly transaction mode 203
readwrite transaction mode 203
versionchange transaction mode 203
identifier, touch object 305, 306
iframe 185
images
drawing 163-165
implementation considerations,
mobile game
about 277
battery life 279
battery life, saving 284, 285
best practices 280
browser differences 279
computing power 278
desktop version, offering 285
finger-friendly design 283, 284
graceful degradation 280
planning, for offline 285
progressive enhancement 281-283
screen size and orientation 277, 278
Indexed Database API 32
indexedDB.open method 199
IndexedDB, snake game
about 183, 197-199
elements, deleting 209-211
elements, getting 204-208
IDBFactory 199
IDBOpenDBRequest 200
IDBTransaction 202, 203
Int8Array, view type 153
Int16Array, view type 153
Int32Array, view type 153
integer argument 149
isFinished() function 99

J

JavaScript
about 59
query selectors 60

tel input type 73
time input type 64
url input type 74
week input type 63
NOT operator 287
number input type, web forms
about 70
attributes 70
nums array 148

O

Offline application cache, snake game
about 141, 173
using 173-175
onClose event 232
onError event 232
onMessage event 232
onOpen event 232
onsuccess callback 208
onupgradeneeded 200
onupgradeneeded callback 204
OpenGL ES 219
OpenGL ES 2 221
Open Web 33
orientation attribute 292, 293
OR operator 287

P

page not responsive warning 141
pageX coordinate, touch object 308
pageY coordinate, touch object 308
pause event 239
physics component 324
PhysicsManager class 339
pixelData array 216
pixels
manipulating 166, 168
placeholder 16
play event 239
playing event 239
polyfills 109
postMessage function 186, 232
progress event 238

Q

query selectors, Typography game
about 82, 84
using, in game 85

R

radiusX attribute, touch object 309
radiusY attribute, touch object 310-313
range input type, web forms
about 71
attributes 71
ratechange event 239
readonly transaction mode 203
readwrite transaction mode 203
rect function 161
reflow 15
regions 59
removeChild method 102
removeItem(key) 193
requestAnimationFrame
function 101, 143-147, 280
resolution attribute 300
responsive design 277
rotationAngle attribute, touch object 313
rotation function 162

S

SASS
URL 24
scale function 162
scan attribute 301
screenX coordinate, touch object 307
screenY coordinate, touch object 307
search input type, web forms
about 72
attributes 72
seeked event 239
seeking event 239
Selector API 32, 59
selectors module, CSS3 26
sessionStorage.key function 196
session storage, snake game 183, 196, 197
setCustomValidity() method 76

Thank you for buying
Learn HTML5 by Creating Fun Games

About Packt Publishing

Packt, pronounced 'packed', published its first book "*Mastering phpMyAdmin for Effective MySQL Management*" in April 2004 and subsequently continued to specialize in publishing highly focused books on specific technologies and solutions.

Our books and publications share the experiences of your fellow IT professionals in adapting and customizing today's systems, applications, and frameworks. Our solution based books give you the knowledge and power to customize the software and technologies you're using to get the job done. Packt books are more specific and less general than the IT books you have seen in the past. Our unique business model allows us to bring you more focused information, giving you more of what you need to know, and less of what you don't.

Packt is a modern, yet unique publishing company, which focuses on producing quality, cutting-edge books for communities of developers, administrators, and newbies alike. For more information, please visit our website: www.packtpub.com.

Writing for Packt

We welcome all inquiries from people who are interested in authoring. Book proposals should be sent to author@packtpub.com. If your book idea is still at an early stage and you would like to discuss it first before writing a formal book proposal, contact us; one of our commissioning editors will get in touch with you.

We're not just looking for published authors; if you have strong technical skills but no writing experience, our experienced editors can help you develop a writing career, or simply get some additional reward for your expertise.

HTML5 Canvas Cookbook

ISBN: 978-1-84969-136-9   Paperback: 348 pages

Over 80 recipes to revolutionize the web experience with HTML5 Canvas

1. The quickest way to get up to speed with HTML5 Canvas application and game development

2. Create stunning 3D visualizations and games without Flash

3. Written in a modern, unobtrusive, and objected oriented JavaScript style so that the code can be reused in your own applications.

4. Part of Packt's Cookbook series: Each recipe is a carefully organized sequence of instructions to complete the task as efficiently as possible

HTML5 Mobile Development Cookbook

ISBN: 978-1-84969-196-3   Paperback: 254 pages

Over 60 recipes for building fast, responsive HTML5 mobile websites for iPhone 5, Android, Windows Phone, and Blackberry

1. Solve your cross platform development issues by implementing device and content adaptation recipes.

2. Maximum action, minimum theory allowing you to dive straight into HTML5 mobile web development.

3. Incorporate HTML5-rich media and geo-location into your mobile websites.

Please check **www.PacktPub.com** for information on our titles